THE
GODDESS
OF THE
STONES

By the same author

THE CIRCLES EFFECT AND ITS MYSTERIES (*Artetech*)
CIRCLES FROM THE SKY (*Souvenir Press*)

THE GODDESS OF THE STONES

The Language of the Megaliths

GEORGE TERENCE MEADEN

Foreword by Marija Gimbutas

SOUVENIR PRESS

To those ingenious peoples who developed the peace-loving rite
of the Sacred Marriage, and left signs that thousands of years
later we might rediscover their secrets in this warrior age—
a rite that was likely founded at a time of equality
between sexes, of friendship and peace between peoples.

First published 1991 by Souvenir Press Ltd,
43 Great Russell Street, London WC1B 3PA
and simultaneously in Canada

ISBN 0 285 63031 8

Printed and bound in Great Britain by
WBC Ltd, Bridgend, Mid Glamorgan
Photoset by Rowland Phototypesetting Ltd
Bury St Edmunds, Suffolk

Contents

Acknowledgements

It is a pleasure to thank the archaeologist Dr Marija Gimbutas, world-renowned for her erudite studies of Neolithic symbolism in Eastern and Mediterranean Europe, for showing so much interest in my work and for enthusiastically agreeing to write the foreword to this book. I should also like to express my appreciation to Dr Aubrey Burl, author of so many valuable studies on megalithic circles, for the attention and encouragement he showed me in 1987 and 1988 when I revealed to him the secrets of my discoveries concerning the origins of stone-circle shapes and the consequences that they would have for Alexander Thom's much-debated geometrical interpretations; Dr Burl has patiently guarded these secrets while awaiting their release in this book. I may add that I enjoyed and profited from the archaeological study tours made with Dr Burl to Brittany in 1987 and Professor John Coles and Bryony Coles to Scandinavia in 1988, which gave me the opportunity to identify numerous Goddess stones and other signs of Goddess worship, some at little-frequented sites, which were helpful to my inquiry. I also record my thanks to Riane Eisler whose influential book *The Chalice and the Blade* was published in 1987. This innovative, timely work sets the prehistory and history of men and women in a context which approaches the truth more closely than any overview of world history that was ever prepared by a man. Riane Eisler graciously welcomed me into her Californian home in March 1990, and listened with excitement to the implications in my work for improving our understanding of the spiritual fabric of the Age of the Goddess in Britain, Ireland, France, and indeed the rest of the world. The great Romanian historian of religions, Professor Mircea Eliade, died three years ago, sadly before I could meet him. His books were my foremost inspiration in religio-philosophical matters. By his works, above all *Patterns of Comparative Religion* and *The Sacred and the Profane*, I came to understand the Neolithic mentality sufficiently well to be able to look afresh at grave goods, stones and tombs, and begin to recover from them the sense of adoration and awe that they once engendered in the minds of our ancestors. I also express my gratitude to my wife and family who gave me their steadfast support throughout the 1980s, for this allowed me to pursue my archaeological and crop-circle research programmes across the world in a relentless endeavour to solve age-old megalithic mysteries; this quest is continuing apace, and enough material is already to hand for the preparation of at least four further books on stone age archaeology, one of which is finished. Finally I thank David Ashwell, Ernest Hecht and Brian Thomas for providing help in their various ways immediately upon learning of the discoveries reported in my first two archaeological books; farmers Stephen Horton (Beckhampton), David Stanier (South Wonston) and Bernard Elliott (Norton Bavant) who allowed me on to their land to study crop circles and to construct the first stone circles by the ancient methods for well over three thousand years; Bradford-on-Avon artist June Peel for skilfully attending to 33 of the illustrations sketched for this book and Tim Cornford for preparing eight of the line drawings. All other illustrations are by the author, as well as all photographs except for those credited, with my thanks, to Keith Mortimore, David Banks, Terry Clewes, Peter D. Rendall, Mary R. Shaw, David C. Smith and Geoffrey A. Smith.

Foreword

by Marija Gimbutas

Megalithic monuments have been studied for hundreds of years. The main achievements in the latter part of the twentieth century have been the thorough descriptions and excavation reports of important constructions such as Newgrange and Knowth, both outstanding sanctuaries in the Boyne valley of Ireland. The megalithic art of western Europe has been systematically catalogued, and the shapes of stone rings mathematically analysed. The questions raised, however, are endless. Why did our ancestors carve spirals, lozenges, zigzags, circles, cups and other motifs on the big stones? How did they succeed in making perfect ellipses or circles when setting up their big stone rings, and why should they want to make perfect geometrical shapes anyway? The building of awe-inspiring monuments such as Silbury, Avebury, Stonehenge, Newgrange and hundreds of others were undertakings of a magnitude which would have engaged most of the local workforce over a period of many years. There must have been a deep motive for this creation. The monuments and symbols are part of religious expression and bear witness to the spirituality of ancient Europe. What Professor Terence Meaden does is show us the means by which we can open up the secrets.

Prior to his work, and characteristic of the twentieth-century mind, the building of the megalithic structures was linked with 'megalithic science', not with religion. In the 1960s and 1970s studies on ancient astronomy and mathematics appeared with a message that megalithic society revolved about mathematical and astro-nomical thought. The pioneering work was by Alexander Thom in his fruitful *Megalithic Sites in Britain* and by Thom and his son Archibald in *Megalithic Remains in Britain and Brittany*. Their studies suggested that many megalithic sites acted as solar and lunar observatories, and it was proposed that in designing megalithic circles the builders used a standardised unit of 2.722 feet which the Thoms called the megalithic yard.

Most of these suggestions were tested and some accepted by Douglas Heggie in *Megalithic Science* and by Clive Ruggles in *Megalithic Astronomy*. About the same time Martin Brennan, in *The Stars and the Stones*, saw alignments of monuments and their symbols as being connected to solstices, equinoxes, lunar risings and settings, and lunar cycles. The importance of this cannot be denied, but the symbolism must not be interpreted as an expression of astronomical and mathe-matical knowledge unrelated to religion. The monuments are to be viewed in a ritual context. The issue is *why* such monuments were so orientated. The answer can only come from analysing megalithic symbolism. There must have been a magico-ritual background to the physical settings in the landscape of these extraordinary constructions. In this regard Michael Dames' pioneering work should not be forgotten. His books on Silbury and Avebury opened the way towards associating the monuments with the Goddess religion and with large-scale ritual celebrations of the Goddess's life-bringing, life-taking and regenerating powers.

Terence Meaden provides quite a new key in the ongoing explanations of the meanings of the Neolithic symbols, how the perfection of the geometry of the monuments was achieved, and what the monuments mean. His book begins a new period of co-operation between meteorology, religion and archaeology.

Everything follows from this: the puzzles of the Neolithic era are explained, Thom's conundrums are solved, and astronomy is set in its proper context, one that is subservient to religion. Much of this book involves the spiral and its meanings which are explained along with the other symbols. An ideology based on belief in an unending and returning cycle is disclosed—birth, life, death, rebirth. The tombs and sanctuaries are permeated with the idea of regeneration of life powers which depend on the Cosmic Mother. As in my own work on the symbolism of prehistoric art, She manifests in the aspect of the Goddess of Death and Regeneration. Rituals and ceremonies must have been practised in associa-tion with the belief in regeneration of life and the Goddess in whose domain were the powers of regeneration. As we know from European folklore, the atmospheric changes and lunar cycles, and the renewal of the sun, were in Her powers.

Step by step we are gaining a deeper perception of the symbolism of these extraordinary monuments and engravings of the flourishing period of megalithic culture in the British Isles. With it the religion and spirituality of our ancestors are revealed. The linking of the monuments with the atmospheric phenomena, presented analytically and systematically in this book, is a big stepping stone, a major clue to the solution of a lot of unanswered questions.

Department of Archaeology,
University of California,
Los Angeles.

Preface

To people in the twentieth century AD the Neolithic and Bronze Ages are times so remote that, as John Aubrey wrote three centuries ago in his unfinished work *Monumenta Britannica*, 'no books do reach them'. To look back so far—to a period stretching from 4600 BC to 1000 BC—in order to unlock its secrets we have to sift the fragments gathered by archaeological work and with the help of modern science examine the evidence in the light of what we know of the customs, folklore and religious faith of agrarian cultures throughout the world. Nowadays it is appreciated that only by transcending interdisciplinary boundaries can we increase our understanding of the beliefs of lost peoples; otherwise the discoveries of archaeologists, however carefully studied, can never be wholly comprehensible.

I came to archaeological research via physics and meteorology, being already, since boyhood, an antiquarian, and it was by applying my discoveries in those fields to the world of five thousand years ago that I began to realise what it was that had motivated the spiritual lives of our ancient forebears: a mystic vision so powerful that it dominated spiritual thought in Britain for two thousand years, at a time when the governing deity was female, the omnipotent Great Goddess. In this, the megalithic age, there arose throughout the land almost a thousand stone circles and the prodigious masterpieces that are Newgrange, Knowth, Avebury and Stonehenge.

Beginning in 1980, my investigations led me to discover that Neolithic life and religion were bound up with a natural phenomenon which inspired a deep devotion and permeated every aspect of worship, culture, art—even day-to-day living. I began to understand the religious experience which directed the building of stone circles, henges, round barrows and round houses, and the cryptic and previously meaningless carvings engraved on megaliths became intelligible, their powerful symbolism radiantly clear. A new world opened up, providing amazing insights into the cult of the Great Goddess and her consort, the Sky God.

As a result I have unlocked the secrets of several major monuments, including Newgrange, Ireland's finest passage-grave, and Silbury Hill, the world's biggest prehistoric mound. I have described the art at Newgrange in the order in which I deciphered it during the years 1984–1986, which led me eventually to uncover a fairly complete iconography of the monument. I also tackled the relatively few stones at Knowth whose art has been published, and my interpretation is given in this book. At the same time I was studying megalithic art at other sites in the British Isles, especially in Wales and Scotland, and from 1985 onwards I was travelling frequently to museums and Neolithic sites as far afield as Malta, Brittany, Crete, Greece and Mycenae, Norway, Sweden, Hungary, Egypt and California—even to Japan and Indonesia. Over three years, from 1983 to 1986, I came to understand the origin and meaning of Silbury Hill and the underlying significance of round-barrow burial, and I also explored chambered barrows, especially at Stoney Littleton during the winter solstices of 1985–1987 and in 1987 when the 18-year moon cycle peaked. Although my first thoughts concerning the spiritual origins of round barrows and stone circles entered my mind in August 1980, I did not start my fieldwork on them until 1983 and my research is still going on.

A consequence of my discoveries is that the glory and stature of the monuments are greatly enhanced, and the skills and technological abilities of their builders can be set in a framework realistic for the times in which they lived. We can begin to retrieve the outline of a religion and perception of life which is appropriate to the British and Irish Neolithic and Bronze Ages. A window opens on the harmonious world of the Great Goddess, a world of peaceful coexistence which lasted for thousands of years until it was overthrown by sword-wielding invaders who devised, for the purposes of self-respect and the exploitation of the female half of the population, the unforgiving gods of war, and thereby initiated a warrior age ruled by male gods, which has lasted to this day.

The illiterate peoples of those far-off times left nothing in writing and nothing by way of sagas and oral traditions. Besides their monuments and stone engravings we have only those of their tools, grave goods and bones which chanced to be imperishable. By reading their symbols and understanding their rituals we can learn how they viewed the wonders of Nature and came to terms with the uncertainty of life. They lived in a silent, dangerous world—so sparsely inhabited when compared with our own. The stars shone brilliantly against the deep, dark sky—pitch-black until the rising of the moon which like Nature was regarded with the minutest attention that few people today appreciate. Sun and moon, earth and sky, animals, plants and humans, all enjoyed a complex interdependence, the result of long evolution.

The former inhabitants of these islands rise in our esteem. The monuments emerge from the mists of time to stand more imposing than ever. We are reunited with a forgotten age: the Age of the Goddess.

The principal prehistoric sites and some other place names mentioned in this book.

1

Stone Age Mysteries

Until about 4600 BC the British Isles were inhabited by nomadic tribes, hunter-gatherers who had roamed the country since the end of the last ice age in about 10000 BC, camping for a while in areas where game, fish and edible plants and fruits were plentiful, and moving on as the seasons dictated. Although traces of their encampments have been found, these peoples had little or no lasting effect on the landscape.

In the middle of the fifth millennium BC the Neolithic or New Stone Age peoples began to settle in the islands, bringing with them a way of life which was to have a profound influence on the landscape and to establish a pattern of living that would prevail until the industrial revolution of the nineteenth century AD. They were the first farmers, living in settled communities, rearing animals for food and clearing land to grow cereal crops, and the results of their labours can still be seen in Britain's now treeless uplands where the land was easier to clear and the soil easier to till.

They have left other traces, too—evidence of a culture which for centuries has puzzled scholars and ordinary people alike—in their causewayed enclosures, barrows, cursuses and henges and, later, in their megalithic circles and rows, many of which still dominate the remote areas of the British Isles, silent witnesses to rituals and beliefs long forgotten. It is the purpose of this book to uncover the

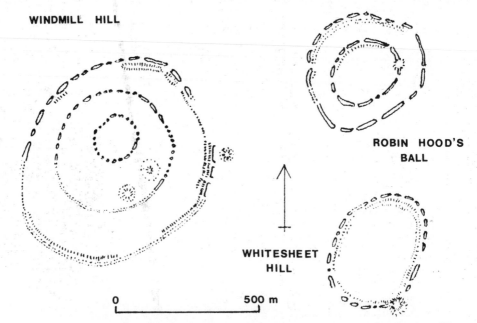

WINDMILL HILL

ROBIN HOOD'S
BALL

WHITESHEET
HILL

0   500 m

Banks and ditches demarcate the circular areas known as causewayed enclosures. They date from the fourth millennium BC. These are from the chalk hills of Wiltshire. Later round barrows lie upon some of them.

mystery of those monuments, and to reveal the secrets which have reached out, across the millennia, to our own time.

Those early farmers encountered harsh conditions and ceaseless problems in their efforts at clearing forests, tilling the soil, establishing crops, and improving yields, while meeting the dangers from wild beasts and submitting to the vagaries of the weather. Trial and error taught them about land-use, soil impoverishment, crop improvement, fertilisation, drainage, stockading, breeding, and so on. It was a life of the utmost austerity, at the mercy of the elements.

At the beginning of the Neolithic Age communities were thinly scattered, each consisting of several individuals or a few families. But the agrarian way of life was less harsh than that of the hunter-gatherer. The population gradually increased, acquired a sense of ownership of the land they cultivated, and slowly developed technological skills. During the course of the fourth millennium BC, earthworks began to be constructed, on a scale so massive that many of them have survived to this day, although their purpose has yet to be satisfactorily explained.

The so-called causewayed camps, or interrupted-ditch enclosures, were earliest. Ditch-and-bank constructions with access causeways surrounding roughly circular sites often of enormous acreage, such as the one at Windmill Hill near Avebury on the North Wiltshire Downs, are found mostly in the southern half of England. The first were built around the start of the fourth millennium BC and a few stayed in use until the start of the second millennium. The one nearest to what later became the site of Stonehenge is called Robin Hood's Ball. Four kilometres to the north-west of the famous monument, it pre-dates the bluestone-

Megaliths fronting the forecourt of the chambered long barrow at West Kennet near Avebury. Silbury Hill can be seen in the distance. The great stones were placed in position at the time of sealing the barrow, around 2500 BC.

circle phase of Stonehenge by some 1,500 years. The purpose of these causewayed enclosures has been much debated, but it seems likely that they served as places of assembly or as cult centres.

Several fourth-millennium enclosures have been excavated in England. Although surviving material is meagre we are able to glimpse the unsophisticated character of Early Neolithic life by the plain domestic pottery and artefacts, the quantities of animal and human bones, and several unpretentious objects of stone, flint or chalk, some of which were certainly of profound religious significance.

Also dating from this period, the middle and late part of the fourth millennium, are the earliest-known surviving monuments to the dead. Remnants have been found of earth-covered timber mortuary houses, as at Fussell's Lodge in South Wiltshire, but many earthen long barrows had less complicated interiors than this. In the stonier regions of the country the earthen-barrow idea came to be superseded by more substantial megalithic chambered barrows. Many were used for hundreds of years before being closed and sealed in the third millennium.

In Ireland a passage-grave tradition developed, with access to a central chamber within a circular mound along a slab-lined gallery. The great tumuli of the Boyne Valley at Newgrange, Dowth and Knowth are splendid examples. In these imposing places another aspect of the prehistoric world is richly represented: megalithic art. The walls of galleries and cells, and the sides of external kerb-stones, are decorated with an extraordinary abundance of symbolic engravings—notably spirals, circles, zigzags, lozenges, cups, and cups-with-rings.

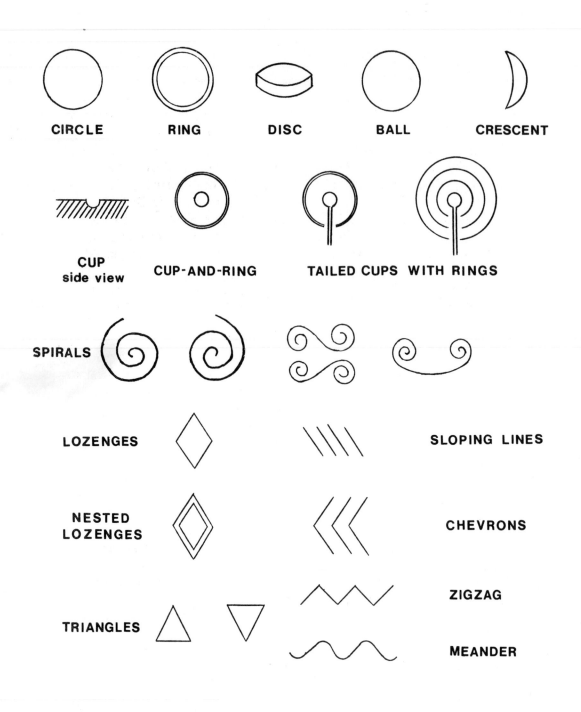

CIRCLE **RING** **DISC** **BALL** **CRESCENT**

CUP
side view **CUP-AND-RING** **TAILED CUPS WITH RINGS**

SPIRALS

LOZENGES **SLOPING LINES**

NESTED
LOZENGES **CHEVRONS**

ZIGZAG

TRIANGLES **MEANDER**

The chief symbolic elements of Neolithic art explained in this book.

What could have been the meaning of these symbols? And what significance can we attach to the *shapes* of stones (whether perforated, pointed, or rhomboid) and their arrangement in circular or imperfectly-circular rings, or in rows or as sentinels? The spiral particularly, unquestionably the most striking of stone age art motifs, remains the most baffling, and yet it may hold the key to the very heart of primitive religion. It has been found in stone age cultures all over the world, right down the ages to the present century in some—for instance in New Zealand, Oceania, Indonesia, India, Central Africa, and Indo-America. In Britain it had such tenacity that its use has persisted in some form even into our own era—despite the attempts of persecuting male-dominated religions to obliterate all memory of the spiritual environment in which the spiral had once played its essential role.

Besides their obvious preoccupation with the spiral and the circle, the Neolithic peoples left evidence of a serious study of the movements of the sun and moon. The architecture of the Irish passage-graves provides clues of early date, but there are good, though less magnificent examples in British long barrows.

At the same time as the megalithic long barrows were being constructed, monuments of another kind began to appear—the most extraordinary of all constructional feats to have scarred the prehistoric landscape. These are the mysterious linear *cursus* earthworks, some forty of which have been found in England and Wales, but in no other part of the British Isles. What possible reason could drive a community to labour for months or years on end to prepare pairs of parallel ditches and banks, often a hundred metres apart for distances of one, two or more kilometres across country, over hill and down dale and sometimes traversing deep water-courses?

The Greater Cursus at Stonehenge, almost three kilometres in length, was laboriously cut into the white chalk of Salisbury Plain through a thin layer of turf. The longest of all cursuses, in Dorset, was hacked from the chalk for a distance of ten kilometres, using nothing more than the unrefined tools of the period—chiefly stag-horns—as picks and levers. It has been estimated that its construction occupied some 450,000 man-hours.

Another mysterious undertaking of great magnitude, which must have engaged the local able-bodied work-force over a period of many years, took an estimated four million man-hours to complete. This was the raising of the gigantic mound of Silbury Hill in the territory of the Windmill Hill people at Avebury. Silbury's date, at about 2700 BC, is towards the end of the cursus-building era. It is much the biggest earthen mound thrown up by human hand in ancient times. Three excavators have been to its centre, hoping a burial might be there. But Silbury is no tomb. Just what did the excavators find there? The answer is nothing but a pile of turf—and yet the turf, which had been brought there from some distance away,

Henge and stone ring at Arbor Low in Derbyshire, third millennium BC. All the stones have fallen, including a specially arranged central group known as a cove.

was ritually consecrated and rated by the builders as meriting preservation for eternity.

Earlier than Silbury, and again in the category of ceremonial rather than burial monuments, were the first henges. These were earthworks of bank and ditch, usually circular with one or two entrances. Like the cursuses they seem to be a wholly 'British' invention. They were used over a period covering many centuries—from the mid-Neolithic to the mid- or late Bronze Age. Some 65 are known, from the south of England to Scotland, and there are others in Ireland and two or three on the part of the Continent nearest to Britain. Some of them appear featureless, as at Knowlton and Maumbury Rings (Dorset) and Marden (Wiltshire). Others were garnished with rings of standing stones, either natural boulders or quarried stones which had been hauled with toil and perseverance to the site—as at Arbor Low (Derbyshire) and Brodgar on Orkney and, above all, at Stonehenge.

What religious zeal possessed those ancient peoples to cause such prodigious works to rise? What organised power ensured their completion? What rituals and ceremonies attended their use?

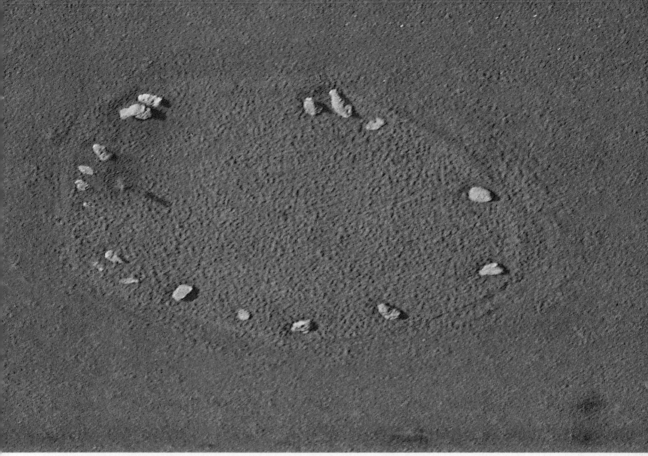

The Kingston Russell stone ring near the Dorset coast in the south of England. Its outline
is that of a 'flattened circle type B', according to Alexander Thom.

Many rings of stone had no accompanying henge—such as the Castlerigg Circle
(Cumbria), the Rollright Stones (Oxfordshire) and the Stanton Drew Circles
(Avon County). Nearly a thousand were built in the British Isles, and there are
others on the Continent. Not unexpectedly, many are *circular*. More remarkably,
the majority of those in Britain and Ireland which are *not* circular disguise a non-
circularity that is so slight as to be unnoticeable except by modern surveyors
wielding theodolites and tape-measures. Nevertheless, it is at once astonishing
and perplexing that between 4,000 and 5,000 years ago non-circular rings were
being laid out with outlines which followed good ellipses or 'egg-shapes' and yet
deviated from true circularity by such small amounts that few people could ever
tell it had been done.

How was this precision achieved? What could the intentions of the stone ring
planners and 'temple' designers have been? These problems were raised by
Alexander Thom three decades ago, and have been disputed ever since. Thom,
and later his son Archibald, insisted upon the accuracy of the surveying and
argued that the Neolithic planners must have understood the principle of the
Pythagorean triangle two thousand years before its formulation by Pythagoras,

otherwise the near-perfect ellipses, the flattened circles, and the egg-shapes could not have been prepared. Many archaeologists, however, have misgivings about this theory, although no wholly convincing argument has been offered in its place. The same applies to Thom's extraordinary claims that the megalith raisers used a fixed unit of length, which he called the megalithic yard, measuring exactly 2.722 feet. He proposed that it was in use throughout England and Scotland, but not all his colleagues have accepted the idea.

In the third millennium BC a major change took place in burial practice which left a lasting legacy on the landscape. The chambered and earthen long barrows which had been in use for hundreds of years were sealed up, and the higher-ranking dead were thereafter buried in mounds of circular shape. Known as round barrows, these earthen mounds were raised over a single burial located at the barrow's centre. Quite often, totally concealed beneath the grass-covered heap, was a circular ditch or a ring of small stones. Like the megalithic circles, these hidden rings were not always exactly circular; some were elliptical or egg-shaped and some were really flattened circles, echoing the puzzling shapes of their mightier cousins. Why should anyone trouble to mark out these geometrical designs, only to cover them over soon afterwards?

During the Neolithic period this preference for circles began to be reflected in domestic dwellings also. The previous rectangular houses were replaced by circular ones, and not until the Iron Age, more than two thousand years later in the first millennium BC, was rectangular housing reintroduced into Britain on a wide scale. Was this change dictated by strong spiritual beliefs rather than mere practicalities? What else can explain the persistence of the universal round house to the total exclusion of log-cabin and stone-wall squareness throughout part of the Neolithic and the entire British Bronze Age? On the Continent rectangular houses never gave way to round ones during this period.

The stone circles, whether true circles or ellipses, lie at the heart of the mystery, and to solve it we need to know not only *how* they were constructed, but *why*.

In itself, marking out a true circle requires no sophisticated geometrical knowledge—a single person, using a rope and stake, can mark a circle swiftly and accurately—although, to be sure, transporting ten-tonne megaliths and setting them into holes around the perimeter is another affair, entailing the co-operation of a dedicated team of enthusiasts.

So why are not all stone rings stone circles? Why, moreover, do so many of the ellipses, egg-shapes and flattened circles have such small deviations from true circularity that most people are unlikely to notice them? Is it possible that such geometrical oddities could have had any significance for the primitive societies which raised the megaliths so industriously?

The few attempts to answer this question have been unconvincing. Andrew

A series of Bronze Age round barrows on Overton Down adjoining the Sanctuary, a concentric-circle monument close to Silbury Hill and Avebury, Wiltshire.

Fleming suggested that flattened circles might have been designed to heighten the impact of ceremonies that took place in them, being more impressive for both the 'performers' and the spectators. But, again, it is plain that any improvement for the spectators would have been insignificant, the differences from circularity being virtually unnoticeable in most cases except in a carefully-sketched plan. Others proposed that non-circularity might result from attempting to mark out a circle by the judgement of eye alone, and Aubrey Burl has endorsed this idea by pointing out how imperfect is the bluestone circle of Stonehenge, a circle which could so easily have been made faultless if it had been accomplished by simple radial offsetting from the perfect outer sarsen circle. Its non-circularity seems to be evidence of the effect of using eye alone.

Alexander Thom's attempts to find answers are deficient, as Douglas Heggie's criticisms cautiously imply. Thom claims that the megalith builders may have been trying to achieve a shape whose ratio of perimeter-to-maximum diameter would be as close to 'three' as possible, whereas a true circle correlates with pi (π)—the ratio of the circumference to the diameter.

Another proposal is that non-circle geometry has the effect of creating a major axis which can be used for orientation purposes. The axis of egg-shaped Woodhenge, about two kilometres from Stonehenge, is aligned quite close to north-east/ south-west, and so has been claimed to be orientated in the direction of mid-summer sunrise. But was the orientation of the axis intentional, or did the builders merely take advantage of an accidental alignment? Looking at all non-circular megalithic rings, the orientation of every one can be explained equally well by chance as by intent, which suggests that, whatever the circumstances, there will always be some axial directions which appear to have significant alignments.

Aubrey Burl has put forward the interesting proposal that flattened circles may result from a lack of sufficient level ground to construct a true circle. He has noted some sites (Long Meg at its north-east, Castlerigg to the north-east, Swinside to the south-south-east, and Brats Hill to the north-north-west) where the flattening is at the side where the gradient alters. At Penmaenmawr (the elliptical Druid's Circle in Gwynedd) there is a flattening at the side where an ancient trackway passes close by. Such a suggestion may at first seem oversimplified compared with the mathematical complexities evolved by a professor of engineering, but in my opinion it comes closer to the reality of the past than do Thom's conjectures.

After a lifetime of work Alexander Thom concluded that the extraordinary geometrical secrets he had revealed proved that, as well as providing stone rings of particular shapes for unspecified purposes, the shapes had been constructed with the aim of expounding mathematical knowledge and demonstrating surveying skills. Wisely, however, archaeologists who are better acquainted with the level of learning and technical abilities attainable at such an early stage in the evolution of western Neolithic communities doubt that this is likely. An explanation for the mysteries of the ring-shapes must lie elsewhere.

And it does: the answer falls beyond the bounds of conventional archaeological study and lies outside the expertise of astronomers, too. In fact, the solution belongs to the realm of the life-supporting, environmental science of *meteorology*—that often-neglected non-life discipline whose atmospheric components synthesise to produce the most impressive of natural phenomena which were, nonetheless, for the vulnerable, weather-dependent farmers of ancient Britain and Ireland at once needful and alarming.

Throughout agricultural history the weather has played an eternally ambivalent role in human lives—one day bestowing the benefits of gentle rain and sunshine, the next day unleashing harm and destruction through wind and flood. The atmosphere was the realm of the gods intermediate between sky and earth.

'Thro' all the circle of the golden year' (as Tennyson put it) the atmosphere brought the clouds and the rain—and it bore the storm and the whirlwind, conflicting manifestations of a loving and vengeful deity.

2

The Spiralling Whirlwind

The Neolithic newcomers to the British Isles, pioneers of agriculture on the backbreaking virgin land, found themselves at the mercy of a temperate maritime climate. The forests, chiefly of oak, ash and elm, had to be cleared, small areas at a time, using fire and basic tools fashioned chiefly from stone, bone and wood. The easiest land was farmed at the outset, generally upon the lighter, well-drained soils of the higher plains and slopes where the vegetation was also less dense.

Although the climate was better than it is now, the difference was not that great. From about 6500 BC to 4000 BC there had been a post-glacial warming phase called the Atlantic, by the end of which deciduous trees were growing even at altitudes of 750 metres above sea level where none grow today. But from around 4000 BC annual mean temperatures fell to approach levels that were, at best, no more than a couple of degrees Celsius above the averages of today—and they remained so until about 1400 BC.

For Neolithic and Early Bronze Age Britain, especially in the north, there was rather less cloud, rather more sunshine and probably a little less rainfall than we are familiar with in our own century. It is probable that in England and Wales the climate of this period, known as the Sub-Boreal, may have resembled that of the northern third of France as it is today.

After 1400 BC, from the Middle to Late Bronze Age, there was a noticeable deterioration in the climate, with less sunshine and more dampness. This led to the gradual spread and deepening of peat on the western and northern moors of Britain and Ireland, and explains why, long after their abandonment, so many of the Scottish and Irish megalithic structures came to be submerged beneath deep layers of peat. This climatic period continues to the present day and is known as the Sub-Atlantic.

Whatever the average weather in those times, there would always have occurred, as nowadays, the familiar vagaries of the elements and their occasional extremes. We know too well the dismal sequence: flood, drought, heat, cold, snow, hail, gales, thunderstorms—with damage to crops and endless suffering for frail humankind in the struggle for survival. Because of primitive housing, combined with the inescapable dampness and frequent exposure to the elements, life must have been harsh and life-spans short. Studies of skeletal remains taken from grave barrows, ditches or pits, especially on the chalk hill areas, show that even the leading members of society suffered and died from rickets, osteoarthritis and osteoporosis, some at an early age.

The weather must have been a constant source of anxiety for the peasants of these agrarian communities—much as it is for the farmers of today, particularly those who toil in the world's more arid zones. They must have monitored the weather daily, for it governed their lives and regulated their futures. This period probably saw the birth of weather lore as we know it and the prediction of local trends and changes. Fears of crop and stock failures must have been an everyday concern, especially as, with the passage of time, the crude farming methods caused a progressive impoverishment of the once-rich soil; as part of this there would have developed an awareness of deities who must be placated to ensure abundant harvests and fertile breeding stocks.

The air and the sky, from which the weather came, were the obvious abodes of the gods, and the movements of sun, moon and stars would have been closely monitored. It was chiefly because of its changing shape and its monthly cycle, so similar in period to that of women, that the moon early acquired a mystical character associated with femininity, which led sooner or later to its securing the status of goddess, and the Moon Goddess came to receive devout recognition from primitive societies worldwide. However, she was but one manifestation of a universal and more resplendent female divinity known as the Great Goddess.

The moon's ascendancy into spiritual thought seems to have begun in the Upper Palaeolithic period and lasted through the Neolithic, but the major advance toward civilisation which came in the Neolithic—that of farming—directed people's attentions, more than ever before, to the soil of Earth. So, within the all-embracing scope of Goddess worship an increasing reverence came to be reserved for Earth itself, a devotion which was manifested through the concept of an Earth Mother who in turn became a major part of the Great Goddess triad.

Despite the authority wielded by these female divinities, there is also evidence for the existence of a parallel although unequal force in the masculine divine sphere. A bull-cult seems to have prevailed in ancient Britain, associated with the Sky God as well as the Great Goddess, and it is not hard to see how the idea of 'marriage' between Sky God and Earth Goddess was arrived at, and came to be proclaimed as the origin of all that was luxuriant and bountiful in the universe. This tender and serene theme of a Divine Cosmic Marriage lies at the heart of this book.

Separating Earth from the celestial vault is the zone of the atmosphere. As the medium of life-sustaining air it was valued as the bearer of the 'creative breath of life'. Air (and hence wind and storm) was, like fire, active and masculine, whereas water and earth were passive and feminine. The air transported the clouds and brought the rain; the clouds tempered the scorching sun; the rain nourished the thirsty crops.

These very elements provided the means by which the gods could descend to the plane of man's habitat on Earth—for instance the storm god arrived by the clouds at the time of the thunderstorm and the 'great whirlwind' or tornado, accompanied by flooding rain and hail. Mystical evidence for this survives in later religious practices and folklore. Neolithic society, at least in the countries of north-western Europe, was obsessed with the role played by the atmospheric elements in mortal life, and the element claiming a considerable mystical attention was the whirlwind.

Whirlwinds have occurred in the earth's atmosphere since time immemorial. They must have been regarded by those early farmers not just with curiosity and puzzlement but with mistrust, from the first time they influenced or endangered their lives or livelihood in any way.

There are many conditions under which whirlwinds can form, and several distinct types have been recognised, but the Neolithic people would have been aware of two kinds: those of a peaceful disposition, and those which were manifestly violent. The most placid whirlwinds appear to be little more than inoffensive, frolicsome imps. They announce their arrival on a quiet summer's day with a rush of wind and whirling mischief, invariably provoking surprise if not alarm in the minds of unforewarned bystanders. In total contrast, the most turbulent whirlwinds descend from storm clouds in the form of twisting waterspouts and tornadoes; they portend rough weather and are potential sources of total destruction to life and property.

Whether the whirlwind is the innocuous species or whether it erupts as the palpably dangerous kind, it is even today regarded with a mixture of awe, suspicion and foreboding. It is no wonder that in prehistoric times, in societies imbued with the sense of an all-pervading divine influence, it was nothing less than a spectacle to be marvelled at and feared. Whirlwinds were accorded a substantial degree of respect and acts of propitiation were performed in their honour.

The heart and core of a whirlwind is a spiralling column of air ascending in rapid motion. Buoyant air, a result of the sun's heat warming the ground and the layers of air closest to it, is drawn into the base of the rotating air column from every direction. When the air temperature increases, its density falls. This destabilises the heated air nearest the ground so that it acquires an ever-increasing tendency to move upwards. But not for long can warm air underlie the heavier, cooler air above. What normally happens is that a thermal plume of warm convective air develops, and a balance is maintained as air lost by convection is replenished at ground level with supplies from the surrounding air-mass. Sometimes the plume sports a white cumulus cloud at its summit, which drifts away to be followed by others, so that together they resemble a line of sheep on a mountain path. In this airborne age, glider and hang-glider enthusiasts profit from their practical under-standing of the benefits of rising columns of light air, in the way that soaring birds have always done.

When a thermal starts rotating, a fair-weather whirlwind bursts into life. The gyratory motion usually begins in the in-flowing warm-air layer at ground level; the effect of the rotation then winds its way up the thermal plume. Its beauty emerges when sufficient dust, sand, smoke or debris is drawn into the perimeter where the airflow is fastest and is carried upwards in visible concentrations. This type of whirlwind is popularly called a 'devil', with the appropriate qualification of dust, sand, or what have you. An impressive photograph of a 'dust-devil' whirlwind, taken in Jersey in July 1984, appears on the opposite page.

Eyewitness accounts of thousands of devil whirlwinds have been assembled by the Tornado and Storm Research Organisation, and are catalogued in its library. This has enabled the organisation to examine the formation and life-and-decay characteristics of devil whirlwinds. In typical British summer conditions fair-weather whirlwinds last from a few seconds to a few minutes. In the desert regions of the world the superheating of the air-layers at ground level can be so great as to induce much longer-lived, even dangerously boisterous, whirlwinds under a clear sky. In such conditions quite minor variations in the landscape are enough to trigger local gyrations of the inflowing air. The result is a towering pillar, or more precisely a hollow tube, of spiralling dust which, in the arid zones of America, Africa, Asia and Australia can persist for long periods of time. There are occasions when these lofty dust-devils or sand-devils impress eyewitnesses by standing in one place, sometimes for hours on end. But more often they are to be seen traversing the ground with a stately allure at a pace about equal to that of the

A whirlwind with a well-defined cylindrical column. These natural atmospheric vortices were objects of fear and reverence in prehistoric times, and even today attract the wonder of passers-by. *Photograph by Mary R. Shaw at Jersey*

prevailing wind of the day. They can rotate in either direction, clockwise or counterclockwise.

Devil whirlwinds are sometimes silent, sometimes noisy. They are most eerie when invisible yet accompanied by an unearthly sound which has been variously described by witnesses as humming, buzzing, swishing, rushing, rustling, screaming or roaring. The noise originates from internal electric-discharge effects, because whirlwinds are electrostatic generators. Whirlwinds of this type cannot develop at night, but if they did it is probable they would emit a feeble glow of light.

The belief that devil whirlwinds were the embodiment of a spirit was common in many parts of the world until fairly recently. The Arabs regarded a sand-devil as the flight of an evil djinn, while Irish peasantry believed whirlwinds marked the passage of fairies or spirits who were undertaking a journey. Similar ideas once prevailed in Scotland, England, France and the remainder of Europe. Indeed, so many sources could be cited for this widespread belief that it is clearly of very ancient origin.

The impulse of the nineteenth-century Russian peasant to destroy the whirlwind—said to be 'wizard wrought'—by hurling his hatchet at it suggests a degenerate survival from prehistoric times, when the axe was the guardian instrument of spiritual people, being emblematic of the omnipotent Sky God of the Indo-Europeans and long before that of the Neolithic Great Goddess. A similar gesture was formerly made by sailors who cast a spell when they sighted a waterspout and made as if to cut it with a black-handled knife. Breton peasants used to hurl a knife or fork at a whirlwind, whilst those of eastern Europe threw a knife or a hat.

Again and again in folklore and in popular usage throughout the world the devil whirlwind is depicted as mischievous, if not malevolent, and linked to the presence of spirits of the dead, for it was a sign not only of aerial spirits but of those from the netherworld as well.

How does a typical whirlwind behave? The following account appeared in an Irish newspaper, the *Western Journal*, on 1 July, 1977, and gives a good description of a 'fairy breeze' as it is still called:

> That curious summer phenomenon, the fairy breeze, cursed by farmers because of the playful way in which it whisks cocks of hay skyward, brought astonishment to the faces of residents in McHale Road, Castlebar, at 2.45 p.m. on Thursday. One moment it was calm and humid, and then a dense cloud of choking dust was seen to hover around the Bacon Factory before advancing as far as O'Malley's Supermarket, sending pedestrians scurrying for shelter and residents scuttling to conceal doors and windows. Finally, the dust cloud reversed its course midway down the street, gathering even more dust from dry topsoil on the newly-made embankments in McHale Park.

Another recent Irish report of a whirlwind, dated 1985, gives the name *Si Gaol* as the Gaelic for this so-called 'fairy wind'.

In her book *The Gobi Desert*, Mildred Cable paints a vivid picture of the rotational characteristics of dust-devils:

Travellers call them dust-spouts from their likeness to an ocean water-spout, but the desert dweller, certain that these waterless places are peopled by *kwei* (demons), calls them dust-demons. The pillar of sand gives the impression of an invisible being daintily folding a garment of dust round its invisible form. Some whirl from left to right, and some from right to left. 'This one is the male and that one the female kwei,' said the men; 'you can distinguish them by the way they fold the dust cloak round them, right to left and left to right; see how they come in pairs.'

For people caught unawares the passage of devil whirlwinds can be menacing, and must have been more so in earlier god-fearing centuries than now. A story from the *London Magazine* of 1748 describes the panic that could ensue:

Sat., July 2: About two in the afternoon, a whirlwind carried off from a field at Fenham, near Newcastle, nine or ten cocks of hay, in about a quarter of an hour, in sight of several spectators, who say that the whirlwind came from the S.E. corner of the field, and went to the N.E. and lifted each of the cocks entire as high as St. Nicholas's steeple, when they were observed to break and disperse in small pieces. Several women rakers were in the field at the time, who being terribly frighted shriek'd out and run off; the day was quite calm before it happen'd.

It must be remembered that devils and fair-weather whirlwinds are completely invisible unless, or until, something movable is touched, because cloudfree air is nothing but a transparent gaseous medium. The vast majority are never seen, but if one is close enough, at least some of them can be heard, as mentioned earlier.

Most devilish whirlwinds are of the mobile, venturesome type, which meander about like blithe spirits in otherwise tranquil weather conditions in the presence of a gentle wind-of-the-day. I did, however, indicate at the start of this discussion that conditions can exist under which whirlwinds are able to stand still. An account from Sussex illustrates what happens:

This afternoon (Aug 6), about 4 o'clock, the hay was being turned in one of our fields when that close to a worker *began to whirl round in an increasing circle until the whole of the crop within an area of 30 feet was lifted up to a height of over 100 feet. It ascended in a spiral*, but afterwards spread out, resembling a small cloud, as it disappeared in the distance. [The italics are mine.]

The way the gyrations began is worth noting—at a centre and across a steadily widening circular area until a diameter of some ten metres (30 feet) was reached. Apart from the immediate vicinity of the whirlwind atmospheric conditions must have been calm, or nearly so, at ground level. In general it can be said that whirlwinds are able to retain their ground positions without becoming travelling devils in the presence of a wind-field that is below 1.4 metres per second (three miles per hour). In recent years similar standing whirlwinds have been observed and recorded in many counties of the British Isles.

A more spectacular example was seen by Mr and Mrs Ganter in Cumbria on 13 August, 1976:

> . . . a monstrous slow-motion sort of whirlwind about 50 yards across, slowly whirling up countless wisps and bundles of straw to a most colossal height in the sky. No matter how high one looked there were always ever-smaller bits still higher up. No breeze at all where we were, about two fields away. After an hour or two, during which we went to Ardee and back, we found that straw was still falling in the same place, and it continued for another hour or so.

This description conveys the stillness of the overall air mass, the consequence of the strong anticyclone which was so persistent in the year of Britain's greatest drought of the century.

A good many of the fair-weather whirlwind diameters reported for the British Isles span the range two to 50 metres. Bigger ones are described once in a while. The biggest diameter whirlwind described in any communication to the Tornado and Storm Research Organisation was almost 200 metres.

Another fundamental and significant characteristic of fair-weather whirlwind activity is the irrefutable, arresting observation that quasi-stationary whirlwinds sweep out a practically clear circular area from the field of grass or hay which they assault. When this happens in connection with an uncut cereal crop, the crop receives a circular impression of damage whose shape is akin to that of a dish, or more accurately that of a 'cup'. Still more significant are those astounding occasions when the swirling air at ground-level leaves a spiral pattern in the field of grass or corn. When this is the result of spiral inflow into a thermal or eddy whirlwind, patterns made in grass are generally short-lived because the grass soon regains its normal upright stance.

A photograph in *Weather* some years ago, taken in Suffolk while a whirlwind was in action, showed such an impression caused by the anticlockwise inflow of air over a grass surface. A more recent photograph of a circular impression formed by a summer whirlwind at Pucklechurch, near Bristol, was reproduced in *The Journal of Meteorology*. The investigator, Peter Rendall, concluded that the anticlockwise swirl had been caused by the *descent* of air. This implies that the up-spinning thermal whirlwind had suffered a phenomenon known to fluid-flow experts as 'vortex breakdown', or had reformed into a spherical vortex like the one witnessed by Jackie Pearson on Roundway Hill in Wiltshire in July 1989, and interpreted by George Bathurst as a Hill's spherical vortex.

There is, however, another up-spinning vortex phenomenon—of the lee-eddy type—which develops naturally in the atmosphere, by night or by day, and under certain critical conditions creates spiral patterns of the most exquisite beauty in crops or grass. These ground patterns display perfectly the effects of spiral *outflow* when the up-spinning vortex gives way to the outward swirling of a parcel of *descending* air. Spiral patterns of this type have been studied in recent years in crops of many kinds, ranging from cereals, rape, rice, beans, and mustard to root crops (sugar beet, potatoes) and grass. The spirality is daintily and methodically described by the recumbent stalks, and, even to the modern eye, is aesthetically pleasing, although completely mystifying. Neolithic people, however, could well have fancied the spiral-circles to be the work and signs of passing spirits issuing from the womb of the Great Goddess.

3

The Circles Effect

It is only since 1980 that scientists have become aware of the exceptional meteorological phenomenon distinguished by the forced *descent* of a spinning volume of air which leads to a spiral-centred circular mark on the ground or in a standing crop.

Recent research has shown that the motion originates from air currents overhead, most commonly the result of a species of eddy vortex or trailing-vortex system generated by airflow across hills or rugged terrain. Once triggered, a parcel of air, rotating about a vertical axis, strikes downwards, the airflow being in the opposite direction to the rising currents experienced in conventional whirlwinds. Eventually the vortex, which may have the character of a ring or sphere, hits the ground and reveals itself by creating a pattern of circular-symmetric damage, the details of which depend upon the nature of the substance obstructing its path. The most impressive spectacle for the bystander appears when the vortex strikes a growing crop. This is known as the 'circles effect'.

New though the discovery is to meteorological science, the circles effect in crops and grass was undoubtedly a familiar sight to the men and women who toiled the ancient fields of Britain in the Neolithic and Bronze Ages between 4000 and 1000 BC—and to farmers in the circle-prone areas ever since.

The first case of this type to be studied scientifically was found in a field of oats at

Bratton, Wiltshire, in July 1980. It was the first of more than a thousand circles which I had personally investigated by September 1990. All occurrences of this type (totalling 1,700 circles worldwide) are now monitored, surveyed and catalogued by the Circles Effect Research Unit (CERES) of the Tornado and Storm Research Organisation. The name CERES is particularly appropriate, since it was also that of the Roman Goddess of Fertility and Agriculture. She bore an ear of corn and a phallus-like column as her emblems.

The unusual damage to the crop is the result of the stalks being bent over and pressed hard against the ground. They follow a spiral path outwards from a centre and continue until the sharp cut-off is reached at the perimeter. Because of the circular symmetry of the spinning volume of air, under ideal conditions the perimeter of the damaged area is also circular.

Apart from the circular shape, obvious even from a distance, the most distinctive feature is the beautiful, yet mathematically complex, outward-swirling spiral. Spirals have a hypnotic effect on the eye, drawing it in decreasing circles towards the centre; and then back out again—and in again—in alternating rhythms.

Of all the basic symbols associated with archaic times and primitive beliefs, the spiral is the most difficult to draw well, yet it came to dominate the art motifs and megalithic inscriptions of the first agriculturalists, and so well has it survived the passage of time, carved into the hard mineral of stones and rock faces, that five thousand years later we are still able to study and admire it. The deep mysticism of its simple, single line motivated those early farmers to Herculean feats, causing them to move megaliths and mountains; and they found their inspiration in the hard-won crops and the grass-fields of their own landscape, where Mother Nature—a loving, fertile aspect of the universal Great Goddess—drew her entrancing spirals for the wonder and veneration of the pious.

Spirals, as we have seen, may rotate in either a clockwise or an anticlockwise direction. During my investigations of crop-damaged circles in Wessex in 1987, I recorded a total of 73 circles and actually visited and surveyed 66 of them; 36 were anticlockwise and 30 clockwise. In 1988 113 circles were archived, of which 52 were clockwise and 35 anticlockwise. For 1989 the number of known circles in Britain totalled 308, and in 1990 there were more than 700, roughly equally divided between clockwise and anticlockwise examples.

The most rewarding spiral-circles to study are those formed in cereal crops—wheat, barley, rye and oats—and they are also the most common; but similar circles have been reported in recent years from fields of rape, beans, mustard, spinach, maize, tobacco, rice, sugar beet and potatoes. Others have been found in reed beds and in grass, but the pliable blades of grass quickly recover, within a few days as a rule, whereas the stalks of cereals retain evidence of the flattening spiralled effect until harvesting time.

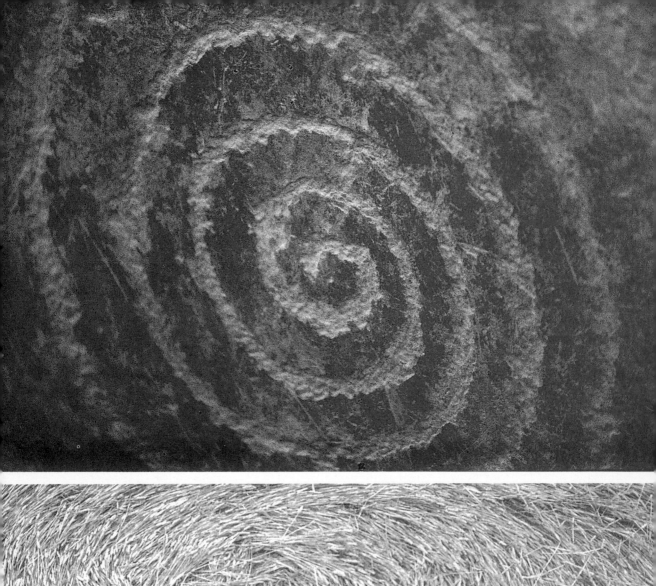
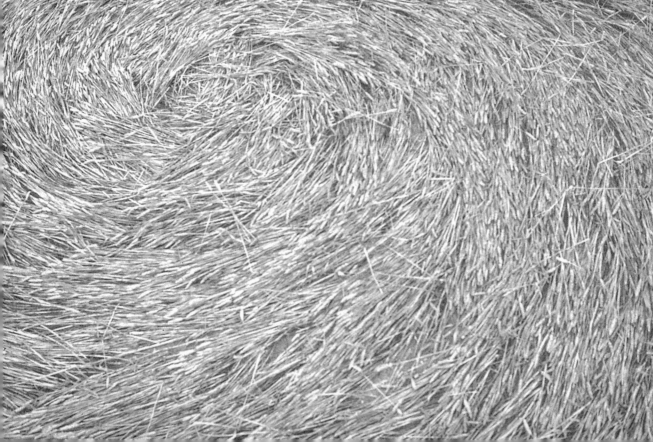

Opposite, above: The eye-catching spiral. This detail from a kerbstone at Knowth (fourth millennium BC) shows that the technique used was hammering of stone upon stone.

Opposite, below: Detail of the strong, spiralling, outward flow found in natural crop circles. This clockwise example with sharp-edged perimeter was photographed at Bratton, Wiltshire, in 1987.

Above: An anticlockwise spiralled crop circle in wheat, also from Bratton.

A number of eyewitnesses have recorded descriptions of spiral-circle formation in daylight hours. The first to come to my attention, of a sighting made near Warminster, Wiltshire, over grass, dates from the 1970s.

One evening there were about 50 of us sky-watching along the Salisbury Road. Suddenly, the grass began to sway before our eyes and laid itself flat in a clockwise spiral, just like the opening of a lady's fan. A perfect circle was completed in less than half a minute, all the time accompanied by a high-pitched humming sound. It was still there the next day.

This is precisely the kind of happening which would have awed the ancient observer. Unlike the population of today, everyone in those remote times inhabited the countryside, and the herdsmen and crop-growers would have had every opportunity to witness such events. Their working day was dictated by the sun, from dawn to dusk, and they would have been greatly alarmed by the vision of a spiral-centred circle flattening itself in their laboriously-prepared crops of emmer wheat or barley.

A recent witness to a similar circle-forming feat was Ray Barnes, who watched while a huge spiral-centred circle, more than 30 metres in diameter, appeared before him in a ripe cereal crop at Westbury, Wiltshire, one summer's evening. The whole process, which took only some four to five seconds, was accompanied by a steady humming sound.

Another witness watched on horseback as a spiral-circle appeared in a field of ripe wheat late one sunny evening in August 1983. It happened on the slopes of an elevated dry valley near Great Cheverell Hill, part of the Westbury–Lavington escarpment of western Salisbury Plain. The observer, Melvyn Bell, was fifty metres from the invisible vortex as it spiralled dust, dirt and debris into the air, and it was only a matter of seconds before a ten- to twelve-metre circle had been flattened into the wheat. Like all the other crop circles, its perimeter sharply delineated the clockwise spiral bed from the upright standing corn.

A fourth eyewitness, near Dundee in Scotland, was out at dawn in August 1989 when, only 15 metres away, he heard a peculiar sound and 'quite suddenly the crop went flat over a circular region estimated as 15–18 metres across'. In all, CERES has listed more than a dozen good eye-witness accounts of crop circle formation by natural means.

On 16 June, 1988, vortices of a similar character, three in all, were witnessed in the parish of Avebury in a field of wheat one-and-a-half kilometres south-west of Windmill Hill. These short-lived vortices, seen by a farm-hand in the humid air of early morning, were made visible by the sudden condensation of fog- or cloud-droplets in the envelopes and spinning cores. If interpreted as ghosts of the dead or as divine emissaries, the land would have been deemed truly sanctified by the fearful believers who farmed these fields in ancient times. Such visions may have been a relatively common occurrence near Windmill Hill, and some may have been nocturnal rather than daytime occurrences, in which case the spectacle would have been no less astounding—and prodigious.

It is because of the electrical effects accompanying these vortices that night-time events are sometimes, perhaps often, luminous. Two such occurrences were observed quite recently.

On 29 June, 1989, an orange-coloured ball of light over ten metres in diameter was seen descending into a field of wheat south of Silbury Hill. The next morning a 15-metre diameter spiral-centred clockwise circle was found at that exact spot. Two months later, near Manston in Kent, a spiralling vortex of flashing light landed in a field of wheat and extinguished itself. Immediate inspection revealed an 18-metre diameter anticlockwise spiral circle on the precise spot.

Such extraordinary happenings are regarded with awe even in today's educated world. Similar events in historical times were ascribed either to the work of angels—for example, the religious visions reported in the mountainous region near Fatima, Portugal, in April 1917—or to the devil, as this next case, taken from a contemporary pamphlet, shows.

In the year 1678 in Hertfordshire, the night after a rich farmer had fallen out with a poor reaper over the price to be paid for harvesting his oats, several passers-by noted the 'field of oats . . . to be all of a flame'. In the morning this was reported to the farmer who 'no sooner arriv'd at the place where his Oats grew, but to his Admiration he found the Crop was cut down ready to his hands; and as if the Devil had a mind to shew his dexterity in the art of Husbandry, and scorn'd to mow them after the usual manner, he cut them in round circles, and plac't every straw with that exactness that it would have taken up above an Age for any Man to perform what he did that one night.'

The seventeenth-century publisher's illustration of the devil at work (p. 42) leaves little doubt that these were the result of spiralling vortices.

Unlike thermally-generated whirlwinds, therefore, the atmospheric vortices which give birth to the majority of spiral-circles are not related to specifically diurnal effects such as the sun's heat. As they have been known to form on cloudy days and wet days as well as under sunny conditions, it follows that they must originate as a 'forced wind'—in other words, the source of energy is some coexisting wind-system arriving from elsewhere.

Whereas crop-damaged circles have so far been found only in the spring and summer months, from April to September, this is chiefly because these are the only months in Britain when the cereal stalks are sufficiently strong for vortex-induced damage to be lasting and so permit later discovery. Evidence suggests that the spiral-making vortices are able to occur all the year round, although they are likely to be much more frequent in the summer months. In winter they have been seen over snow-covered surfaces.

Spiral-centred crop circles are often found near escarpments, usually below but sometimes above them. This indicates that an eddy effect on the lee side of the edge of the hill is responsible, and confirmation has come through numerous well-documented cases describing prevailing weather conditions at the time of circle formation. These include the appearance of circles close to isolated conical hills, as for instance the round chalk hill in Wiltshire called Cley Hill, with its Iron Age fort and two Bronze Age round barrows. Research by Andrew Hewitt, David Reynolds and myself has shown that 85–90 per cent of all circles occur within two kilometres of hilltops.

THE MOWING-DEVIL:
OR, STRANGE NEWS OUT OF HARTFORD-SHIRE.

Being a True Relation of a Farmer, who Bargaining with a Poor Mower, about the Cutting down Three Half Acres of Oats: upon the Mower's asking too much, the Farmer swore *That the Devil should Mow it rather than He.* And so it fell out, that very Night, the Crop of Oat shew'd as if it had been all of a Flame; but next Morning appear'd so neatly mow'd by the Devil or some Infernal Spirit, that no Mortal Man was able to do the like.

Also, How the said Oats ly now in the Field, and the Owner has not Power to fetch them away.

Licensed, August 22nd, 1678.

The Mowing Devil. The front page of a pamphlet written in August 1678 concerning a dispute between a Hertfordshire farmer and a mower and the subsequent arrival of crop circles on the farmer's land. In those days any such happenings were ascribed to the work of the devil, so it is ironic that the word 'devil', invented by the Christian Church to account for earthly evil and obscure happenings and disasters, is traceable back to the Sanskrit *devi* meaning goddess, a sense which it has to this day for the Hindus.

The escarpment of Salisbury Plain showing the Westbury White Horse and spiral crop circles in the wheatfields below. On the right, within the ramparts of Bratton Iron Age hillfort, is a Neolithic long barrow.

The work of CERES, together with meteorological evidence concerning airflow over isolated hills, proves that eddy-induced vortices can develop even at considerable distances from the hills themselves. In one verified case in July 1989, at Aylesbury, circle-making vortices formed on the plain six kilometres downwind of the creator-hill in the Chilterns.

This allows one to understand how any undulating landscape may trigger such activity, not just in the vicinity but well beyond, where the topography is less uneven; and how eddy effects, caused by distant variations in topography, must be the best explanation for the fair-weather formation of whirling vortices over lakes and over the sea near coasts. This type of vortex system appears to be formed in stable layers of airflow, and a subsequent breakdown or other change in airflow causes a ground-seeking ring-vortex or spherical vortex to damage the crop, leaving its tell-tale circle. I should emphasise that spiral-circle traces are capable of appearing anywhere that vortices form, and that on occasion freak conditions of the atmosphere do give rise to such phenomena even in flat areas where there are no hills.

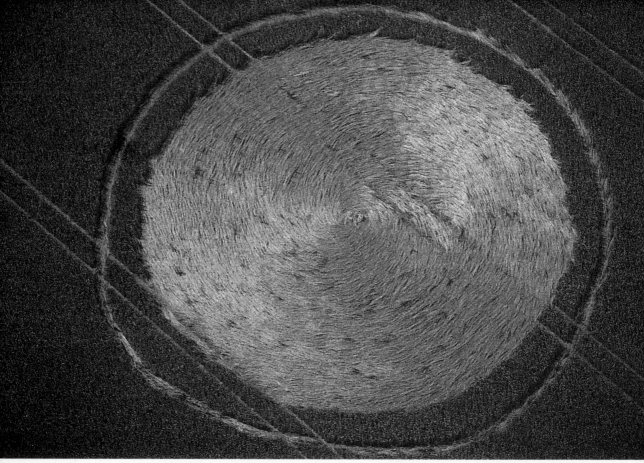

A ringed spiral-circle at Beckhampton, Avebury, in 1989. Main circle diameter 32 metres (104 feet), overall diameter 39 metres (127 feet).

The fast-spinning vortices are also known to emit a humming noise, besides appearing luminous at night—manifestations which must surely have had a profound effect on the spiritually-susceptible bystanders of Neolithic and Bronze Age times.

Multiple sets of circles are occasionally found. They may be formed simultaneously, or within seconds, minutes or days of each other. Interrelated groups of up to ten are known, and some circles may have outer rings as well—sometimes as many as four in perfect formation. Single circles range from one metre diameter to 61 metres, with ringed ones reaching a diameter of 95 metres and bigger ones thought to be awaiting discovery.

There are two other significant points about circle shapes. The first is that, whereas the spiral centre is sometimes located at the geometrical centre of the circle, this is not always so. Even with a perfectly regular, circular circumference the spiral focus may be slightly off-centre, and on most occasions close inspection and exact measurement prove that this is the result of the spiral centre drifting from its starting position.

The circumference of the anti-clockwise circle found at Headbourne Worthy in

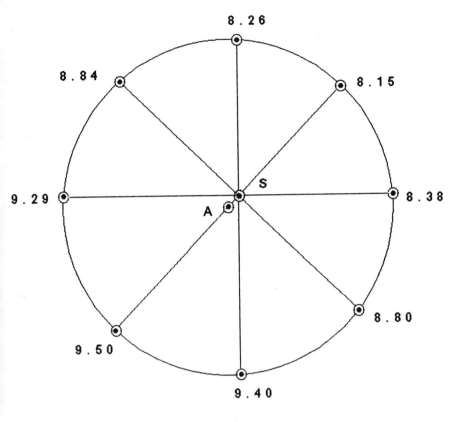

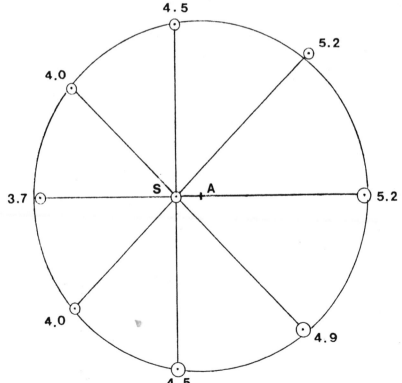

Above: A near-perfect circle, diameter 17.66 ± 0.02 m, formed in Hampshire in 1986. The spiral centre S, to which my eight survey points were directed, is displaced a distance of 800 mm from the geometrical centre A. The circle of radius 8.83 m is centred on A.

Below: A nine-metre anticlockwise spiral-circle at Beckhampton, Avebury, 1987. The survey points were directed to the spiral centre S which proved to be displaced 700 mm from the geometrical centre A.

Hampshire in August 1986 was precisely circular; the mean of eight measurements gave a diameter of 17.66 ± 0.02 metres, and yet the spiral centre to which the eight measurements were made was offset from the geometrical centre by 0.80 metres. At an anticlockwise single circle surveyed in 1987 at Beckhampton, near Avebury, the spiral centre was displaced 0.70 metres from the centre of the nine-metre diameter circle. (See diagram p. 45.)

The second important discovery is that many of the so-called circles are not circles at all: they are better classified as ellipses, egg-shapes, flattened circles, and hybrids of these.

The *simple ellipse* can best be described through the example of a spiral-circle found on Beckhampton Down in Wiltshire. A plan is given opposite.

Next, we come to the *egg-shape*. In his various publications on the shapes of megalithic circles Alexander Thom introduced two basic forms for the egg, calling them Types I and II. Examples of each type of egg-shape are also found in natural spiral-circles. The first is sketched in the diagram opposite, from measurements taken from a ringed circle at Bratton in 1986, and a Type II egg, drawn from a spiral-circle discovered in Wiltshire in 1985, is shown bottom left.

The last specific shape is the *flattened circle*, for which Thom identified three types. A Type A circle, based on a spiral-circle found in a wheatfield near Avebury in 1987, is shown in the fourth diagram. As with the egg-shapes and ellipse above, the geometrical construction for the flattened circle followed precisely the method adopted by Thom.

Hybrids or imperfect circles are common too, as exemplified by the quasi-circle of the last drawing on p. 45. In this case a circle of radius 4.5 metres, diameter 9.0 metres, passes through six of the eight survey points given a tolerance of ± 0.1 metres, or all of them if a deviation of ± 0.2 metres is permissible (and in prehistoric times it is doubtful whether this would have mattered).

Scientists trained in physics and meteorology have no difficulty in understanding vortex-circles and rings, but some non-scientists have attempted to explain spiral-circle formation in terms of paranormal phenomena. This in itself is interesting, because of the insight it gives into the minds of people of the Neolithic Age. This reaction to the inexplicable has an unconscious basis in the psychology of the circular form, which is an innate symbol of the Self and expresses the totality of the psyche and one's ultimate state of unity with the cosmos. Indeed, the psychologist Carl Jung suggested that the circular form of some 'Flying Saucer' or UFO visions could be a fantasy projection of a psychic content of wholeness. However, the spiral-circles in the farmer's crops—and the globular electrified vortices that produce them—are real enough, although spiritually-minded people desirous of mystical solutions may be propelled unknowingly by the psychic symbolism of the circle to suggest that these phenomena have paranormal origins.

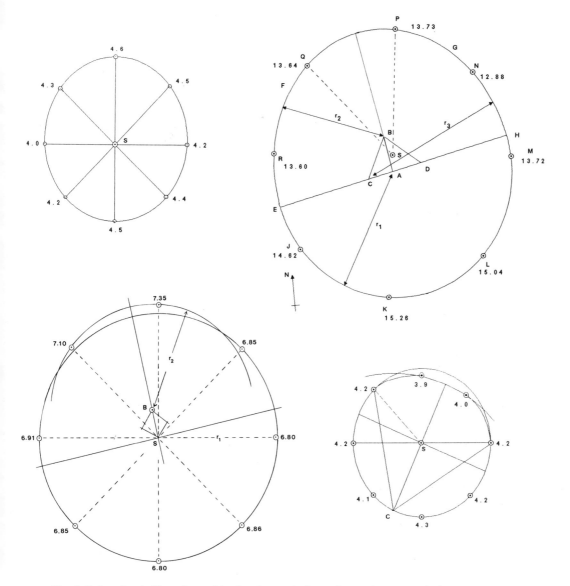

Top left: A natural ellipse formed by the descent of a vortex on to a crop of wheat at Beckhampton, Avebury, 1987. S is the spiral centre from which I measured my survey points. *Top right:* A natural egg formed by a whirling vortex striking a wheatfield at Bratton in June 1986 and spinning out a spiral. Superimposed on my survey points (relative to the spiral centre S) is the Type I geometrical construction initiated by Alexander Thom. Axial lengths are 29.2 and 27.2 metres. The arcs of four circles (centres A, B, C, and D) make up this figure. *Below left:* An egg-shaped spiral-circle of Type II, surveyed in Wiltshire in June 1985. The egg is based on a principal radius of 6.85 $\pm$ 0.06 m, centre S (the spiral-centre) and a subsidiary circle of 5.80 m radius, centre B. The axial lengths are 14.2 and 13.7 m. This remarkable shape resulted naturally from atmospheric motions interacting with the crop. *Below right:* A spiral-circle of the 'flattened-circle type', found in a wheatfield near Avebury in 1987, upon which is superimposed Thom's geometrical construction for a Type A flattened circle (measurements in metres from the spiral centre S). The main circle has a radius of 4.2 m; the flattened arc centre C has a radius of 8.0 m.

The reasons for devoting so much space to the formation of crop circles must by now be apparent. Research has shown that most vortex-flattened areas in corn-fields appear to be circular. To the eye few are obviously non-circular but careful measurement reveals that many of the shapes, when they are not circles, are not just imperfect circles either. They are usually better described by other geometrical forms—at least to within a degree of accuracy similar to that accorded by Alexander Thom and his followers to stone-circle design. There is field-based evidence of naturally-formed rings whose shapes, to use the terminology of Alexander Thom, are circles, ellipses, egg-shapes, and flattened circles, ranging in diameter from as little as one metre to nearly a hundred metres. Moreover, the greatest reported diameter for any standing whirlwind in Britain has been estimated as close to two hundred metres. If we consider the locations of all known stationary vortices of atmospheric origin, we can rightly say that every part of the British Isles is represented.

This leads to an inescapable conclusion: that whirlwinds, whirling vortices and their spiral-circles are as ubiquitous in the British Isles as are the ancient stone circles, the round barrows and the round cairns. The shapes correspond and the sizes harmonise. Our spiritual ancestors solemnly initiated an enterprising scheme, monumental in concept and execution, which would endure for eternity, but whose secrets would vanish with the last worshippers of their age.

Their age was the Age of the Megalithic Rings.

4

The Mark of the Goddess

The Neolithic farmers knew their fields intimately. They venerated their land as only a primitive agrarian society could—through devout worship of a Great Goddess, whose rule of Heaven, as of Earth, regulated both wild and cultivated life of all species. In her guise as Earth Mother she possessed all the virtues of a maternally sustaining body; she was the origin of all life and its nourishment, commanding the fertility of crops, and animals, and women. She was the divine archetype, universal to all peoples regardless of her local name.

She created life from her own substance, and at death re-absorbed the flesh into her body. Hence the Great Goddess had the power to regenerate life from the dead. Death was seen as a rebirth, founded on the belief that life would return—as it does to sown seed—although not necessarily on earth but in an eternal after-life. It was from her abode, and by her grace, that spirits could rise from the dead. For it was universally understood in all the sacred mythologies of archaic times that mankind would regain the paradisiacal existence enjoyed before the dawn of real time, before he fell and was forsaken by the deities with whom he had earlier dwelt. As in the much later mysticisms of the world's great religions, immortality was the aspiration of temporal mortals.

People observed how plants die, noting how the essence of life is retained by the soul of a seed which, when buried in the soil, is born again with renewed strength and vitality. The burial of the dead in the bosom of the Goddess became a custom based on the conviction that the human spirit also outlasts death and returns to life in a new form when the flesh has decomposed.

The farmers were acquainted with every part of the fields and pastures which they tended so carefully. From planting to harvest, the crops were watched attentively and protectively. The appearance of a large circle with the crop flattened in the manner of a spiral would have been greeted with awe, as evidence of divine intervention. The actual formation of a spiral-circle in conjunction with a whirling wind might have been noticed, or it might not. For some farmers, circles appeared in the daytime; for others at night. Sometimes, their sounds were heard, or their spinning lights seen.

In any event, all farmworkers would have been familiar with the sight and action of the common whirlwind, usually mobile but occasionally stationary, sometimes unseen and noisy, sometimes visible and silent. Their response would surely have been one of fear and bewilderment, if only because the whirlwind tends to appear from nowhere, as though emanating from the ground. Moreover, the capacity of the fair-weather whirlwind to ascend is so conspicuously and impressively a normal trait that it cannot fail to have contributed to the widely-held cosmological belief in ritual ascension.

The idea of the fair-weather whirlwind as a spirit rising from a subterranean abode makes sense in a culture ignorant of physical laws. At one moment the air is tranquil; at the next, a gyrating wind commences—gentle at first, and often from a point, as if issuing from the ground. It gathers force, apparently from no other source than Mother Earth herself. Its motion is swift and bounded by a spinning cone, the energy concentrated within a limited, neatly-defined volume. Forever twisting and rising, the spinning vortex transports loose matter to heights as far as the eye can see—sometimes to the celestial clouds. And when the spiralling wind weakens and dies, the keen observer notices that it does so from the bottom upwards, the lower part of the circulating dust envelope rising away beyond the reach of humankind and into the domain of the heavenly gods.

This is true of any up-spinning vortex, whether it is ambling capriciously across the countryside or rooted in one spot. Yet the quasi-stationary whirlwinds, the spherical vortices, the breakdown vortices and some of the luminous spinning globes are marked by a further attribute, as we have seen, which decisively sets them apart from the wandering whirlwinds and thereby corroborates the contribution of the Great Goddess to the proceedings. And that is the circular area which is depressed in crops or grass and is so splendidly embroidered with a spiral design, and consequently looked upon in the primitive mind as if it was the Goddess's vulva, opened for the purpose of releasing the spirits of the dead.

During the course of religious prehistory spiral symbolism became increasingly complex, but nearer the beginning, in the early years of the British Neolithic era, we come close to a major philosophical origin of spiral representation in the prehistoric mythology, religion and art of the British Isles. In this the rotational direction of the spiral in the grass or crop played an important part—either as a clockwise rotation outwards from a centre or as an anticlockwise one.

In our own rational times it may at first be difficult to envisage the essential concepts, but it has invariably been understood by spiritual minds that outward spiralling, because the spiral is growing in size, corresponds with the principle of creation or regeneration, and hence with rebirth into a new life. Once we understand the logic behind the allegory, we can see how it arose and how, for the same reason, all life was thought to owe its development to gestation in the Mother's womb prior to its discharge as a newly-born or a reborn individual into either the terrestrial or the divine world.

In later Celtic times springs and wells were regarded as sacred and were the focus of complex rites and votive offerings in honour of their role as womb-openings of the beneficent Goddess or Earth Mother; this was certainly a legacy from the Neolithic and even Palaeolithic Goddess religions. In the same way, in the Neolithic and Bronze Ages, the spiral-circles were seen as womb-openings which released the spirit, or what may be termed the Creative Breath. The correlation between moving air or wind and the creative breath or creative exhalation may, as a general principle, have been almost universal. Indeed, as noted by Carl Jung, it can be no accident that in Arabic, as in Hebrew, the word *ruh* means both 'breath' and 'spirit'.

The concept of outflowing spirals signalling the generation of life has its counterpart in the values attached to the significance of inflowing spirals. To these, tradition has assigned the principle of death and destruction. Again, the evidence of the spiralling whirlwind can clarify the reasoning: destruction is the domain of the twisting tornado—a manifestation of the Sky God—and tornadoes always turn with an inward-flowing motion and an anticlockwise rotation of their spirals.

The significance of this symbolism makes clearer how appropriate is the name CERES for the scientific unit investigating the circles mystery. Ceres, a Graeco–Roman goddess descended from much older traditions, was Nature's Creatress; the corn and the column which were her emblems were the instruments of creation. That phallus-like column can be equated with the circle-making vortex which is centred on the womb-opening of the spiral-circle, itself an integral part of the body of the Earth Mother—Ceres herself. In this sublime imagery of vortex-circle interaction we have an early hint from prehistoric times of the Sacred Marriage, the Marriage of the Goddess and her God.

The concept of the whirlwind-spiral-spirit manifestation impressed the Neolithic observers so greatly that it inspired a complete magico-ritual system within

Tornado photographed at Ganol, Carmarthen, South Wales, in 1968. The inherent phallic symbolism of tornado funnels was certainly noted by the Neolithic people and ascribed to the majesty of the Sky God. Tornadoes like this one are much more common in the British Isles than is generally realised. The windflow is always inwards and upwards.

the overall Great Goddess religion. Its influence on the lives of the communities of Atlantic and Northern Europe can still be seen in their monumental earthworks and megalithic constructions.

The sight of whirling vortices and the appearance of natural spiral-circles in grasslands and cultivated fields was, for the societies of ancient Britain, a religious experience of deep intensity. To them the vortices were either impregnating the earth at the instant of circle creation or were seen as spirits released from the earth by means of the spiral-circles. It was a highly imaginative idea, the imagery startling, brilliant, absolute. Every circle ordained by the Goddess in the fields promptly assumed sacrosanct status; the primary objective of the dutiful believer would be to prevent the dispersal of the mystical powers at the centre, and to guard them from the forces of evil without. To achieve this it was sufficient to erect a symbolic barrier as a magical deterrent, by preparing either a bank-and-ditch or a ring of stones; or both. Sometimes, the spiral ground-trace may have been preserved, quite literally, by protective concealment—by covering the sacred site with a layer of soil or turves, an act which led to an artificial raising of the ground. This does seem to have been likely at some stone-circle sites.

The middle point of the spiral was the centre of attraction, the spiritual core, just as in Islamic tradition the Ka'aba at Mecca is the central point and goal of the pilgrimage. We know from anthropological studies of shamanic and American Indian religions that the Centre is spiritually sought and has to be attained. Only from it, as Tom Chetwynd has written, 'is it possible to rise on a pole or whirlwind to the upper-world of Divine Powers'.

We know that a few stone circles were given a central megalith, while others had a post—perhaps a totem. It is probable that this was positioned at the spiral centre of the Goddess's circle. But because the middle of a spiral does not necessarily correspond to the geometrical centre of the circle, the central megalith was often placed off-centre, as both Alexander Thom and Aubrey Burl observed.

We do not know why some communities felt a need for a central stone. It has been suggested that they formed part of an alignment system—astronomical, for instance. Or a stone may have been positioned at a spiral-centre to allow spirits, or a kind of 'aura of holiness or Godliness', whether coming from above or below, to suffuse it and occupy it. If that is so, most societies seem to have feared that any such action would have the opposite effect—that of blocking discourse with the deities of earth and sky. This would help explain why so few circles had stones placed at their centres—they number less than forty out of a thousand, according to Aubrey Burl—and why the sacredness of the natural spiral-centre decreed instead that it was better left unobstructed.

With these variations, dictated by evolving local customs and the character of regional geology, over a period of two thousand years there arose on the landscape of the British Isles a host of novel types of monument to be used by the religious leaders for the purpose of the living as well as the dead.

Where a circle was constructed near an isolated hill, it is likely that the hill was included as part of the overall mystical site. One such example is at Swinside in the south of Cumbria, west of Broughton-in-Furness. Here 55 stones remain, with 32 standing; a formerly-reported centre stone is missing. The view of this circle, 28.5 metres in diameter, is framed by the mountain beyond, the domed hill locked geometrically with the circle for eternity, the former a likely topographical source of the latter.

The setting of another stone ring, which recalls the hill-circle relationship so often noticed by crop circle investigators, is that at Castlerigg, near Keswick in the central Lake District, a few kilometres south-west of the hill of Blencathra. This ring, which at one time had 42 stones, is flattened on its north-east side, the axial ratio of its major and minor axes of 32.9 and 29.9 metres being 91 per cent. There

Swinside stone circle (Cumbria) standing in the lee or 'wind-shadow' of the domed hill beyond for a south-west wind. In many cases of crop circle formation there is an obvious hill/circle relationship.

are traces of a four-metre round barrow or cairn which was formerly constructed inside the ring.

In the past it has been assumed that the stone circles and some of their earthen counterparts (the henges and earthen circles) must have been designed with some kind of measuring system. The problem was heightened when Alexander Thom declared that only a race led by skilled geometers could have laid the stones around the perimeters of non-circular rings. Yet now we can see how, for some 'circles' at least and perhaps for a great many in total, Mother Nature—the prehistoric Great Goddess—marked the outlines herself; the human contribution amounted to little more than preserving the outline, which was done by using stakes or small stones until such time as permanent megaliths could be raised.

This theory explains why true circles predominate over non-circular shapes and why, in so many of the stone-ring settings, variations from true circularity are so slight as to be unnoticeable by eye alone. The imperfect circles are but aberrations from true circles, caused by descending whirling vortices straying from their point of impact with the ground. The egg-shapes and the ellipses result from onward movements taking place while the swirling vortex is strengthening or decaying. The same may be true of flattened circles, but with these there is the additional factor that on sloping ground distortion might affect that part of the ground-pattern where the angle of the hill changed. Besides this, an ellipse has a tendency to appear whenever the spiral of a cylindrical vortex is inclined to the ground, which it also does when cut obliquely by the slope of a hillside.

In the summer of 1987 I carried out experiments to build three stone circles using the ancient technique. The last of the three, at Beckhampton near Avebury, was an 8.4-metre diameter ring constructed about the perimeter of a clockwise spiral circle. Although I waited until the wheat-crop had been harvested in order to perform this experiment, the spiral pattern could still be seen because the combine-harvester does not cut the stalks when they are pressed hard against the ground.

I used twelve stones, in imitation of the 12-post 10-metre outer ring of the first phase of the Sanctuary, three kilometres to the east, which is dated to around 2900 BC. The job took less than a minute, merely the time to carry the stones from a previously-dumped heap. Without applying any mathematical, surveying or engineering skills, the result was a flattened Type A stone circle (using Thom's classification) with a long arc of 4.2 ± 0.05 metres and a short arc of 8.0 ± 0.05 metres. The stone circle therefore incorporated, without any effort on my part, the inbuilt measurements which I knew from my earlier survey of the spiral-circle were invested within the outline of Nature's own crop circle.

Earlier that year, in June, I constructed a 32-stone ring around the circumference of a clockwise spiral-circle at South Wonston in Hampshire. As at Beckhampton, for the purpose of this experiment the stones were simply laid on the surface of the ground; the time taken to carry and deposit them was a few minutes. The speed in placing the stones made no difference to the accuracy of the quasi-egg/ellipse which resulted, for I had previously measured the spiral-ring and found it to be an elongated figure with major axis 15.28 metres and minor axis 14.42 metres.

In August 1988, at a site on the edge of Salisbury Plain in West Wiltshire, I used a clockwise spiral-circle to mark out another modern stone ring—this time a Type I egg. The placing of the eight stones took one minute, but the perfection of the design equalled that of the Allan Water stone ring in the Scottish Borders, which has comparable dimensions. The axes at Allan Water are 15.2 and 13.1 metres, while my ring had axes of 16.80 and 15.72 metres.

As for Pythagoras, Alexander Thom would have classified the inbuilt right-angled triangle as being one of the '10, 15, 18' type, because $10^2 + 15^2 = 325$, while $18^2 = 324$. But the builder of the stone circle of AD 1988 did not use Pythagoras as Thom did. And neither did our Neolithic predecessors.

Building a stone circle at South Wonston, Hampshire, in June 1987, using the Neolithic technique to delineate the perimeter. One stone was placed at the spiral centre. Using 32 stones, the laying out of this 'flattened' circle with its major axes of 15.28 and 14.42 metres took about four minutes.

An examination of Woodhenge, the Neolithic timber structure near Stonehenge, which was formerly regarded as one of Thom's most successful analyses, makes the point very clearly. Radiocarbon testing dates this multi-ringed monument to the twenty-third century BC. Thom's construction results from superposing upon his survey a series of six egg-shaped rings, using a right-angled triangle with sides in the unlikely ratio of 12:35:37. 'The discovery of this triangle,' he commented, 'must be considered as one of the greatest achievements of the circle builders. That they considered it important is shown by the use they made of it at Woodhenge.' As a starting point he arbitrarily chose the axis of the egg-shapes as that of midsummer sunrise, that is, 49.2°.

It is amazing how well the geometry seems to fit. Since no natural explanation for the appearance of monstrous eggs in the landscape was known at the time of Thom's work, he thought that the ancient farmers must have been capable of designing the egg-shaped project themselves, and he also claimed that his study not only supported his long-standing argument in favour of a near-universal 'megalithic yard', 2.722 feet long, but enhanced his belief that the designers made

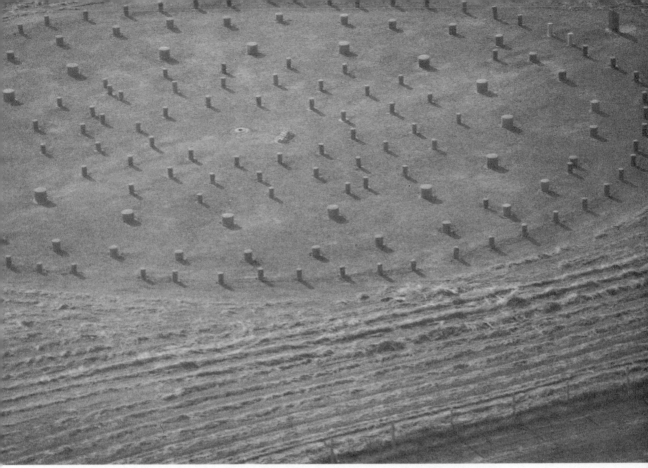

Aerial view of Woodhenge with its concrete markers indicating where the wooden posts used to be.

the circumferences of their sacred circles correspond with another base unit 2.5 megalithic yards long.

One criticism of Thom's work advanced by rightly-cautious archaeologists was that whereas the excavator of Woodhenge, Mrs Maud Cunnington, planned the post-holes, Thom did not have this advantage; he could do no more than survey the concrete posts which Mrs Cunnington had set into them. However, any differences are not enough to matter. In either case the ring which held the biggest posts is a poor fit, but Thom explained this by proposing that, because each post might have been as wide as 2.88 feet, the outine of the egg could have followed the 'inside of this structure' rather than the post centres which he used as guidelines elsewhere.

My approach was to use Thom's survey points as they appear in his published diagram. Unrestricted by the limitations imposed by megalithic yards and the choice of a midsummer axis, I constructed a series of eggs with a common centre A and subsidiary centre B to provide the best fit for the three biggest rings. The resulting axis AB of the eggs pointed 39° east of north, a difference of ten degrees

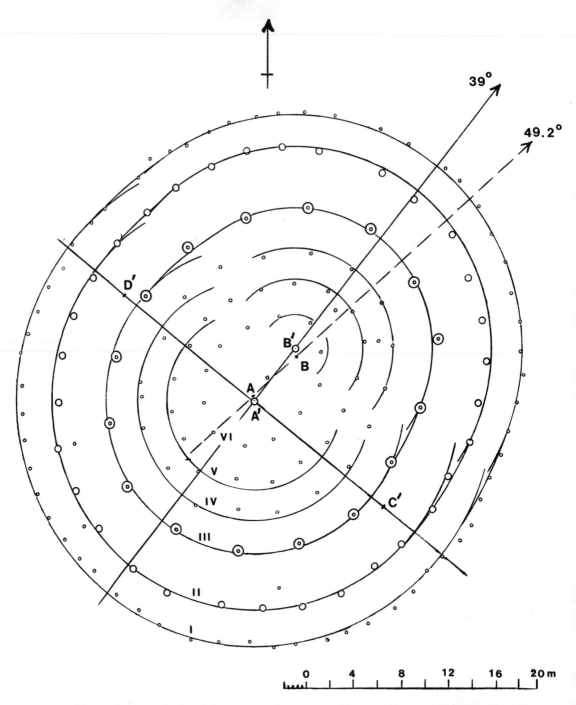

My new attempt at interpreting the post-hole arrangements at Woodhenge. With the main axis now orientated on 39 degrees east of north, the fit of the egg-shapes to the outer three rings is improved. Such a plan could have resulted from Nature's artistry alone, without the intervention of Bronze Age engineers who understood Pythagoras's theorem long before its discovery in Greece.

from Thom's axis. Of course, the nature of the geometrical method ensured that the intrinsic triangles were right-angled, but unlike Thom's the sides were not whole-number ratios. In deciding the position of C, which can be done arbitrarily within certain limits, Thom came up with a line AC which was 2.92 times longer than AB *only because* it produced a right-angled triangle whose sides matched his chosen measurements—his 'meaningful' ratio of 12:35:37.

The eggs of my new diagram for Woodhenge compare very favourably with the natural egg in the wheat at Bratton in 1986. The improved agreement of the new eggs at Woodhenge with the points of Thom's survey has happened at the expense of perfection in the perimeter ratios and in the simplicity of the right-angled triangles. The 49.2-degree axial alignment which Thom picked to coincide with the midsummer sunrise has disappeared, but there was no good reason to suppose that the builders of Woodhenge sought a midsummer alignment anyway. I say this because the causeway across the henge-ditch is not orientated on the solstice but towards 24.5 degrees, almost north-north-east.

If we assume that Woodhenge was based on a natural spiral-circle formed in grass or a crop, what may actually have happened is as follows:

An egg-shaped circle (or circle-with-ring) appeared in a cultivated field or field of long grass; this would of course have happened in one of the summer months, most likely June, July or August.

The edge of the natural egg was outlined, initially with a temporary ring of small stakes. This is the curve that the ring of immense timber posts may have followed.

The three outer rings were marked out by offsetting from this ring, either by pacing or by measurement. Alternatively, the outer ring may have followed the contours of a natural ring-and-circle system formed in the vegetation. In either event the motivation would have sprung from a mystical regard for the marvel of the spiral-circle symbolism of the crop circle. The chance happening that the orientation approximated to the direction of midsummer sunrise may have added to the divine and celestial symbolism attributed to the occasion.

The spiral-centre of the egg-shaped pattern was the unmistakable focus of the system, as with all spirals, and the obvious place for a foundation deposit. At Woodhenge, in a centrally-located grave, Mrs Cunnington found the crouched remains of a three-year-old girl whose skull had been cleft in what may have been a dedicatory sacrifice. She was lying on her right side facing, approximately, the midsummer sunrise. My axis passes next to this place, as does Thom's.

The sanctity of the monument was heightened by the digging of an external ditch, so creating a henge with a single entrance. This northern side overlooks Durrington Walls, the enclosed area nearby which appears to have been a village serving both Woodhenge and Stonehenge.

It is impossible to tell whether or not the six timber rings were all built at the same time. It may be that the inner trio of small timber posts was introduced more casually at some later time by offsetting, especially as the surveys of Maud Cunnington and Alexander Thom indicate that these egg-shaped outlines were inexact.

As I discovered when studying the natural spiral-centred crop circles at Bratton and elsewhere, when the shape of an egg is impressed into the vegetation of the landscape, it incorporates hidden right-angled triangles. However, the geometrical egg-shapes proposed by Thom are the creations of a modern hand, not an ancient one. Far from providing unequivocal proof of archaic egg-planning as Thom supposed, the evidence points the other way: it sides with Nature, with her whirling spirals, as divine artist. The Neolithic peoples attributed crop circles to the watchful interest and beneficence of the Great Goddess, and this is revealed not only by Woodhenge but by hundreds of other timber rings and megalithic circles throughout Britain and Ireland.

It is surprising that, despite the vast number of stone circles surveyed by Alexander Thom and the numerous site plans which he published with co-ordinate details, few people have reworked his analyses in order to verify the precise details of his shapes. Doing so reveals that diameters and perimeters have been expanded or contracted by a few per cent—not enough to disturb agreement with stone-holes significantly, but subtly shifting the diametrical lengths closer to multiples of Thom's 'megalithic yard'. Likewise, a perimeter length can be conveniently edged towards a multiple of 2.5 megalithic yards.

In constructing a graph of stone-circle diameters Thom thought the bunching of diameters around particular values derived from the ancient use of a standard unit of length in the setting-out procedure, but Douglas Heggie asked, 'could it not be that the data are really non-random in some other way . . . which has little or nothing to do with a quantum but has a comparable effect in an application of the statistical tests?' Professor D. G. Kendall's conclusion, based only on analysing Thom's true circles, was bolder: he stated that Thom's megalithic yard hypothesis could be accepted only 'if no other natural alternative hypothesis is available'. Such a hypothesis I have presented in this book, which also explains the non-randomness of the stone-circle data mentioned by Heggie. Indeed, a degree of bunching can be seen in my crop circle diameters too, but it is not due to the use of a prehistoric measuring stick, nor indeed a modern one. Instead, it indicates a natural explanation for the non-randomness of the diameters of crop circles and stone rings, although the reasons may differ in the two cases.

In his book *Megalithic Sites in Britain*, Thom published in 1967 a more complete graph based on his measurements of 211 stone rings. Some grouping of the data remains, but it is superimposed upon what may be termed an even level of 'background noise'. I think Thom's results may derive from two sets of stone-ring data—the first resulting from rings whose dimensions were determined by the character of Nature's spiral-centred crop circles, the second from stone rings whose diameters had been decided by an 'architect-priest' or priestess who may have paced out the radius on which each circle was based.

My belief is that Thom's special length results from his selection of a 'best figure' from his graphs, a figure which, by averaging 2.722 feet or 0.829 metres, merely approximates to the human pace. There is no evidence for the prehistoric deployment of a countrywide measuring rod and unit of measure, as Thom asserted, apart from a generalised and somewhat variable use of the human pace or other body unit under limited circumstances.

The ellipse was one of the geometrical forms Thom chose to describe the shapes of megalithic rings. At the time of his 1967 book he claimed that about 20 definite ellipses were known, to which could be added a dozen or so less certain ones. He gave plans of five of the best, which hardly differ from the shape obtained by rolling a circle a distance of one or two metres. This suggests that the field-marking mechanism, whose end-product was the 'elliptical' stone ring, resulted from the slight drift of a circular mark caused by a moving vortex.

I must emphasise that I am not suggesting that all stone circles were created by the methods I have described here, merely that these procedures explain very well, without recourse to Pythagorean geometry, Thom's conundrum regarding the perfect marking out of non-circular shapes, and that the simple circle can be designed in this way, too. On the other hand, the correlation with crop circles and their mystical significance does supply a persuasive motive for megalithic ring building. Taken together, this is enough to indicate that many of the sacred circles could have originated in this way, although doubtless some of the others, especially circular ones, could have been created by straightforward marking-out techniques.

Sometimes it may have been enough to mark a circle on the ground simply because a daytime whirlwind or nocturnal spinning ball of light had been reported at that place, or for some quite different reason by a people who, for reasons of local geography, were ignorant of the electrically charged vortex or the circle-making vortex concept, or who were unable or unwilling to await the portent of the spiral-circle vortex in their locality. This approach might discriminate against the fabrication of big stone circles and explain why so many Scottish circles have quite small diameters. Indeed, when a circle is marked out at the site of a vortex which did not leave a clear impression of its diameter on the grass, then an arbitrary diameter was probably chosen; at this stage pacing could introduce a tendency towards 'whole number' development. This might go some way towards accounting for the fairly common circle diameters seen in Thom's histogram at

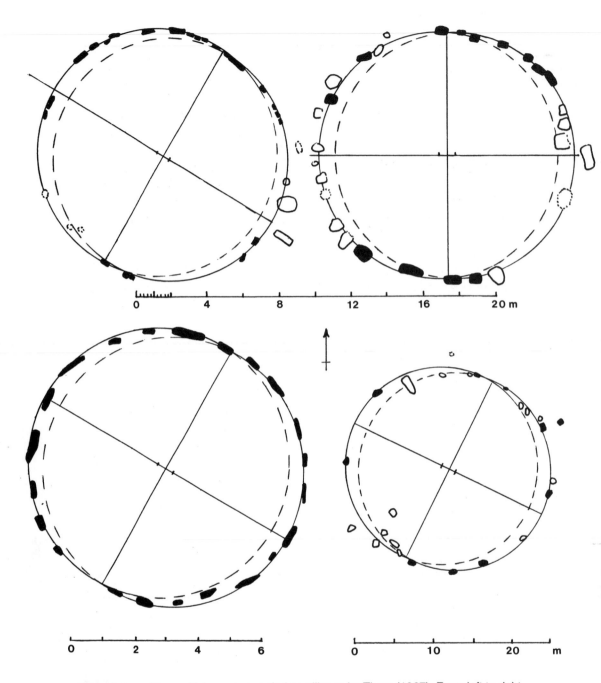

Four stone settings which were regarded as ellipses by Thom (1967). From left to right, starting at the top, are his surveys made at the Sands of Forvie and Daviot (in Scotland), Postbridge (Devon) and Penmaenmawr (North Wales). Upon each survey of the stone positions I have superimposed a double-circle (i.e. a circle which has 'rolled' or shifted sideways) in order to emphasise that the same surveys can more simply be interpreted by the mutual displacement of twin circles whose centres are 1–2 metres apart. In other words, a vortex which usually makes a circular crop-mark can create what Thom took to be an ellipse if the vortex drifts upon impact. Twin-centred circles like these have been surveyed many times by crop-circle scientists.

8 my (= 22 ft), 16 my (= 44 ft), 20 my (= 55 ft), and 32 my (= 88 ft), in which one megalithic yard (my) is reckoned to equal one pace.

A further consequence, noticed by Thom, is that the bunching of diameters at multiples of 4 my (that is, four paces) automatically generates multiples of 2.5 my on the perimeters. Nevertheless, even if, as seems probable, not all circles and not all henges were designed as the result of a spirit-vortex visitation, many of them, especially the non-circular ones, may have originated in this way. Whether or not the henge of Stonehenge came into being like this, its circular bank and ditch, dug about 3200 BC, certainly speak eloquently for the early use of circle symbolism in southern England.

Nature's own impressive spiral-centred crop circles, spawned by the dynamic interaction of a spinning column of electrified air with the erect stalks of the farmers' hard-won crop, simultaneously produced three types of geometrical image which the Neolithic people absorbed into their everyday religious symbolism: the spiral, the circle or ring, and the cup. To these we can add a less tangible fourth: the authentic vision of the spiralling spirit-vortex (or spirit-whirlwind).

The ground hallowed in this way was consecrated by constructional efforts in earth, timber and stone. That this was the origin of so many megalithic circles is suggested by the proven trapping of the circumferential contours by the rings of stone, so preserving the abnormal outlines of the fanciful non-circular rings as efficiently as it did the simpler circular ones.

The process of building stone or timber circles or of cutting earthen circles or rings of pits in the landscape of Britain was only a part of an overwhelming spiritual revolution which spread throughout Ireland, Scotland, Wales and England during the fourth and third millennia—strengthening and maintaining the megalithic cult through two thousand years until its fading in the Middle Bronze Age and extinction in the Late Bronze Age.

5

Pathways to Heaven

For hundreds of years, from almost the beginning of the fourth millennium BC, the inhabitants of the British Isles buried their dead together in a form of tomb to which archaeologists have given the name long barrow. The word 'barrow', meaning 'small hill', is probably derived from the Old English *beorg*, a mound. The length of these sepulchral long mounds was much greater than their width, and many were chambered, the result of using either timber or stone as principal components of an internal framework. The majority were aligned roughly east–west, with the broader entrance end facing east. A variant of the long barrow type commonly found on the Wessex chalklands was chiefly 'earthen' in nature, consisting mainly of earth or materials such as chalk rubble, sometimes with a turf or stone core.

Then, quite suddenly, for no reason which has yet been forthcoming, the practice of building long barrows ceased. An era began in which the time-honoured custom of collective burial was supplanted by a tradition of single burial. Firstly in northern England in the mid-to-late third millennium, and then gradually throughout the rest of the British Isles, there began a practice of interment in round barrows, which was to endure for two thousand years. What caused this change of custom, and what can the internal and external features of the new burial mounds tell us?

A circular halo in the sky above the Oxfordshire Rollright Stones, photographed on 8 June, 1986. Circular celestial visions would have been regarded as exceptionally portentous in the days of the Goddess, just as they were in historical times prior to battles and other events of national importance.

To the ancients everything that was untouchable or extraordinary lay in the realm of the supernatural. This meant all celestial objects and phenomena, and all meteorological happenings and apparitions. Visions such as rainbows, haloes around the sun and moon, strokes of lightning, hailstones and thunderclouds, as well as tornado funnel clouds, were all regarded as portents or divine manifestations sent by the gods. So it was with whirlwinds, as we have seen, and so it was with whirling, circle-making vortices.

Wind is invisible, but it can be sensed by the force of its pressure, and various other effects of the whirling air are discernible, too. Dust rises in a transparent veil; a high-pitched humming or whistling may be heard; a spiral sweeps a circle with a mystical centre upon the ground. To the people of Neolithic and early Bronze Age Britain the apparition would have seemed nothing less than divinely created. They would have reacted with fear and wonder. In the same way that they marked off the hallowed area with henges and rings of earth and stone, I believe that they also saw the circles left by spiralling vortices as sacrosanct places for the burial of their dead.

The following recent account of a whirlwind shows how easily such a manifestation could be seen as a spiritual apparition. Had the witness had poor eyesight or been given to careless exaggeration, a very different interpretation could have resulted.

I was taking the dog for its usual evening walk in Canford Park, Westbury-on-Trym, in Bristol one summer evening in 1963. It was about 7 p.m. Next to the park is a cemetery, and it was while looking towards the cemetery that I noticed what could be described as a whirlwind moving slowly across my field of vision just over the boundary *into* the cemetery. The overall colour seemed white/grey, and I remember remarking to another person watching that it reminded me of the 'white tornado', a popular TV commercial of that time advertising a floor cleaner! It was quite an eerie feeling watching it, heightened by the fact of it being over a cemetery. It appeared to be sucking up leaves mainly. Its height would be about 25–30 feet, and it was witnessed by at least three people near me.

This whirlwind, alarming enough, was of the traditional mobile kind, but it is the descending vortices and breakdown whirlwinds, which leave flattened spiral-circles in the fields or in long grass, that would have impressed our Neolithic forebears most deeply. They would have regarded the circular ground mark as symbolic, at one and the same time, of the subterranean world and the outer cosmos; it would have been the place where the three cosmic spheres intersected—those of heaven, earth and the underworld.

Robertson-Smith concluded that 'all sanctuaries are consecrated by a theophany'. I hope I have shown that a whirling vortex would have been seen by the Neolithic people as a theophany or divine manifestation *par excellence*, as an apparition passing between earth and heaven. The circular ground mark would therefore have been the archetype of sacred space. Ground sanctified in this way was chosen to serve either the living, as with henges and stone circles, or the dead, as with round barrows.

Just as a person and his or her shadow disappear at death when the body crumbles to dust or is reduced by cremation to ash, so does the soul-shadow vanish at the same moment. But our eternal hope of redemption depends upon the unharmed transfer of spirit or soul-shadow from the grave or funeral pyre to the place of paradise long promised by the priests. The ancient inhabitants of Britain and Ireland followed the guidance of their spiritual leaders by perceiving in the aerial vortex their path to salvation.

Vortex ground traces were taken to indicate spirits on the move. They were the points where spirits had escaped from the confines of the earth and had spun away to the heavenly realm of the gods. A vortex was understood to be a spirit or the bearer of a spirit, while the spiral centre symbolised a vertical hole, leading back to the subterranean depths, through which a soul, normally unseen, had passed. The spiralling whirlwind had a continuing link with the atmosphere through its vertical structure, and so between the hole marked in the spiral-circle and the heavens. This, above all, explains why the goal of the barrow builders was to inter their dead at the spiral centre.

It has been estimated that some 18,000 round barrows were erected in the British Isles. Besides the familiar grassy mounds, this number includes several

Bowl-shaped Barrow.   Bell-shaped Barrow.

A bowl barrow and a bell barrow, from John Thurnam's 'Ancient British Barrows' (*Archaeologica* 1870). Standing by the bell barrow is a great bustard, a game bird then common on Salisbury Plain. Some 18,000 round barrows and cairns are known in Britain, the majority built between 2500 and 500 BC.

types of cairn composed wholly or partly of rocky material. The majority were raised in the Bronze Age, but the earliest are Late Neolithic and some even date from the Iron Age and Romano–British times. Six principal types have been identified, the bowl barrow being the most common; they are found with or without a surrounding ditch.

The five other, more specialised types evolved on the chalk downlands of the Wessex counties and are rarely found outside this area. Some five hundred of these barrows are known. Those surrounded by a berm, a flat ring of land between mound and ditch, are called bermed barrows. They include bell barrows, bell-disc barrows, disc barrows and the less common saucer and pond barrows. Many of the disc barrows which have been excavated have disclosed grave goods such as beads, pendants, necklaces, and other ornaments of types that suggest these are the graves of women.

Most round-barrow types measure between ten and fifty metres in diameter, rarely more. This corresponds with the mid- to upper range of spiral-circle ground traces and also the commonest whirlwind diameters studied by CERES and the

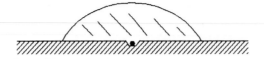

DITCHLESS

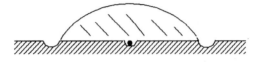

DITCHED

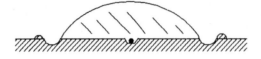

DITCHED WITH
OUTER BANK

Above: Variations in the structure of the common bowl barrow. This is the kind which is found countrywide. *Below:* The principal types of specialised round barrow. These are chiefly restricted to Wessex (after Leslie Grinsell and Paul Ashbee).

BELL BARROW

BELL – DISC
BARROW

DISC BARROW

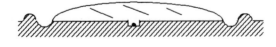

SAUCER
BARROW

POND BARROW

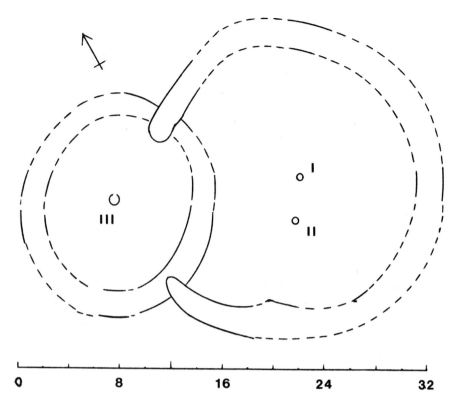

Confluent round barrows near Amesbury and Stonehenge. The earlier bowl barrow *(left)* is overlapped by a larger saucer barrow (after Paul Ashbee, 1984).

Tornado and Storm Research Organisation. After thousands of years of steady weathering, barrow heights vary from about one to six metres. There are a few examples of barrows overlapping one another, for which the term 'confluent' is used. A pair from Amesbury near Stonehenge is illustrated above. One can tell from the ditch configurations that the bigger of the two was constructed later. It has been a longstanding puzzle why some barrows were arranged to overlap when there was so much land available.

Little attention has been paid to the external ground-plans of round barrows. So many appear to be circular that it seems to be tacitly assumed that most, perhaps all, were intended to be circular; so where imperfect circularity is found it has been ascribed to a lack of care or interest by the barrow builders.

Yet there is abundant evidence to show that the builders could always make perfectly good circles whenever they wished, as they did with megalithic stone circles. Why, therefore, were some round barrows constructed on the basis of egg-shaped or elliptical plans?

A saucer barrow at Shalbourne in East Wiltshire offers an excellent ellipse in its ditch and bank geometry. The excavator's measurements, across the ditches, gave

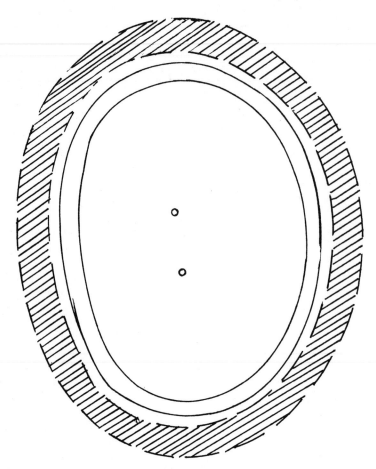

Elliptical or flattened-circle geometry of a round barrow at Milton Lilbourne, Wiltshire, showing inner ditch and outer bank (after Ashbee, 1986). The cremation burials may have been located at the two spiral centres of a natural vortex-generated ellipse.

major and minor axes of 80 and 68 feet. This rather extreme case is equivalent to 24.5 metres and 21 metres, an axial ratio of 85 per cent. Other barrows, although appearing to be approximately circular externally, conceal beneath the surface unequivocal evidence of non-circular geometry. Following Alexander Thom's nomenclature for classifying stone-circle shapes, round barrows have been found in the following primary shapes: circles, egg-shapes, ellipses, and flattened circles.

The materials from which barrows are built are chiefly earthen matter or stone, or both. The simplest consist wholly of turf, chalk rubble, sand, loam, clay and earth. Whereas most barrows are obviously turf-covered, many, more surprisingly, also have turf cores at their ancient centres. On the other hand, soil quite often formed the central core instead. Obviously, when constructing ditchless barrows, all the necessary materials to form the mound had to be brought to the site from elsewhere, but when a perimeter ditch was being dug, the contents of the ditch were thrown upon the central mound, so protecting the interior from

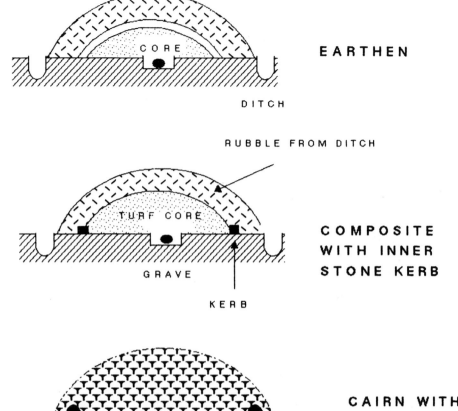

EARTHEN

DITCH

RUBBLE FROM DITCH

COMPOSITE
WITH INNER
STONE KERB

TURF CORE

GRAVE

KERB

CAIRN WITH
INNER KERB

KERB

CIST

Internal details of typical round barrows and cairns (after Ashbee, 1960). *Top:* the common earthen barrow; *centre:* a composite barrow with a concealed circle of stones and turf core; *bottom:* a cairn, wholly built of stones, usually with a concealed ring of stones.

weathering. As the antiquarian William Stukeley remarked in 1740, freshly raised barrows on chalk lands would have been a splendrous white.

The irregularity or incompleteness of so many ditches around barrows suggests that they were often dug with the main objective of obtaining spoil to complete the covering of the mound rather than for the purpose of surrounding the barrow with a circular valley. Nonetheless, on some occasions at least, ditches were dug with care, and the shapes of some were not merely imperfectly circular but, for example, quite precisely elliptical.

Many stone-built cairns had an inner low wall which was totally concealed as the cairn rose in height, and a few, like the 30-metre diameter cairn on Kilmartin Glebe, apparently covered two concentric circles. A number of similar cairns have been opened on Dartmoor.

It is significant that not only many cairns but also earthen round barrows possess an internal retaining wall or stone-kerb. In some other cases careful examination has shown that material derived from the ditch or elsewhere was used to demarcate a provisional or definite boundary of the mound before construction commenced. It has been suggested that these low stone boundaries, generally between three and fifteen metres in diameter, were built in order to help maintain the shape of the inner mound—yet they could only have had a minimal effect at best in most cases. In fact, some of the stone blocks of megalithic size used in this subsurface construction were clearly too big for such a purpose. In some instances, the rings may not have been hidden when laid down; they may have been constructed as visible kerbs which subsequently became soil-covered. It is interesting to note that a good many of these hidden stone rings or kerbs enclose stacks of turf with a central grave or stone-built cist.

Measurement has revealed the shapes of many of the kerbstone rings to be non-circular. Egg-shapes, ellipses and flattened circles are easily identified among the published plans of skilled barrow-excavators. One may ask, as with the free-standing megalithic rings of preceding chapters, what motive could have been responsible for this, and why some round barrows, at the time when their construction was planned or begun, had stake or wooden-post rings in them instead or as well.

The evidence for stake or post rings within British round barrows has been assembled by Paul Ashbee. Stake-circle diameters range from three to fifteen metres. The bigger, or peripheral, rings seem generally to have coincided with the barrow's perimeter, while the smaller diameter ones lie much nearer the central part of the main mound. In every case except one, excavation has proved that the stakes were removed before the earthen mound itself was raised, but under a barrow at Sheeplays in Glamorgan, South Wales, the former presence of stakes could be traced to a considerable height inside the mound. There is also a Cornish composite barrow in which stake withdrawal had undisputedly been effected because the stake-hole positions were overlaid by an internal stone wall.

Concentric rings of stakes or posts in association with barrows have also been found, up to four in number. Ashbee classified them into three categories. In Category A are single-ring settings with posts widely or closely spaced. Those of Category B differ only by the trench that was dug before the insertion of posts into pits in the trench bottom. The third category was reserved for the multiple-ring settings consisting of two, three or four roughly-concentric rings.

No clearly defined function for these stake or post settings has been agreed, despite several proposals. These include the continental work of Glasbergen who studied Dutch examples. On the basis that the settings resemble, in some measure, wooden-post henges, the idea was mooted that mortuary huts or houses were erected on the occasion of funerary ceremonies or feasts. The wooden stakes were certainly temporary, and were often replaced by permanent stone settings,

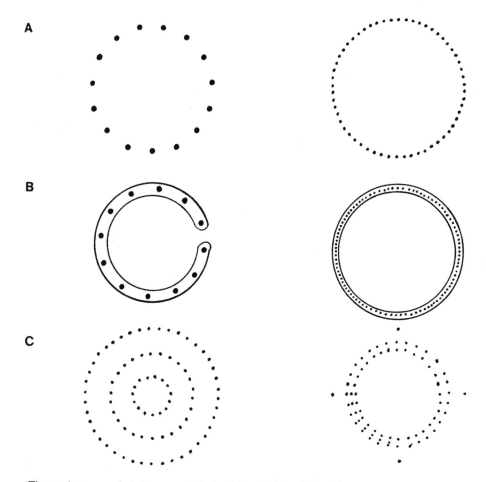

A

B

C

The main types of stake or post circles (after Ashbee) found beneath round barrows, some of which were set into circular ditches.

so they may have been intended to demarcate the limits of intended barrow building. Beyond this, good support for earlier theories is lacking, and no one has been able to explain why stake settings should have been made to follow elliptical outlines (like the one beneath bowl barrow 61 at Amesbury) or egg-shapes instead of circles, sometimes with difficulty when stakes were driven into underlying chalk, only to have them soon destroyed and sealed away for ever. Furthermore, why should the mourners have gone to the trouble of digging a trench for the stakes or for the 'palisade', if it was to be as rapidly filled in?

Why do some barrows, like the Amesbury 61a disc barrow (this one is devoid of stakes), have an oval outline within an oval ditch? And why, above all, did a few barrows never receive their intended primary burials, while others, despite all the planning and the toil, have a grave that is not centrally placed? I believe that the spiral-circle hypothesis can provide answers to these questions.

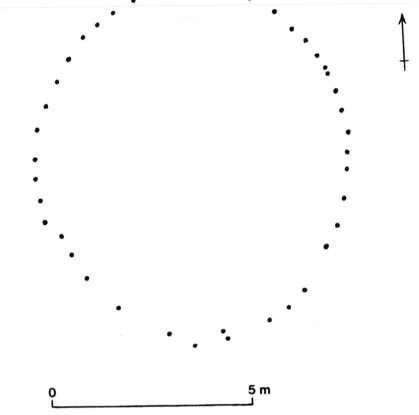

The ring of stakes beneath bowl barrow 61 east of Amesbury. Despite all the preparatory work there was no central burial. The excavator's plan shows that the ring was not truly circular; it was more oval, like that of an egg, with major axes of 8.8 and 8.0 metres (Paul Ashbee).

If one accepts that to the Neolithic and Bronze Age people whirling vortices were apparitions representing the souls of the dead, and that the sites where they occurred were regarded as the pathways followed by souls on their journey to heaven, then one may suppose that any place where a spiral-circle was discovered or a stationary whirlwind was sighted might have been marked out for retention as a site suitable for a future burial. The placing of a standing stone or post, or a circular setting of posts or stones, would have served the purpose well enough. Certain regions or even particular fields appear to be more favourable than others to descending vortex or whirlwind action; such areas would in the course of time have acquired a reputation as ideal burial places and eventually would have developed into cemeteries. While even mobile or travelling whirlwinds would have contributed to a locality's reputation for supernatural power, a high frequency of crop circles or stationary whirlwinds would have attracted the most attention as a hallowed site.

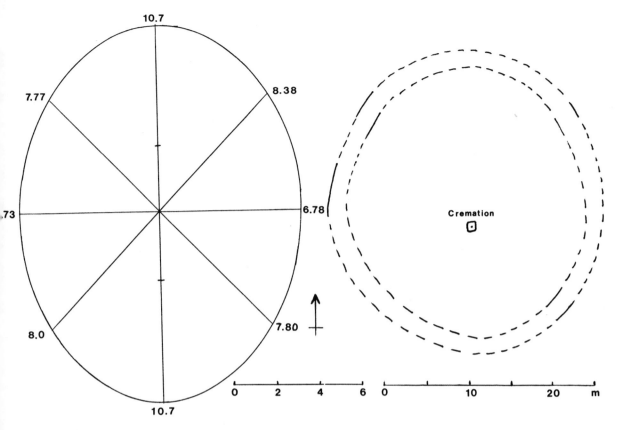

Left: Plan of a spiral-patterned crop circle 21.4 m long, with an oval or quasi-elliptical outline. This example, from Bratton in 1987, with axial ratios of 63 per cent, is the most extreme case so far known. Most ellipses formed in crops by vortices have axial ratios of 90–98 per cent. *Right:* Plan of the interior of Amesbury 61a, an oval-shaped disc barrow (after Ashbee, 1984). Note the ex-centric location of the cremation deposit.

How would the ancient inhabitants of these islands have responded to the discovery of spiral patterns in fields of grass or crops?

A plain circular or non-circular flattened spiral pattern could have been outlined by a kerb of stones or by stakes driven in around the circumference. This would faithfully record the exact details of the perimeter. Circles, ellipses, eggs or any other shape could be precisely marked out, and the shape retained while a mound was raised to conceal it or while a ditch was dug closely around it to match the contour. The common bowl barrow, whether ditched or ditchless, could have originated very simply in this way. So could the ditched bell, the bell-disc and the disc barrows of Wessex.

The outer-ringed versions of the spiral vortex pattern, which were mentioned in Chapter 3, could have been the source not only of bowl barrows but of several other barrow types too.

A comparison of the quasi-circular outer-ringed field pattern found at Winterbourne Stoke, west of Stonehenge, in 1987, with Paul Ashbee's excavation plan of the Amesbury disc-barrow 61a, makes the point clearly. Besides the similarity in shape, the resemblance extends to the non-centrality of the focus (spiral centre for the crop circle, cremation grave for the barrow), axial ratios (crop circle was 98 per cent, Amesbury barrow about 91 per cent) and order of dimensions—the maximum lengths are within the range 24.76–25.28 metres for crop circle and 33.5–37 metres for the Amesbury barrow. If the origin of the Bronze Age disc barrow lay in the site of a natural vortex pattern, then the diggers followed the ringing bands of the spiral-centred crop pattern with their trench and outer bank.

The same vortex patterns (plain and ringed-circle types) could have been variously interpreted to create other barrow forms, such as bell-disc, bell and saucer barrows and outer-ditched bowl barrows. The ubiquitous bowl barrow of ditchless and ditched forms could have been prompted by plain-circle pattern discoveries, or even by direct whirlwind observation in the absence of a clear pattern, although the diameters of bowl barrow and vortex patterns do match very well.

Composite barrow types could also have derived from field-vortex patterns. The natural positions of the ring-systems would have determined the positioning of stone-kerb settings and some stake settings.

The experiments I described in the previous chapter, in which I set stones around the circumference of spiral-centred circles, are equally enlightening in the context of barrows. In 1987 I placed ten stones round the edge of a nine-metre circle near Avebury, in which the wheat had been flattened in an anticlockwise direction. The experiment was done after harvesting. The circle had an ex-centric spiral centre displaced by 0.7 metres from the true centre.

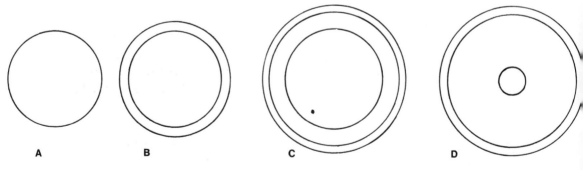

A   B   C   D

Simplified plans of all types of Neolithic and Bronze Age barrows grouped to emphasise their common circular features and hence their possible relationships with natural vortex crop circles. (A) Ditchless bowl barrow and cairn; (B) ditched bowl, bowl with kerb, cairn with kerb; (C) ditch-and-banked bowl, composite bowl with kerb, bell, bell-disc, saucer, cairn with inner kerb; (D) bell-disc barrow, disc barrow.

In the spirit of the long-lost round-barrow customs, in which a ring of posts or stones was laid out before the mound was raised, I prepared a kerb of stones along the perimeter of a crop circle. The floor pattern of this circle, while swirling out from a centre, followed the rarer S-shape format. Commencing as an anticlockwise spiral it progressively reversed itself to finish clockwise, or nearly so, at the circle's edge.

Another spiral-circle in which I constructed a stone ring (see above) was elliptical in shape, and its dimensions corresponded closely with those of the stake-ring found by Ashbee beneath bowl-barrow 61 near Amesbury. The major axes were 8.8 and 8.0 metres for the stake-ring and 8.9 and 8.2 metres for the vortex crop-mark. It, too, had an ex-centric spiral centre.

The type and location of the primary or main burial in round barrows can tell us a lot about the funerary practices of Late Neolithic and Bronze Age times. If barrows were sited on spiral circle traces one would expect the grave to be at the spiral centre. This is because outflowing spirals are the common factor in the spiral patterns of the circles effect and the outward-flowing spiral denotes spiritual birth or rebirth. By contrast, inward-flowing spirals equate with death. The whirling vortex can also be interpreted as an exhalation or spirit issuing from the earth.

In some perfectly circular vortex patterns spiral-centre and circle-centre coincide. At such times it would be normal to position the grave at the spiral centre, in which case this would also become the centre of the circular barrow. Most graves occupy this prime site, yet sometimes the grave is rather strangely but undeniably off-centre. Harder to understand is why the primary grave is at times placed in a peripheral position, and why a few barrows have never had any primary burial at all.

Off-centre graves seem impossible to explain except in terms of crop circle theory. Ex-centric spirals are natural happenings in vortex formation—for example, the Headbourne Worthy crop-pattern of 1986, in which a nearly perfect circular perimeter surrounding a 17.65-metre diameter circle had its spiral centre 0.8 metres from the circle centre. A devout believer in the spiritual properties of circle-making vortices would wish to pinpoint the spiral centre of the crop-mark for the exact location of the future grave, and to mark the perimeter with stakes or stones in order to demarcate the limits of the holiest ground. When the pattern is egg-shaped or elliptical, it is usual for the spiral centre to be displaced, often along the major axis. The primary grave in the disc-barrow illustrated on p. 75 is off-centre along the major axis of the elliptical/oval disc.

Crop circle theory is also needed to explain why the prime, central positions of some round barrows were never occupied, and at the same time it explains why some small stone-ring settings never had barrows raised over them. It is likely that, following the discovery of a spiral-circle pattern or the direct observation of a nearly-stationary whirlwind, the site was marked in some way and held in reserve until a personage worthy of burial should die. The majority of whirlwind sightings or field vortex-pattern discoveries would have been summertime events, whereas the majority of deaths by natural causes would have happened at other seasons. Preliminary work had to be carried out on a barrow at once, however, because only by covering the spiral pattern with turf sods or a protective layer of clay or loam would there be any hope of preserving the spiral picture for a reasonable length of time. Skilled excavation can show that, on occasion, a barrow must have remained open for some months after work on it had begun.

Over the centuries local memories must sometimes have lapsed, so that it was forgotten that the prime site of a barrow had not been used, and the same barrow would have secondary burials inserted on the periphery or in other less important places. Rings of stones are to be found where barrows are common or where they adjoin barrow cemeteries, which could well represent the first stages of barrows abandoned without completion. Stake settings, possibly with a central post, may also have been raised as a temporary measure, but those that were never converted into finished barrows have subsequently been lost. If that is true, some unfinished barrows may yet await rediscovery on chalk downlands by virtue of

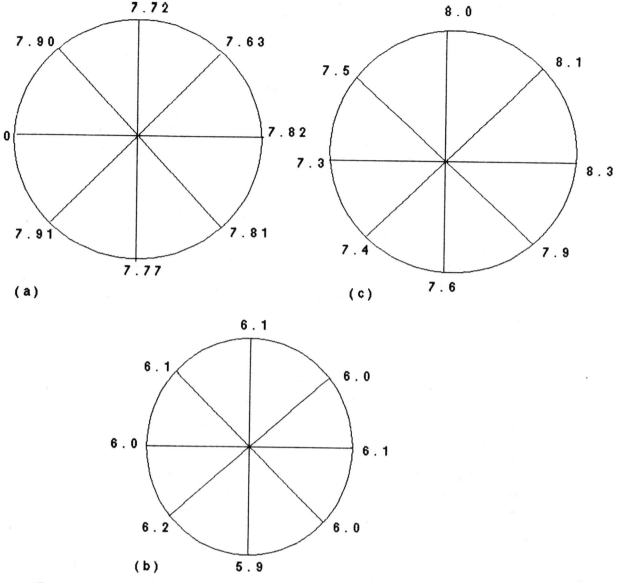

Examples of spiralled crop-marks made by the circles effect in which the geometry was nearly circular. For (a) Alresford 1987 and (b) Corhampton 1987, there is near coincidence of the spiral centre and the geometrical centre, whereas for (c) Westbury 1987, there is a non-central spiral centre.

their post-pits, if these were made deeply enough into the chalk not to have vanished through the action of chalk solution over subsequent millennia.

It is nevertheless certain that some barrows were erected not as graves but as holy sanctuaries, while others, their centres void, had very complex construction motivations, for in some the grave or cist was located at the circumference on a stake circle or stone kerb.

The Beacon Hill barrow in Sussex was shown by its excavators, Earl Cawdor and Cyril Fox, to have been completely built before any of the burials had been inserted. The suggestion that it might have formed a cenotaph in honour of a distinguished person whose body was unavailable is not acceptable. It must have been raised because the site had been sanctified, probably by some manifestation of religious significance.

At Six Wells Farm in the parish of Llantwit Major near the coast of Glamorgan, at a height above sea-level of 83 metres (271 feet), stands a 28-metre (90-foot) diameter bowl barrow which was excavated by Cyril Fox in 1940. Beneath it lay a stake circle with a diameter of 15.5 metres (50 feet). In contrast to the care with which the radius and diameter of the circle had been maintained, the great variation in spaces between the stakes showed that the importance lay in marking the line of the circumference, not in spacing out the stakes. These appeared to have been driven deeply into the earth, but most had been withdrawn before the barrow was raised. For those where measurement could still be made, their height above the ground had formerly been 7 to 10 centimetres (three to four inches).

At the centre of the turf barrow a dome of clay and earth had been fashioned to rise over and enclose a circular pit, 30 centimetres in diameter; it was a virgin pit devoid of any burial, and betrayed no sign of burning, trampling or other activity. The supreme Centre, the usual *raison d'être* for toiling away on barrow-building, had been left empty—or at least it was empty to profane eyes. Instead, another surprise awaited the excavator at a point on the circumference of the stake circle south-south-east of the centre. Here, there was a stone cist, obviously lozenge-shaped, and eminently suitable as a receptacle within the abode of the Great Goddess. The long axis of this box lay along the edge of the perimeter of the stake circle and its symbolic form was further emphasised by the addition of pointer stones at each corner of the long axis.

The axis of the cist ran deliberately just outside the stake circle but one of the stakes lay inside the cist, for a stone had rested upon it while it decayed. Evidently the cist had been built after the stake circle had been laid out but was planned in conjunction with it so that the cist would lie on the circle—a small part in, the larger part out. And it was in the larger part that a cinerary urn with the remains of a cremated adult was found. The urn was of a rare type; its only known predecessor came from a West Somerset barrow, at Elworthy, southwards across the Bristol Channel in the Brendon Hills. The Elworthy urn was decorated with running chevrons and a continuous zigzag (both generalised symbols of rain/waters/life/fertility), horizontal grooves, and four pairs of moulded dimples. The Six Wells urn had only the horizontal grooves and the four pairs of dimples but there were close similarities in other ways. As to the burial place beneath the barrow, the Elworthy report stated that it 'contained a circle of upright stones, about six feet in diameter, enclosed with flat stones, containing this urn, with

1. *Above:* At almost sixty tonnes the lozenge-shaped stone at the northern entrance to the great circle at Avebury in Wiltshire is the monument's heaviest standing stone. Known as the diamond stone or 'Swindon' stone, it resembles a four-pointed diamond or lozenge with one point in the ground. Why do so many stones at Avebury and elsewhere in Neolithic Britain have this particular shape?

2. *Below:* The high circular bank of the third-millennium henge of Maumbury Rings in Dorchester. This anciently sacred place was refashioned by the Romans as an amphitheatre and used by the residents of the town in more recent centuries.

3. *Above:* A whirlwind spiralling up dust and straw on the Beckhampton Downs of Wiltshire, near Avebury, on a fine hot day. Whirlwinds are a major natural manifestation of the enigmatic spiral in both two and three dimensions. *Photograph by David Banks*

4. *Below left:* A powerful stationary whirlwind with a column reaching to the sky. The great length of these spiralling columns brings celestial symbolism into the interpretation. *Photograph by Terry Clewes*

5. *Below right:* A circle with an impressed spiral pattern formed by a natural atmospheric vortex striking a field of wheat. The ramparts of the Iron Age fort on Scratchbury Hill loom in the background.

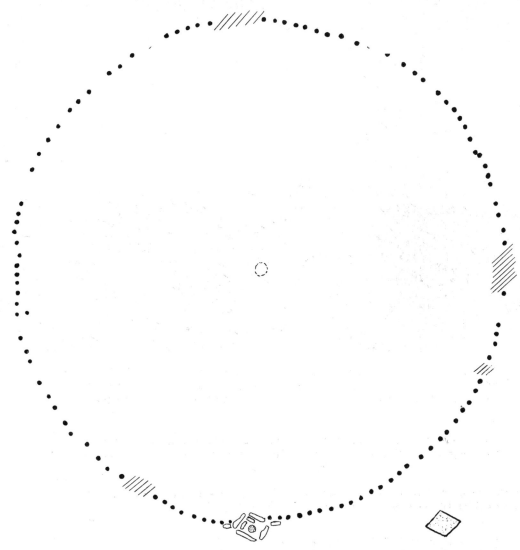

The below-ground structure of the barrow at Six Wells, in South Wales, showing the stake ring and the peripheral siting of the lozenge-shaped cist with its cremation deposit (after Cyril Fox). The cist cover is shown removed, inset lower right of sketch.

fragments and ashes of burnt bones.' Another turf barrow on the Brendon Hills, with a concealed stone kerb three metres (ten feet) in diameter, was found to have a burial-free pit 60 centimetres deep.

As Fox stressed so clearly, the construction of the Six Wells barrow was directed around the central domed pit, itself surrounded by a surface area which must have been treated with respect, since it had not been hard trodden as elsewhere. But the near-central pit was vacant, whereas another pit, peripherally sited outside the stake circle although within the cist that straddled the circle, was occupied. Fox concluded that 'the stake circle was in effect the precinct wall of a shrine or sanctuary; burial would pollute an area "occult, withheld, untrod", and could not be permitted. A votary, marginally interred, might however expect favour from the Power to whom the pit was dedicated, or with whom contact was established by libations, food-offerings, or other ritual centred on the pit.'

Fox saw in the vacancy of the central pit a means by which 'a chthonic [or earthly] power was approached, consulted or appeased . . . and that we may have here a barbarous version of the sanctuary with its tenemos.' It was a temporary shrine, soon covered to house the dead man, but wherein, according to Fox, he had been 'ousted from the central and dominant position which we have good reason to believe he held in the earlier (megalithic) religion of the Highland Zone. Whatever authority the man . . . wielded during life, in death he was a suppliant. The concept involved in the worship of the dead is here visibly overthrown.'

On the basis of the vortex theory I feel that I can go farther than Sir Cyril Fox could in his day. I see the Six Wells barrow as a local variation on the theme of burial within the realm and comfort of the Goddess's protective shroud, with the same yearning for eternal life and rebirth as is expressed in all round barrow constructions. The cremated remains are set on the vortex-spiral's outer limb. The position of the cist allows the spirit of the deceased to penetrate the sanctuary where cist and circle overlap; the stake hole arrangement west and east of the cist suggests a clockwise spiral entry. The rites were to allow the spirit to spiral inwards to the centremost pit which had been left vacant for that purpose, with free access to the subterranean realm of the Goddess. During construction and the performance of later rites much trampling had taken place, because Fox remarked that a widespread layer, which he called hard-pan, had developed. The level of the hard-pan 'floor' suggests that the ancient grass surface had been earlier protected by a temporary covering of soil. Why should this have been, unless to safeguard the spiral-laid grass?

In some of the stony, upland areas of the British Isles straight rows of stones, sometimes megalithic, are found in association with cairns or cists. Round stone cairns take the place of earthen round barrows in these regions.

Single or double rows are most common, but triplets have been found as well. Some 70 stone rows are known on Dartmoor, for instance, and there are others in Cornwall, on Exmoor, in Scotland and Ireland. Some rows are short, others surprisingly long, extending to two or three kilometres. The longer ones meander over hill and dale with less-than-perfect linearity. The origin of some of the rows may be linked to that of the cursuses. With double rows one naturally thinks of avenues and processions, but a single line of stones is more puzzling.

Straight settings of posts have been found in connection with the stake circles of some barrows, and more will probably be found in the future with today's improved excavation techniques. A bell barrow at Poole has an entrance alignment of posts along a causeway across the ditch. Several barrows have similar

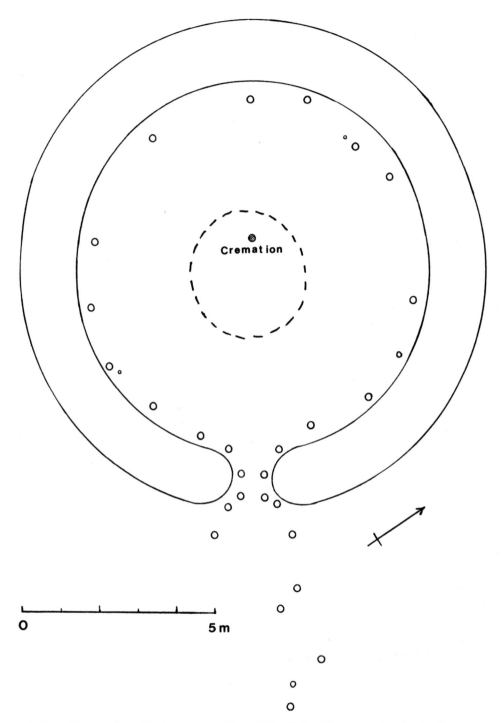

Round barrow from Poole, Dorset, with an internal ring of posts and a short entrance avenue of posts (after H. Case). The avenue crosses the causewayed ditch to arrive at the inner sanctum where an off-centre burial was discovered within a ring of stakes beneath the inner turf mound (indicated by the dotted line).

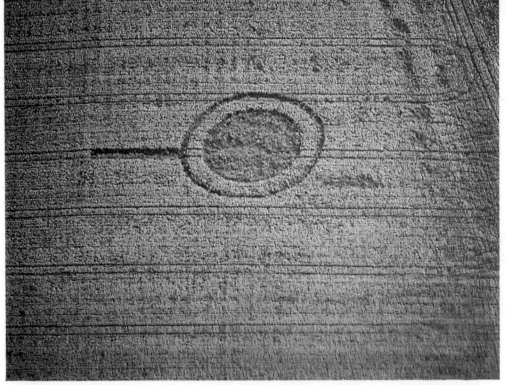

Aerial photograph of a natural spiral-circle with outer ring and exit spur (Pepperbox Hill, Whiteparish, south of Salisbury, Wiltshire, 1987). Elsewhere in Britain crop circle spurs or 'avenues' have been found as well, the longest at 40 metres appearing close to Stonehenge in 1990.

circular trenches interrupted with a single causeway—at least eleven are known in southern England alone. The idea of the single-causewayed circular fosse is reminiscent of henges—but henges were built to be used by the living, and they continued in use over very many centuries. So why would the causeway be introduced to the interior of a sepulchral mound—a causeway that was to be used briefly, and most likely just once? A possible explanation may lie in a type of 'causewayed' spiral-pattern circle formed naturally in crops, several examples of which have been studied in southern England.

The main features of these naturally-formed meteorological oddities seem to be copied in the Poole bell barrow construction—including the causeway! By a means as yet unknown, the forces that provide flow and counterflow in the circular aspects of the natural vortex systems can also produce an incidental linear feature radial to the main circles. If Neolithic and Bronze Age people had discovered such a pattern, they might have decided to mark out the main features with stakes and posts, and the result would have been a barrow like the one at Poole.

On the other hand, the stone rows found on Dartmoor, often with a cairn as a focus, may indicate actual paths along which narrow-path whirlwinds had been moving, the location of the cairn occupying some special zone, such as a place where the 'spiritual vision' halted temporarily or the point at which it parted from the earth's surface.

6

The Cult of the Round Barrow

The fourth millennium had seen the flowering of the cults that produced the causewayed enclosures, the cursuses, the earthen long barrows, the chambered long barrows and the passage graves; but the last of the long barrows were constructed about 3000 BC, and chambered long barrows did not continue in use beyond the middle of the next millennium. By about 2500 BC the Cotswold–Severn tombs had been used for the last time and sealed. One of these, the West Kennet barrow of the Windmill Hill people, was deeply filled with 'occupation earth' (that is, earth seemingly taken from dwelling areas); some farewell deposits were ritually set in place (a roe deer horn was laid at the threshold of one cell), and the tomb's entrance and façade secured with colossal megaliths as guardian deities of the ancestral dead. The area's first round barrows had been built in the preceding centuries, and nearby Silbury Hill had been finished, too.

The changeover from long barrow to round barrow burial customs happened slowly, appearing first in Yorkshire and spreading progressively over the whole country as the power of the new ideas took hold. In many areas the old ways continued for a while beside the new before they were displaced. It is likely that in regions where crop circle and vortex activity were particularly strong, round barrow burial was adopted sooner rather than later, but over the next thousand years round barrows, or their stone equivalents, cairns, came to be seen throughout Britain, with every part of the country participating in this burial cult by the time of the Beaker period in the late third millennium. Single barrows and small barrow groups abounded, but clustering into large cemeteries was more limited, and restricted to the more favourable areas within the ancient occupation zones.

Spiral-pattern formation is most commonly seen in summertime over fields of growing crops or in long grass, the most favourable regions being the undulating country of the upland hills and downs. Ordinary whirlwinds occur in the flatter regions, too, and they also choose hill ridges, plateaux and summits. The proximities of hill crests are favourable because of wind-shear effects. Where the siting of round barrows was governed by vortex systems, this can explain the apparently incongruous barrow constructions found upon ridges or along so-called false crests, which have often aroused comment among British archaeologists. These very features tend to encourage and increase the forces necessary to trigger and sustain vortices of the eddy-type. The following modern eye-witness account by Mr C. G. Ward describes a whirlwind seen on Pilsdon Pen, a hill-top which was occupied in prehistoric times and is the highest point of the present-day county of Dorset. There are at least two bowl barrows on Pilsdon Pen.

On 3 September 1955 a picnic party was lunching about 25 yards from the Triangulation Point, at a spot where the ground slopes sharply down to the east. Suddenly at about 1205 GMT a sound was heard from the west like sand being loaded into a truck. But only a level stretch of coarse grass was to be seen. Some of the grass in the direction of the sound was then observed to be moving and becoming flattened, while bits of paper were seen whirling in the air, though the wind was light where the party was. In a few seconds the miniature whirlwind was upon the picnickers. It removed a small paper bag, and lifted an umbrella which had been left open on the ground. This was moved in an anticlockwise manner away north-eastwards over the earthen rampart of the prehistoric fort and about twenty feet into the air. It was then brought back almost within reach of the owner who was by then standing up, but it was lifted away eastwards and finally deposited about fifty yards down the hill. At the time the nearest cloud was a rather dark cumulus which seemed to have passed before the whirlwind occurred.

In the eyes of the Late Neolithic and Early Bronze Age people, living in a world dominated by magic and religion, sightings like this would have been regarded as sacred signs—divine manifestations of a moving spirit. The weird sound, the obvious spiralling in the air and flattening in the grass, would have proclaimed the sanctity of the place and its suitability as a future burial site. A temporary marking-out of the ground would doubtless have followed, and on some later occasion a typical bowl barrow would have been raised there. In the absence of a well-defined flattened area with a definite circumference, the barrow would probably have been made circular, using peg and rope, and its diameter selected more for convenience than geometrical accuracy. The place on Pilsdon Pen where the whirlwind was seen, besides being on the hill-top, was also the point where the slope changed rapidly, as it does on ridges or hill-crests. This is a common occurrence and many examples could be cited.

Barrows were raised on many hill-tops—including Cley Hill (West Wiltshire) and Hambledon Hill (North Dorset), as well as Pilsdon Pen—and along prominent crest lines or ridges as at West Overton near the Sanctuary (North Wiltshire), Priddy Nine Barrows on the Mendips, and Nine Barrow Down, not far from Rempstone Stone Circle near Swanage (Dorset). The concentration of barrow building in these and other regions may have been due partly to commonplace whirlwind formation and partly because the areas were more thickly populated. Where the land was suitable for cultivation, spiral-circles may have appeared in the summer crops, and it is obvious that the locations of the Neolithic and Bronze Age barrows would have been linked to the regions colonised and farmed by the inhabitants of the times—the better-drained upland parts. In certain areas barrows abound in great numbers; in others, they are isolated or appear in unconnected groups, having been constructed in a seemingly random manner, sometimes at intervals of decades or even centuries.

Both Britain and Ireland have many sets of grouped barrows, so much so that the term 'cemetery' often seems appropriate. Yet even here most barrows are scattered, without evidence of any preconceived plan. The Oakley Down group in North Dorset is typical, as is the Poor Lot group of 44 barrows in the south of the same county. The Poor Lot barrows spread across the borders of what are now three parishes in the neighbourhood of the elliptical megalithic 'circle' of Winterbourne Abbas (to their east) and the Long Bredy long and bank barrows (to their west), and include 22 bowl barrows, seven bell barrows, six disc and two bell-disc barrows, two triple barrows and five pond barrows. There are some purely earthen circles also, as at Litton Cheney. The variety and numbers suggest a Bronze Age population-centre close by for several centuries. Yet even here there is no evidence of planning—no 'chess-board' patterns with rows and ranks of barrows, as with the more ordered megaliths of Carnac in Brittany; no barrow avenues as with the double stone-rows at Avebury and other monumental sites. Where seemingly linked groups exist, there is never a perfect geometrical arrangement; barrows are not set at the points of a triangle or a square or about the circumference of a circle. Apart from a small number of double or triple barrows enclosed within a single ditch, barrows appear to have been built one at a time over

Part of the Bronze Age barrow group on Oakley Down, North Dorset, close to the Dorset Cursus (not visible in this photograph). The barrows are not arranged in orderly fashion as in modern cemeteries.

a long period, without any advance planning. Indeed, in terms of simple geometrical forms, the most perfect are those which archaeologists term 'linear cemeteries'.

There are several of these in the neighbourhood of Stonehenge, obviously built with some underlying logic, but not according to geometrical measurement. Of the 27 round barrows at Winterbourne Stoke, eleven are roughly aligned with a more ancient long barrow to the south-west. A certain degree of progressive planning appears to have developed over the centuries, based loosely on this alignment, and it is possible that it was used in the absence of a convenient whirlwind or spiral-circle vortex discovery, perhaps in cases of accident or epidemic, when several important burials had to be carried out together or one after the other. The sacred area near a disused long barrow—a place that had served the community's ancestors for centuries—would have been an eminently suitable alternative. There may also have been some degree of mystical sanctity linking the long barrow with the western end of the Stonehenge Cursus, because round barrows began to appear along or very close to the line between the two.

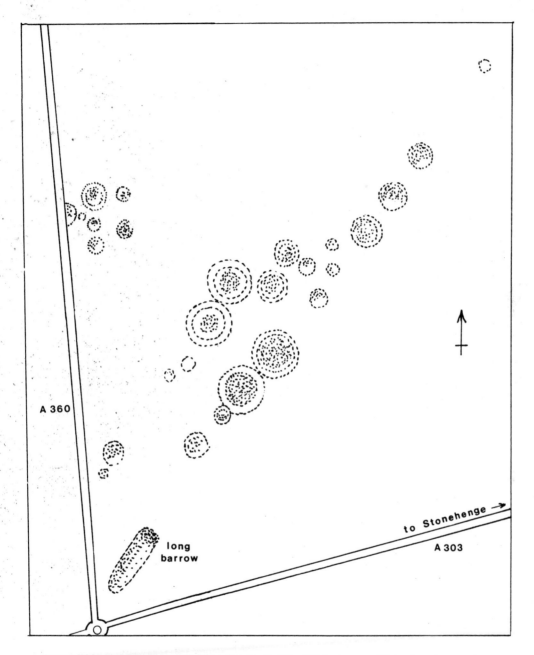

A round-barrow cemetery adjoining the much older Winterbourne Stoke long barrow two kilometres west of Stonehenge. Some of the barrows have an almost linear orientation north-east from the long barrow.

Of the round barrows at Winterbourne Stoke, some are obviously fairly early, around 2100 BC, and two had been built as a pair. Five held inhumations as primary interments, and so would appear to predate the cremated burials of the other barrows of the linear set.

Another type of cemetery is the Seven Barrows group south of Beacon Hill, near Litchfield in the north of Hampshire. Close to the ancient mounds six cropfield spiral-circles are known to have appeared in the years from 1981 to 1990. The recent crop circles are the result of vortex formation, downwind either from the conical hill a couple of kilometres to the north or from the hill to the west, and the barrows may well owe their origin to similar happenings in the Bronze Age. Over the years, in many parts of Wessex, numerous cases have been noted of spiral-circles in crops which formed in the area of round barrows.

Unlike the simplest bowl barrows and cairns which are ditchless, barrows with peripheral ditches occasionally intersect one another's ditches, and sometimes a single ditch or a ditch and bank will surround two or three barrows. Whereas the latter were obviously planned as such and built together, the former may well have been built at different times. The occurrence of double or triple cropfield spiral-circles makes one wonder if double or triple barrows were so planned because adjacent double or triple cropfield circles were found in the field. The site of the second barrow may have been chosen either because of a later vortex event which chanced to overlap the first, or because the place was thought to share the sanctity emanating from the first barrow.

There is considerable evidence that many round barrows were raised on a grass surface or in cultivated fields; cores consisting of turf heaps or stacks are quite common. Sometimes the ancient vegetation is well preserved, and the types of snail-shell found amongst the soil have proved that construction took place in a generally open landscape. When a barrow is built, it preserves the ancient soil and protects the sub-surface rocks from further weathering and water dissolution. As a result, beneath long barrows and round barrows built upon chalk downland, the chalk surface beneath the sub-soil has been found to retain evidence of primitive arable farming before a decision was made to build barrows.

In more than a dozen cases, round barrows seem to lie on the boundary of or inside a field which already existed, and in several barrows from Cornwall to Yorkshire, weeds and cereal remains have been found, indicating nearby cultivation. Paul Ashbee has published an aerial photograph showing round barrows sited upon ancient fields on New Barn Down and Earl's Farm Down, about four kilometres east of Stonehenge.

Of course, cultivated fields provide the ideal landscape for the display of vortex patterns or any other whirlwind motion. Religious pressures and the logic of the burial rite can explain why a prehistoric farmer would allow a barrow to be built

A Beaker inhumation contracted in the foetal position, from a barrow near Roundway, Devizes in Wiltshire (John Thurnam). The drawing of the articulated bones is a little fanciful but it recreates well the aspect of the corpse at the time of burial. Note the attendant drinking vessel or beaker.

upon what had been for him a perfectly good arable field; nor, presumably, would he object to a certain hindrance in his routine work that would ensue forever more. Sometimes this would be the beginning of the growth of a notable barrow cemetery on what had been, until then, excellent cultivable land of the highest quality. At other times the pre-existing field may have been left fallow, or had perhaps arrived at the hay-cutting stage when the circle-making vortex or the mischievous whirlwind passed by.

Certain zones, fields included, seem to have more than their fair share of vortex activity. Round barrows may have come to identify the places of past circle traces by marking the positions of spirits seen rising from the earth, and suggest how barrow cemeteries could develop in a region known to be congenial to spirits and therefore suitable for the recent dead as well. The agricultural element is important here. Farmers may have been disposed to display a degree of unusual goodwill towards these manifestations because the activities of the spirits were *on their land*, the land they knew well, the land that assured their livelihood, and which had been cultivated by their forefathers in earlier times.

What do we know about burial practices from the start of the round barrow stage of the British Late Neolithic period to the end of the Bronze Age? Primary burials in the earlier round barrows involved a crouched or contracted inhumation. Cremation was not common before the approach of the Middle Bronze Age, say around 1700–1800 BC, after which it came to be the dominant burial rite until the start of the Iron Age. Admittedly, cremation did occur in the British Late Neolithic period, but as a general practice the rite seems to be linked with the spread of a people who used Corded-Ware pottery and certain axe types.

Crouched inhumations were accomplished by curving the corpse into the foetal position in a manner reminiscent of a new-born infant—evidence of an intent to seek rebirth after death, strengthened, most probably, by the thought of physical contact with the womb of the Goddess or Earth Mother. Often the corpse was laid facing east or west, but other directions have been recorded as well. It was laid on either its left or right side; both positions are equally common, and no theory has previously been suggested to explain why one direction was chosen rather than the other. However, the theory of burial at the centre of spiral-circles at once offers a very good reason.

Spiral-circles are made by outwardly moving air. If a corpse is buried at the spiral centre of a clockwise-rotating (right-handed) spiral, so that the body lies along the direction of *outflow*, then it must be laid on its left side. For an anticlockwise circle the body would need to be on its right side.

In 1987 I carried out some experiments at Beckhampton near Avebury, within sight of Windmill Hill and Silbury Hill. I started from the premise that the eyes would *face* east, so it followed that in a clockwise direction the head was to the north, and in an anticlockwise direction it was to the south. This could explain the main recorded variations in the style of the burial rite. Alternatively, the body might be in-turning instead of out-turning, as if to permit the spirit to enter the ground for the purpose of rebirth through the spiral hole—which therefore becomes a womb-opening! This would mean laying the body on its right side in a right-handed spiral and on its left side in a left-handed spiral.

In many of the later round barrows the primary cremation was deposited in an urn. This may seem rational enough, except that a great number of the urns were carefully arranged upside-down! In his statistical analysis of collared urns in Great Britain and Ireland I. H. Longworth found that 23 per cent of cremation urns were inverted. However, an explanation for the meaning of this long-standing custom seems possible on the spiral-circle theory of barrow consecration.

Because the spiral centre is at the vortex centre and shares its vertical axis, it occupies, in primitive mysticism, a common path between heaven and earth. The inverted, lidless urn has the function of directing the spirit downwards, perhaps to a meeting with the Goddess as a prelude to rebirth and the promised resurrection. So cremation becomes the means of reducing the body of the dead person to a formless, primaeval substance (the ashes) and of releasing the spirit into free air. By means of the surface spiral the soul-shadow is transported into the ground for reunion with the Goddess, after which it can begin its ascent to the heavens.

Not all social groups in the country may have known of the custom of inverting urns, or wished to adopt it. Certainly many secondary burials were urned, and a lot were inverted, but even more were arranged the conventional way up. Accurate

The way in which the two senses of spiral revolution may have been used at the time of round-barrow interment, demonstrated in 1987. *Above:* The right-handed spiral (clockwise out); *below:* the left-handed spiral (anticlockwise out).

dating is virtually impossible at present, but there does seem to have been a later progression from inverted urn cremation to upright urn cremation, suggesting a change from an earthward- to a skyward-dominated religion—a part of the ideological change that took place all over Europe and is evident in other ways in the British Bronze Age. Urn inversion was intended to guide the spirit into the dominion of the Goddess; reversing the rite sent the spirit directly skywards to the realm of the solar and celestial deities.

At the time of burial on chalk downland, the corpse was either laid on the ancient surface or was interred in a chalk-cut grave. Sometimes a wooden coffin was provided. In stonier, rocky regions a grave was cut into rock—as at Llandow in Wales, and in Scotland—or built of stone slabs in the form of a cist. What is significant is that the bereaved members of some early societies carved symbols on slabs or stones incorporated into the burial place. Although any religious inscriptions which may have been cut into wooden objects have not survived, a wealth of symbolic markings remains on stone slabs at some of the undisturbed sites.

Best known among the symbols are *cup-marks*, which have been found extensively in western and northern England and Scotland. Although they can be seen on other sepulchres, like the interiors of Irish passage-graves, they are more usually found at outdoor locations, such as in association with megalithic circles and rocky outcropping slabs in Scotland and northern England. As with the spiral motif, although some of the cup-marks occur in places associated with death, they are unlikely to be a death *symbol* in any direct way. In fact the opposite is more probably the case: their more general symbolism seems to be a deeply spiritual identification with the awareness and purpose of life.

The *spiral* is a symbol of birth and rebirth. It bridges the abyss of darkness between life and life-after-death. By countering the fear of death it expresses the optimistic reinstatement of life. In a funerary context it symbolises hope. Spirals have been found on stones beneath cairns and barrows. The returning spiral from a cist slab beneath a barrow at La Mancha, Peeblesshire, effectively symbolises rebirth.

The underside of a stone in a layer covering a Beaker-age cist at Catterline, Kincardineshire, itself secreted beneath a gravelly mound, bore two separate spirals and a concentric oval ring. Because this surface had become heavily weathered prior to its incorporation into the structure of the cist, the pecked slab must have originated elsewhere. Another slab from the same cist carried a cup-mark which had been carried to the logical limit of total perforation: the drilling of the hole had been achieved by countersinking from opposite faces. This stone appeared to be unweathered, and the crouched inhumation within the cist lay on its left side facing south-east.

I believe that the sepulchral meaning of the cup-mark is linked to the basic ideas discussed in this book, and I shall return to the whole subject in more detail in Chapter 13.

Many interments beneath barrows were accompanied by furnishings as part of the burial goods. Some belonged to the deceased as personal ornaments, weapons or objects associated with prestige or power. Barrows at Avebury and Normanton even yielded musical bone flutes. Additional objects were introduced as part of the funeral rites and the awaited afterlife or the journey thereto—such as tokens of food and drink suggested by the survival of ceramic vessels. Beaker pottery is characteristic, and the well-shaped pots or 'drinking vessels' often bore symbolic decoration inspired by aspects of the contemporary religious beliefs.

Evidence of ritual practices survives in various ways. A barrow at Radley, Oxfordshire, covered a Beaker burial accompanied by the horn core and metatarsus of an ox or bull. This hints at some form of bull worship. Offerings of a similar nature have been found in round barrows at Crichel Down (Dorset) and Linch Hill Corner (Oxon) among others. The more ancient long barrows, too, very often housed the bones of ox or bull.

Necklaces and pendants of shells and fossils had a high degree of symbolic significance. Pierced cowrie shells, particularly, signified fertility and rebirth.

Further evidence of a developed ritual tradition was the ceremonial breaking of prestige and/or personal objects. A pot or beaker would be smashed and the pieces laid round the head, or fine flint implements would be deliberately cracked and shattered. Axes and daggers have also been found broken. The intention was to release the spirit from the stone or vessel or weapon, so that it could accompany the departing spirit of the deceased.

Sometimes the burial place was covered with loads of occupation material—earth impregnated with pottery sherds, stone chippings, flint artefacts and other domestic waste products like animal bones—as though the floor of an occupation site had been removed and transferred to the barrow. Sometimes a whole range of pottery types appears in this manner as a single deposit, the oldest dating back centuries to the Late Neolithic period. The rite seems to have been performed because of the importance and sanctity of the site to the deceased. The occupation material may have been removed from a dwelling or place of worship and used to cover and enshrine the spiral image that had been formed in the grass or the crop, in order to give it an absolute and lasting protection.

Pond barrows have long puzzled barrow archaeologists. The very name is a contradiction, the words pond (a depression) and barrow (a mound) being opposite in meaning. Pond barrows are circular hollows which range in diameter from ten to 40 metres, including the regular external bank. Two pond barrows have recently been examined. One at Winterbourne Steepleton (Dorset) had 34 pits in it, of which eleven held substantial quantities of human remains, one pit

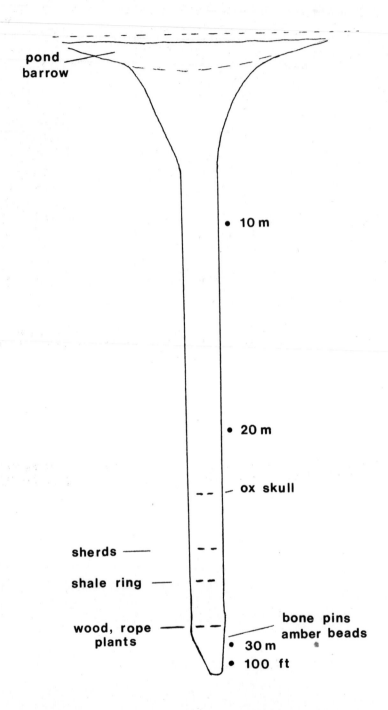

pond
barrow

• 10 m

• 20 m

ox skull

sherds

shale ring

wood, rope
plants

bone pins
amber beads

• 30 m
• 100 ft

A Bronze Age shaft, 30 metres deep, at Wilsford near Stonehenge, found at the time of excavating a pond barrow (after Paul Ashbee). It was carefully dug with round walls using broad-bladed axes.

6. Flattened crop circle at Woolstone, Gloucestershire, in the Cotswolds, formed on 21 July, 1989. The effect of vulvar symbolism is heightened by the size and position of the bare-earth patch.

7. Castlerigg stone circle with the dome of Blencathra in the distance. In many cases of crop circle formation there is an obvious hill/circle relationship. *Photograph by Geoffrey Smith*

8. Aerial view of the circle with 'flattened' perimeter at South Wonston in which the author built the first of his AD 1987 stone circles.

9. Three natural crop circles in a line, photographed at Bratton, Wiltshire. Doubles occur occasionally as well, sometimes touching, as with round barrows.

being central and ten peripheral. The other 23 pits were either empty or held pottery or cremations. I feel that the main purpose of this sanctified area could not have been sepulchral; I see it as a place designed for vigil, worship, and ritual offerings. It suggests that at least some pond barrows can be regarded as subterranean shrines in a local cult unique to Wessex.

Excavation of the pond barrow at Wilsford, a couple of kilometres south-west of Stonehenge, produced something totally unexpected. What began as a careful but rather routine excavation, estimated to last a few weeks, managed to take three summers (1960 to 1962) to complete. The initial removal of the contents of the primary 'pond shape' led to further and further deepening of the hollow and a progressive descent into what seemed to be an inverted cone. When the cone had been emptied to a depth of six metres (20 feet) below the ancient surface nothing older than a single Iron Age pot had been found (and that was at three metres). At the six-metre point the cone ended and a vertical shaft began. The shaft had a nearly constant diameter of 1.8 metres (or nearly six feet) and continued through the solid chalk to an extraordinary depth of 31 metres, close on 100 feet.

At a depth of 22 metres an ox-skull was found, and below that a shale ring and the remains of Mid-Bronze Age pottery, but from the waterlogged lower sections came considerable quantities of wood including wooden vessels, stitched composite vessels, rope, miscellaneous vegetable matter, bone pins and several amber beads. Radiocarbon dating based on seven pieces of wood gave a date of about 1600–1700 BC, which puts the latest use and construction date of the shaft as Early to Mid Bronze Age.

What was the shaft for? So much labour for a well seems unlikely in the Bronze Age. It may be yet another variation on the theme of ritual monuments—this time an inversion of the customary above-ground varieties. The cutting of the chalk had been done with broad-bladed axes which may indicate some kind of ritual, and if this was so the aim may have been to create a means of making contact with underworld deities.

Whatever the intentions of the diggers, the resulting shaft is basically another circular monument, the subterranean equivalent of the spiralling whirlwind. Inquisitive people may have wished to explore the origin of the whirling vortex— perceived as an exhalation from subterranean depths; by digging through the surface circle, or crop-field spiral-circle, they were approaching the lower abode of the Goddess. The enterprising attempt was beyond their capabilities—indeed, it would be no easier today using workshop hand-tools. The Wilsford shaft was as futile an exercise in terrestrial descent as it would be to climb a hill in order to get nearer to the moon.

7

The Sacred Centre

In modern Britain we are so accustomed to the square-cornered ground plans of houses and public buildings that we tend to think the rectangular shape is the only acceptable one. Since the end of the Iron Age and Romano–British times it has been our basic constructional design. For thousands of years before that, however, round houses predominated. What is more unexpected is that the buildings of Britain's earliest Neolithic farming communities, built in timber 6,000 years ago, were based on rectilinear architecture as they are nowadays.

The oldest known rectangular dwellings in the British Isles, at Ballynagilly, County Tyrone, with hearths, pits and pottery, are dated to the middle of the fifth millennium BC. A later one, measuring 6.5 × 6 metres, had walls of split oak planks set in trenches and supported by packing stones. Throughout much of the Neolithic era the building of rectangular houses and huts continued with no obvious improvements until, fairly abruptly, a circular design was introduced. The new style gradually spread all over Britain, and from the Late Neolithic period, through the Bronze Age into the Iron Age, round dwellings were the norm. Although some Bronze Age structures based on straight-line architecture have been identified, most of these seem to have been intended as huts or stockades for animals or storage.

The custom of the circular house has no obvious contemporary parallels on the

Continent, so how can we explain this decidedly insular tradition?

Rectangular construction is the most rational; it simplifies the process of planning, building, and subdivision into rooms, reasons quite sufficient in themselves to explain its universal use in most ages of mankind. Because of this, and for other reasons, the square and the rectangle came to stand for earthbound stability and order in the symbolic imagery of early societies.

Although circles may be the most natural shape for wigwams, circular construction in timber and stone presents many problems. Besides the difficulty of working around a circle and having to build upwards with essentially straight materials (such as timber or flat-sided stones), round buildings of large diameter also create roof-drainage problems, especially when the run-off is directed into a central courtyard; nor is it easy to build beyond ground-floor level. Nevertheless, in spite of the drawbacks and the proven success of the early rectangular building methods of the fifth and fourth millennia BC, the new fashion for circular dwellings became so entrenched as to resist change over the next two thousand years. It can be no coincidence that this period corresponded with the advent of the era of circular public monuments—henges and passage-graves, megalithic and earthen circles, circular barrows and man-made Silbury Hill. They are all aspects of the religious cult which worshipped and sanctified the circle and saw it as the epitome of divine symbolism. Through the tornado, the whirlwind and the crop-circle vortex, deities were brought closer to humanity because heaven could be seen interacting with Earth; it must have been the thrust of these spiritual forces which fuelled the desire to create circular buildings and which determined the shapes of stone circles and henges, including the henge of Stonehenge at its founding.

Moreover, just like the megalithic circles and round barrows, a number of so-called hut circles are not actually circular. For instance, a stone circle at Sands of Forvie, Grampian, which Alexander Thom saw as a designed ellipse but I believe to be the result of a drifting crop-circle vortex, is probably a hut circle. Whatever could have motivated people to erect buildings on the basis of ground plans that were elliptical or egg-shaped?

Primitive and archaic societies are known to have regarded their houses symbolically as the 'Centre of the World', sacred retreats where men and women could communicate with the deities. Within their familiar boundaries space was ordered and secure; outside, it was unknown, chaotic and dark. The house was a microcosm of the world within the larger microcosm of the whole community, and as each village had its own sacred Centre, so too did each house, consecrated according to custom and belief by some divine manifestation, or by an approved ritual or method of construction. Each of these 'Centres' lay on its own axis of the world, which passed through all three cosmic levels—the heavens, the atmosphere and the earth.

The symbolism of a Cosmic Axis is extremely ancient and enduring. In recent times the stone age cultures of the Arctic and North American peoples regarded the central post of their timber cabins as corresponding to the Cosmic Axis. Offerings to the celestial deities were deposited at the foot of the post since this was the route to heaven. When the Central Asian nomads wished to perform similar rites in their *yourts* or huts, they set up a tree to project through the central smoke-hole, its seven branches symbolising the seven celestial spheres.

This idea seems to have been common to all ancient societies, and one suspects that it is part of that human condition which feels a 'nostalgia for Paradise'. Spiritual comfort and the eternal hope of salvation come from having a sacred refuge and a home that is always at the 'Centre', in direct communication with the deities of the other cosmic levels.

It is my theory that the ancient Britons, too, lightened the heaviness of their arduous lives by pursuing religious beliefs which raised their expectations of attaining Paradise in the next world. Such aspirations can be seen in their barrows, and now we find them in their housing.

Some houses or public buildings may well have been founded on whirlwind sites and made circular in consequence. A few would have been raised on vortex-circle field markings, after staking out the circumference; these ended up circular, egg-shaped or elliptical. But the majority were probably set out on circular plans, in imitation of the circular cosmological symbolism of the prevailing religious beliefs, and were consecrated by rites whose character we can piece together from the small clues left by dedicatory tokens and sacrificial remains which survive to this day. That the sun played a part is evident from the seemingly high frequency with which the entrances to dwellings were positioned to face east or south-east.

The plan opposite, of a farmhouse on New Barn Down near Worthing in Sussex, is a good example. Dating from the Middle to Late Bronze Age, it has a diameter of about five metres for the post-hole circle C–K if that is regarded as standing for the positions of internal roof-supports and therefore the inner circle of a double-ring roundhouse, or a length of six metres if viewed as an oval building using the post-hole series A–L. Whether single-ring or double-ring, it was one of the most common types in southern England in the Middle Bronze Age.

Circular dwellings persisted through the Iron Age as well, but with a gradual decline in totals as the numbers of rectangular buildings increased. There is a palisaded Early Iron Age enclosure at High Knowes, Alnham (Northumberland), constructed in the earlier and middle part of the first millennium, in which the element of circularity remains wholly dominant.

One of the most important—or perhaps *the* most important—of the buildings dating from the Late Neolithic and Bronze Age periods is Woodhenge, the multi-

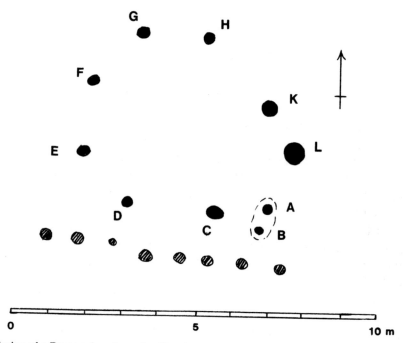

Post-holes of a Bronze Age farm dwelling (with an adjoining section of palisade) from New Barn Down, Clapham, Worthing, Sussex (after Guilbert). As so often in those days, the entrance faced south-east.

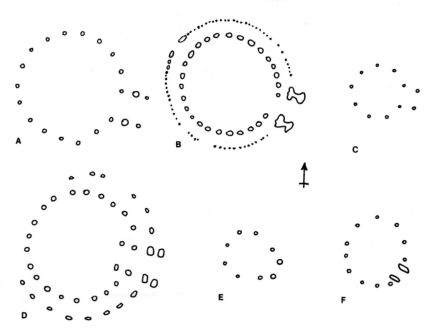

Simplified plans of roundhouse dwellings of various diameters showing post-hole positions (after Guilbert). In some cases the roof area and hence habitable area may have been rather greater. (A) Little Woodbury (Wiltshire); (B) Pimperne (Dorset), (C) Moel y Gaer (Clwyd); (D) Little Woodbury (Wiltshire); (E) New Barn Down (Sussex); (F) Eldon's Seat (Dorset).

ringed timber structure whose shape was analysed in Chapter 4. It seems to have served as a communal meeting place, and, to judge by the evidence of bone-filled pits (the finds include the bones and teeth of pig and ox) was at times a centre for feasting, probably at religious festivals. Radiocarbon analysis gives a date of roughly 2275 BC, making Woodhenge two centuries younger than the early phase of adjacent Durrington Walls, and older than the sarsen stage of Stonehenge. I showed earlier how the remarkable egg-shape pattern at Woodhenge was consistent with the outline made by spiralling vortices, of the type responsible for crop circles. Such a discovery would have been treated as a powerful omen of divine origin. A timber-post temple shrine or observatory was then built, possibly lintelled, the idea later translated into stone at the centuries-old ceremonial monument of Stonehenge.

Like any other theory, this is conjectural, but whatever the answer may be the dedicatory offering of a three-year-old girl was made and a building raised. Other foundation offerings followed. On the south side of the outermost ring, in post-hole 16, a ceremonial axe of fragile chalk was found, and another in post-hole 21 on the side of midsummer sunrise in the second ring. This use of ceremonial chalk axes is found at other sites in Britain, some of which go farther back into the Neolithic or forward into the Bronze Age (including sarsen Stonehenge). These discoveries, combined with the ox bones found among grave goods, suggest the existence of an axe-cult related to a fairly general bull-cult—both known to be part of Goddess worship. Two post-holes of Woodhenge's main timber ring, one on the east side, the other facing the most southerly moonrise, held ritually-deposited chalk cups, signifying femininity and fertility. One was accompanied by a chalk plaque with a hole through it. Unlike the timber structures at the Sanctuary, near Silbury Hill and Avebury, and some other sites such as Mount Pleasant and Croft Moraig, Woodhenge's rings of post-holes were never later reinterpreted in stone, perhaps because developments at Stonehenge came to serve the spiritual needs of the Durrington Walls community.

The chalk cups found in the main, original, ring are particularly important. Chalk is a porous material unsuitable for cooking and most other domestic purposes, but similar cups have been found in Neolithic and Bronze Age ritual contexts in many parts of Britain. These include foundation deposits, as at Woodhenge and Stonehenge, deposits in the ditches of causewayed enclosures, cremation grave goods in pits, cairns or barrows, and symbolic arrangements at shrines. The nature of the associations sometimes seems to point to rites connected with fertility, rebirth, death and so on. The most moving was the discovery in 1939 of a votive group in an abandoned tunnel at the flint-mines of Grimes Graves in Norfolk, on the right-hand side of a gallery entrance. Flint extraction from these mines was at its peak in the period 2100–1800 BC.

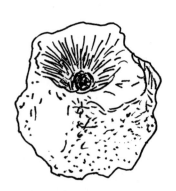

Chalk cups from Wilsford *(left)* and Woodhenge *(centre and right)*.

A roughly fashioned, obese and pregnant chalk figurine of a Goddess, 11 centimetres high, stood on a pedestal of chalk blocks, accompanied by male and female fertility symbols. Beside the figure was a carved chalk phallus and chalk balls, and in front an arrangement of mined flints set in an isosceles triangle with a chalk cup at the triangular base opposite the Goddess. Seven antler picks lay on the flint 'altar'. The whole was interpreted as an appeal to the ruling divinities for the safe discovery of an abundance of good working flint.

Besides confirming the meaning of the carved chalk balls, this collection speaks eloquently for the significance of the triangle and the cup in Neolithic imagery. That the cup equates with the womb opening and therefore female energy brings us back full circle, quite literally, to the natural formation of spiral crop circles. Every crop circle with spiral and axial centre is both vulva and vagina in the earth, through which the spirits are released from the womb of the Great Goddess at the time of their rebirth. The chalk cups at Woodhenge tell us of the fertility and immortality aspirations of the Stonehenge people, as do the cups deposited with cremations or in pits or ditches at causewayed enclosures, as at Windmill Hill, Whitehawk (Sussex), the Trundle (Sussex) and various henges, such as Maumbury Rings (Dorset) and Stonehenge.

N. Thomas, who examined several chalk cups in 1954, including those from Wilsford and Woodhenge, rejected any idea that they could have been lamps, since far more disused cups would then be found in the several known Neolithic flint-mines (chalk cups are so easily broken). In any case, the cups would hold so little oil as to fuel no more than a brief, feeble flame. Thomas concluded that the cups belong 'to the same class of votive or ritualistic objects as the phallic carvings, the ladles and spoons, fabricators, mace-heads, and those other unexplained things with which Neolithic tribesmen attempted to make their corn grow, their cattle multiply, and their trade thrive.'

The imagery of the spiralling, cupped crop-pattern representing the spiralling womb-opening of the Goddess is completed by the parallel of the human foetus. Because the contents of the womb are forever turning if not actually spiralling (as the twisted umbilical cord suggests), it follows that the outward-flowing spirals on the earth's surface are likewise spirals of generation or regeneration and therefore justifiable testimony to the spiral gyrations taking place in the womb of the Goddess beneath the surface.

Before the age of round barrows communal worship and burial had been directed at long barrows. Although the details and mythologies of lost religions can never be retrieved, we know enough to say that the principal divine concept in the earlier long-barrow era was that of the Great Goddess, and that there was a strong tradition of ancestor-worship. The living could communicate with the dead through the ancestral bones retained in the chambers of long barrows and passage-graves. The geometry of long barrows is rather complex but the external outlines are obvious: their rectangular shape resembles that of long houses. In *Bronze Age Round Barrows* Paul Ashbee writes: 'It has recently been possible to see long barrows as the counterparts of long houses, the alliance of round barrow with round house would be equally logical . . . Stake and post circles beneath and around barrows have long been compared with Woodhenge and the Sanctuary, a process still current.'

The natural spiral-circle phenomena marked in fields provide the missing link. They explain the origins of megalithic rings of circular and non-circular shapes, and may account for the origin of earthen circles, henges and round houses too. For this was the age of the round monument, and its interrelationship with the spiral, and in spelling out the relationships, the bond between henges, stone rings, barrows and houses becomes clear. The naturally-created circle was consecrated and put to use not only at all levels of everyday living—dwellings, henges, and temples—but also at the metaphysical level through barrow building. This was the consequence of the mystical significance of the spiral, together with its origins in the atmosphere and upon the surfaces of fields.

Besides generating life the Goddess was responsible for rebirth, for which the spiral was the proper symbol, although its vulvar resemblance was equally important. If the aerial vortex was seen as the means of carrying the spirit of a reborn person to the next world, then the spiral centre or womb opening was a fitting receptacle for the corpse prior to the raising of the barrow. Similarly, if the spiral-circle effect of a descending vortex had been witnessed as it happened, the spinning vortex might well have been seen as a symbol of impregnation. Libations were probably poured into the centre of any sacred monument, and these would have been life-giving liquids, such as fertilising and spermatic fluids. This explains why, in later, better-documented times in ancient Europe, beasts were sacrificed in libation ceremonies to permit their blood (regarded as a vital force) to flow into circular pits.

Every primitive community has its microcosm, limited by the bounds of its known world and within which there is a sacred space marking its supreme Centre for communicating with the divine. It is primarily because of whirlwind symbolism and spiral-circle symbolism that in ancient Britain and Ireland these holy places were circular and were defined by stones or wooden posts, or by a ditch or bank. The outer ditch separated profane space from the sacred, designating the area where the secular was transcended, where contact with the Goddess was closest. Places like this would therefore also have been proper sites for general astronomical and meteorological observations. Additionally suitable as shrines for worship would have been springs, hilltops, and houses, the circular houses conforming to the 'Shapes and Symbols of the Millennium'—the circle and the spiral—and providing devout believers with temporal shelter and divine security.

8

Sacred Marriage

According to what we know of primitive societies, the 'upper realms' may mean the heavens, the moon or some other 'paradise', depending on the nature of their religious concepts. We shall never know exactly what the distant Neolithic inhabitants of Britain and Ireland believed, although enough clues survive for us to glimpse certain aspects of their lost mythology. The starting point must surely be the spiral/whirlwind relationship.

For primitive peoples inhabiting a world of risk and uncertainty, of pain and despair, happenings that were infrequent or unexpected were either assigned to the domain of omens and portents, or were rationalised in more mundane terms that the people could understand. Much evidence has been assembled which proves convincingly that the spiral image came to acquire tremendous spiritual and divine powers, that it gathered about itself a complexity of sacred imperatives and virtues, and that its different meanings came to be simultaneously portrayed and concealed within its directional windings. In the process, it acquired the most profound religious values of any images in the art of the prehistoric world.

Symbolic thought had its roots in societies that lacked the written word, and rules of conduct—social, moral and spiritual—were imposed through the telling of myths, and through visual images and symbols. Religious and moral actions were explained and justified in allegorical stories relating to the familiar world.

Sympathetic magic and the ritual creation of art forms were intended to pacify the gods and subdue Nature's more violent extremes. The use of symbolic practices in forms familiar to us today (such as figurines, inscriptions on portable objects, wall-painting, body-painting, tattooing and masks), dates from the Upper Palaeolithic era. These show careful attempts to explain and control Nature, and reveal a surprisingly advanced development of mythological ideas. But it was the advent of the agrarian and pastoral way of life in the Neolithic period which brought a rapid flowering of symbolic imagery and, in the course of time, a veritable multiplication of divinities and mythologies in the world's Bronze and Iron Ages.

Images and symbols evolve when people begin to create visual representations of their religious concepts and divinities in sculpture or paintings. As time passes, those which best portray the divine attributes and are generally approved become standardised and stylised, so that the images may contain a deep and precious symbolic realism which eludes us today in a world that has little use for symbolism.

Such difficulties are heightened when, in later periods, the stylisation becomes overdeveloped and a sterility of design sets in. Despite this, I feel that in my reinterpretation of the archaic spiral and some of its contemporary symbols (notably the circle or ring, the cup, and the lozenge), I have identified some of the principal components of the lost images from the Neolithic and Bronze Ages.

The most splendid megalithic engravings in Atlantic Europe are among the earliest. These have survived in a good state of preservation in Irish passage-graves in the Boyne Valley of eastern Ireland, some 30 kilometres north of Dublin. The tombs were built in the period 3700 to 3300 BC and continued in use well into the third millennium. The most magnificent are at Newgrange, Knowth and Dowth in the Boyne Valley and within cairns on the Loughcrew Hills (Sliabh na Caillighe) in the same county of Meath. Standing stones in the passages and chambers of these tombs, and some in the encircling kerbs, are richly engraved with motifs and symbols, and many are arranged in strange and beautiful patterns made up of spirals, circles, wavy lines, zigzags, chevrons, triangles, lozenges and cup-marks.

On stones where the symbols are well patterned and neatly executed, the engraver seems to have been following a preconceived design, but on others the arrangement seems chaotic, and occasionally later motifs have been superimposed on older ones. The threshold stone at the entrance to the tumulus of Newgrange, with its interconnecting spirals, both clockwise and anticlockwise, was surely planned in advance, and such well-executed engravings are undoubtedly sacred carvings with definite meanings which would have been perfectly understood by designers and beholders alike.

Radiocarbon dating has shown that the building of Newgrange began about the year 3300 BC, and its first spiral engravings must also date from this time since some of the patterns continue round to the backs of stones; these were not afterwards moved until the excavations and rebuilding of the 1960s AD. Newgrange and Knowth are thought to be the last of the great chambered tumuli of Ireland, so in terms of megalithic architecture, as opposed to art, Newgrange represents the pinnacle of achievement; in art, however, it ranks second because the great tomb at Knowth, whose workmanship was more or less contemporary with that of Newgrange, is supreme in providing the finest set of integrated megalithic carvings in the British Isles. The art at Knowth also provides helpful clues to the level of Neolithic scholarship, besides detailing certain of its achievements, for the archaic peoples of Ireland used carved symbols and images to preserve messages in an ordered code.

Surrounding the circular tumulus of Newgrange, whose diameter varies between 70 and 85 metres, is a great ring of standing stones 104 metres in diameter. We now know that the stone ring was preceded by a ring of timber posts and that the wood of these timbers was later than the foundation date of the tumulus itself. Until this discovery it used to be thought that the stone ring was the oldest in Britain or Ireland. Nevertheless, although the exact date of the stone ring is now uncertain it still remains one of the earliest. It is probable that at least some timber posts were an integral part of the initial design but that as they decayed they were replaced by others, until in the end it was decided to use unchanging stone.

Of the four major engraved kerbstones (numbered K1, K13, K52 and K67) which face the four points of solstice (two for sunrise and two for sunset, in June and December), at least two (K1 and K52) seem to have been positioned to receive shadows from stout posts. Kerbstone K13, which faces the midwinter sunset, has its heavily-decorated face hidden away on its inward side—engraved there before the stone was set in its allotted place—but the secret of Newgrange is not there. It is hidden in the designs which face outwards on kerbstones K52 (midsummer sunset), K1 (midwinter sunrise) and K67 (midsummer sunrise).

That the spirals of antiquity are symbols connected in some way with life and death has been acknowledged for a long time, not only by modern scholars but by ancient writers as well (for instance, Virgil had Daedalus carve a labyrinth on the temple gate at Cumae, a spiral which Aeneas found when he entered the underworld). Some researchers have assumed that clockwise motion equates with creation and growth, whereas anticlockwise movement signifies destruction and death, but the truth is rather more complex. Other symbolic meanings, as we know from the stone circles and round barrows, involve resurrection and immortality, and the concept of both 'breath and spirit'. That the outflowing spiral is a birth/growth symbol seems due to its unvarying nature: from its microscopic origins onwards, as it lengthens, its form is changeless despite endless growth. Intuitively, the spiral was seen to be the key to the universe, and thousands of

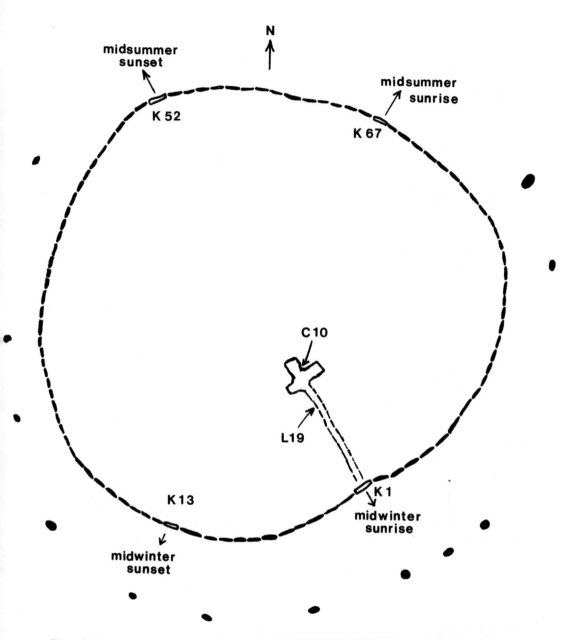

Plan of Newgrange, Ireland's most famous prehistoric monument. Set within the circular kerb are the best decorated stones: K1, K67 and K52 which face, respectively, the midwinter sunrise, midsummer sunrise and midsummer sunset. The midwinter sunset stone K13 is engraved on its hidden side. The gallery is aligned on the midwinter sunrise. The best engraved gallery stone L19 projects slightly from the left wall of the gallery or passage. The famous three-spiral carving C10 lies at the heart of the monument in the farthest cell. A ring of megaliths surrounded the entire monument of which a dozen stones remain today.

BIRTH   DEATH   DEATH   BIRTH

OUT   IN   IN   OUT

The birth/death symbolism inherent in this type of returning spiral accords with observations and deductions concerning atmospheric forces: the inflowing gyrating winds of death (tornado) and the returning, outflowing gyrations (as found in spiral-centred crop circles) of birth and rebirth.

years later we have good reasons to understand why, because the spiral *is* the universal image in its comprehensive embrace of everything from the microcosmic spiral chains of DNA to the cosmic spiral nebulae.

It must be remembered that spirals can be interpreted as either inward- or outward-flowing, and therefore as symbolising either birth or death, inward flow being equated with death. At times of spiritual need, during religious devotion, a worshipper could follow by eye or by finger the winding trail of the spiral inwards and outwards, in endless repetition—a forerunner of the rosary.

At Newgrange spirals are sometimes found in pairs, opposing each other yet in a continuous flow of movement as the returning spiral. This achieves something which a single spiral cannot, a dynamism resulting from the cyclic activity of opposites joined by a single path. Taken separately each part signifies birth or rebirth, whereas reversed they both become paths of death. The ideas of birth, death and rebirth are neatly contained in a symbol which can apply not only to all forms of life, but to the whole cosmic cycle involving the sun, moon and seasons.

The spiral engraving on the splendid kerbstone K67 was set to face the midsummer rising sun, so the path of the outflowing spiral probably stands for the course of the sun from midwinter through spring and on to midsummer, during which the sun's heat strengthens with the lengthening days. This is followed by an inward progression through autumn and back to midwinter, while the sun becomes weaker and the days shorter. The position of the midsummer sun is the

Kerbstone K67 at Newgrange with its returning spirals and attendant lozenges.

point midway between the first spiral and the second; and two lozenge-shapes have been carved here, symbolising a prayer for fertility.

In her book *The Goddesses and Gods of Old Europe*, Marija Gimbutas provides many clear-cut examples of symbolic lozenges, the earliest dating from around 6000 BC. In the eastern Mediterranean, she says, the lozenge is an ideogram for a field; a dot (standing for seed) within a lozenge means a sown field and is an appeal

A figurine from southern Yugoslavia with a dotted lozenge inscribed on its abdomen. Made about 6000 BC, it is similar to others described by Marija Gimbutas from pre-classical 'Old Europe'.

for crop fertility. The lower lozenge on kerbstone K67 has a second lozenge engraved inside it, and Marija Gimbutas suggests that the nested-lozenge stands for the fertile aspect of the Great Goddess herself in her role of fecund Earth Mother.

The lozenge also appears on a sculpted Goddess figurine from Central Bulgaria. Known as the Lady of Pazardzik, it is the work of an early East Balkan or Thracian civilisation of about 4500 BC, and provides a highly satisfactory link encompassing the theme Goddess–Lozenge–Fertility–Spirals. Its divine traits are heightened by the dehumanisation of facial features, by means of a mask, and by the minuscule breasts, so that attention centres on the symbolic messages. The Goddess's enlarged pubic triangle carries the double or returning spiral as a statement of the eternal life–death cycle which she controls—whether animal, vegetable or human life or that of the sun and the seasons. Each buttock is incised with a pair of nested lozenges which Marija Gimbutas notes were 'placed here not as decoration, but to stress the functions of the earth-fertility goddess who is responsible for the germination, sprouting, growing, and ripening of plants'. Apart from this, the absence of pregnant belly and lactal breasts shows that we are in the court of the Goddess of Death and the Earth Mother; this, combined with the fact that the figurine was found in a tomb, led Erich Neumann to conclude that the 'continuous rising and descending spiral—one end rolling upward and the other downward'— showed her to be mistress of both life and death.

Marija Gimbutas's argument is convincing, but the Late Neolithic fertile-field concept seems to me to be a secondary, not a primary, stage in the development of the symbolism of the lozenge. The practical objectivity of the primitive mind demands that the original aim in symbolising the female fertility wish as powerfully as possible was to use an 'open lozenge' to represent the vulva, open in the birth position; in the course of time the early symbolism evolved and widened, so that the lozenge came to stand for the Great Goddess herself.

It is natural to assume that the spread of the lozenge and other symbols related to farming and weather (sloping parallel lines, zigzags, chevrons) resulted from the migrations of the early Neolithic farmers. The same peoples who brought agriculture and pottery to Britain and Ireland carried with them their spiritual beliefs and symbolic representations as well. Provided one goes back far enough into antiquity, one can find helpful evidence to clarify the symbolism, belief and ritual of the British and Irish Neolithic people. And just as the British Isles acquired its original concepts and technologies from the European Continent, so, much later, did Scandinavia. The Bronze Age fertility rock-carving from Hvarlös, Bohuslän, in Sweden, is just as important for the symbolic clues that it enshrines. It gives us the clearest possible portrayal of the lozenge as vulva, for here it is shown joined with the male phallus, whether of a man or a god.

10. *Above:* The entrance stone K1 at Newgrange, with its series of well-planned spiral compositions on either side of a dividing line and with lozenges on the left and a central triangle at the base. Together, these elements carry a symbolic message.

11. *Left:* Stone L19 from the main passage at Newgrange. The upper portion of this stone is covered in running zigzags which merge into three spirals surrounding a lozenge.

12. Snails are the bearers of Goddess symbolism in various ways, but above all they epitomise birth and life. This is the common bulhorn snail, photographed on Silbury Hill, Wiltshire.

13. Silbury Hill, silent witness to a Goddess past. Note the flat area of the summit and one of the causeways on the right. Can we at last explain the hill's origin?

The masked Thracian goddess of fertility, birth and death called by archaeologists the Lady of Pazardzik (central Bulgaria, about 4500 BC).

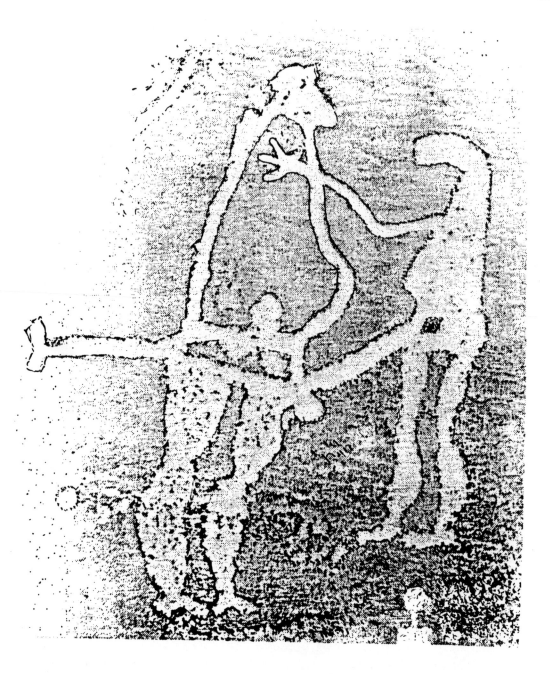

The vulvar lozenge of the female depicted in this Bronze Age Swedish rock carving, together with the ithyphallic god (or man), portrays the fertility wishes of the carver and the essential elements of the Sacred Marriage (Hvralös, Bohuslän).

And it *is* a god that we behold. The mists of time clear just a fraction, and we become aware that we are looking at an ancient rendering, incised in eternal stone, of the Marriage of the Gods.

At Newgrange the lozenges on kerbstone K67 contain wavy lines, which may stand for the fertilising seed of life or may represent water, needed to nurture life in the sown fields of the Earth Mother. Zigzag motifs were used to symbolise rain, water and lightning by many primitive societies from the earliest times right up to the present day, the zigzag representing lightning which issues from the Sky God's clouds and lets fall the life-supporting rain in the thunderstorm. This is believed to explain why a six-stroke zigzag stood for the word 'water' in ancient Chinese and Egyptian hieroglyphics, for in semi-arid zones especially, lightning heralds the awaited summer rain. The Egyptians, incidentally, used the spiral to express cosmic energy, or cosmic forms in motion. They would have been familiar with the peaceful desert whirlwind, and also the foreboding waterspout or tornado in winter thunderstorms, so it is easy to see how the link came about. (The Egyptian deification of the cat may have evolved from another, more abstruse spiral link— the spiralling movement of the cat as it settles down, and its final position of repose, curled up as if in death, like an inward-winding spiral!)

The type of spiral on kerbstone K67, rotating clockwise outwards for growth and known as a right-handed spiral, represents solar imagery, for the sun's apparent journey through the heavens is that of a clockwise spiral. Left-handed spirals flow in contrary rotation, which is anticlockwise when outwards. When the flow is outwards, whether spiralling to the left or to the right, the spiral conveys qualities of rebirth or rematerialisation, and may have been a sign of hope and a potential guide towards a life after death. These concepts apply just as well to anticlockwise outward-spiralling as they do to clockwise outward-spiralling.

When the flow is inward, thoughts turn to death and extinction as signified by the destructive powers of the inturning, anticlockwise tornado. The tornado rotates the same way as its larger relatives the cyclone and hurricane; being destroyers they are viewed as 'major whirlwinds', compared with the 'minor whirlwinds' of fine summer days. Although all tornadoes turn inwards and virtually every one spirals in an anticlockwise sense, a few (but only a very few) have been known to rotate clockwise. It is the principle that matters in spiral mysticism. Death is the zone of inward flow. Therefore clockwise inward-spiralling speaks of death exactly as does anticlockwise inward-spiralling.

Do the ultimate secrets of ancient spiral symbolism lie hidden in the multi-spiralled patterns on the threshold stone K1 at Newgrange, the stone which faces the direction of the sun at midwinter sunrise? This enormous boulder-stone, trimmed to the shape of a fat cigar, lies in front of the entrance to the passage-grave. Only its forward surface was carved, and this must have been done when the stone was in position because the design ends along the lower edge in a way that suggests the remainder of the stone was beyond the mason's reach.

Oddly, the two types of spiral carved upon it are divided by a vertical line. On the right-hand side two complete spirals occupy a central position, carved in the clockwise 'solar' sense. No continuous flow links their centres; each one makes the familiar statement regarding the cycle of birth, death, rebirth, and whereas outward clockwise motion equates with birth, the equation with death, judgement and extinction means going back along the same spiral.

On the left-hand side of the stone, carved in an anticlockwise direction, there are three spirals, cut so broadly that they fill almost all the available space. What does this mean? After all, the basic inflow–outflow significance can be no different: inflow stands for death, outflow for life. So why was a two-handed arrangement of spirals, separated by a line, deliberately contrived?

To understand, we need to go back to Chapter 2 and Mildred Cable's account of the Gobi Desert whirlwinds—that the male ones turn from right to left and the female ones from left to right. The spirals in the right-hand section of kerbstone K1 therefore represent the Sky God in the form of the storm-whirlwind with its pendant funnel and inflowing anticlockwise winds. Inward anticlockwise flow means masculinity, and these spirals symbolise the male principle as well as the solar/sky elements in the cosmic life cycle.

The contrary spirals on the other half of the stone relate to femininity, so that inward-flowing clockwise spirals, as well as outward-flowing anticlockwise spirals, must symbolise the female principle, while still retaining the quality of death and decay with inflow, and of life and creativity with contrary outflow.

The decoration on the stone is completed by a series of lozenges at either end, symbolising the desire for the Goddess to grant fertility or fertile fields, and at the centre of the lower edge, below the vertical line, a series of upward circling lines encloses another fertility symbol, a solid triangle fully pecked out. By its complex symbolism the whole stone reveals a duality of purpose which few Neolithic monuments display so clearly. In its artistry it portrays the opposing sexes, both mortal and divine, in life and death.

The special function of the stone is accentuated by its position which ensures that the midwinter rising sun casts a shadow from a stone of the external stone circle to the middle of the threshold stone, after which, as the sun moves westwards, the morning shadow crosses the solar spirals.

From all this, can we now at last uncover the celestial and divine mysticism which lies behind spiral symbolism?

The powerful phallic significance of the tornado cloud is personified by the masculinity of the Sky God, which imbues both the clockwise outward spiral and anticlockwise inward spiral. The sun shares in this symbolism, for it, too, pursues

The threshold stone K1 at Newgrange, with its complex symbolic design of spirals and lozenges. The solidly-pecked triangle at the centre bottom is another important symbol.

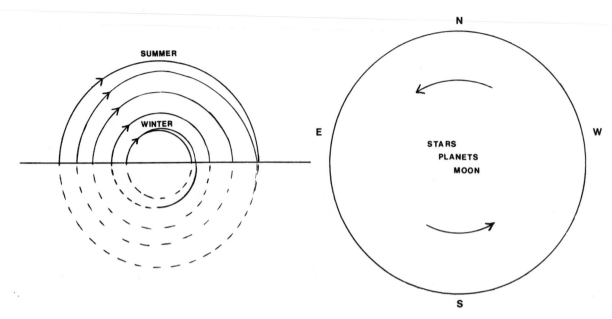

Left: Between midwinter and midsummer the sun's apparent orbit across the sky, although superficially circular, is really part of a growing spiral which is clockwise and outward as expected of the concepts relating to a masculine divinity in its growth stage. After midsummer comes a diminishing spiral which accords with recession and death. *Right:* Looking skywards we see stars and moon moving anticlockwise. This makes the moon symbol, which represents the Great Goddess in her celestial manifestation, an anticlockwise spiral as well. As before, spiral motion is outward for life and rebirth, and inward for death.

an endless, seemingly spiral course through the heavens. On any day the sun's path appears as part of a circle. But the path cannot be circular *and* increasing or decreasing at the same time, so a spiral represents far better the apparent course of the sun. As the year advances and the sun's strength intensifies, it appears to be following an expanding spiral, but after the summer solstice the spiral gradually contracts.

The opposite is true of the moon and its background of stars. Although, like the sun, stars and moon rise in the east and set in the west, to an observer looking skywards the stars seem to revolve in an anticlockwise sense about the zenith. The moon's apparent motion shares in this rotation.

Thus it was that in antiquity moon and stars came to acquire a gyratory meaning opposed in sign and value to that of the sun, and such symbolism fittingly reinforced the feminine qualities that had been attributed to the moon from time immemorial—monthly cycle, waxing pregnancy, passivity (it is a reflector of sunlight), and so on. Consequently, the outward-flowing anticlockwise spiral became a moon-symbol of birth, life and rebirth, and hence the Great Goddess in her celestial, lunar manifestation.

TABLE I

Symbolic meanings behind the Neolithic spirals of Britain and Ireland

Physical aspects or motion   *Attributes*

OUTWARD FLOW CLOCKWISE
Right-handed spirals; outward/right symbolism

sun's strength increasing      male gods; masculinity
  from winter to summer   birth; growth
                                                                 rebirth; reincarnation
ground-trace   rematerialisation
  spiral-vortex effect   generation
                                                                 creative power
snail leaving shell   evolution
(upward spiralling of plants)   activity

INWARD FLOW ANTICLOCKWISE
Right-handed spirals; inward/right symbolism

common tornado      male gods; masculinity
  destructive whirlwind   death; decay
whirlpool   dissolution
sun's strength decreasing   excarnation
  from summer to winter   involution
snail retreating into shell   (spiritualisation)

OUTWARD FLOW ANTICLOCKWISE
Left-handed spirals; outward/left symbolism

moon waxing      goddesses; femininity
                                                                 birth
ground-trace   rebirth; reincarnation
  spiral-vortex effect   rematerialisation
                                                                 regrowth; regeneration
upward spiralling plants   regenerative power

INWARD FLOW CLOCKWISE
Left-handed spirals; inward/left symbolism

moon waning      goddesses; femininity
                                                                 death; decay
whirlpool   dissolution
                                                                 excarnation
tornado (rarely)   passivity or
destructive whirlwind   (spiritualisation)

The position, put briefly, is this:

When the intent is divine, left-handed spirals signify the Great Goddess (Earth Goddess, Moon Goddess, etc.) and her femininity, whereas right-handed spirals denote a male god (Sky God or Storm God, etc.) and his masculinity.

When the intent is cosmic or calendrical, left-handed spirals stand for the moon and right-handed spirals stand for the sun.

The three spirals on the left-hand side of stone K1 at Newgrange could well be indicative of the Great Goddess succinctly epitomised as a divine trinity—the Supreme Goddess in her triple roles as Maiden, Mother and Grandmother/Crone/ Hag, or Goddess of Earth, Moon and Waters. The contrasting spirals on the right symbolise a Male God in his paramount roles as Sky God and Sun God or perhaps Storm or Weather God. It can be no accident that left-handed spirals feature on the left side of the entrance stone and right-handed spirals on the right side.

What is the reason for dividing the spirals into groups standing for female and male divinities and separating them by a vertical line? The answer must be that they represent a Marriage of the Gods, and the strongest clue is provided by the shadow of a megalith of the outer circle which is cast upon this very line by the rising sun at the winter solstice. This shadow has the dramatic effect of uniting the male and female divinities in a midwinter Sacred Marriage, a fertility ritual of divinities. Its rediscovery is the key to understanding the symbolic religious imagery of the monument.

The perfect orientation of the 24-metre length of the passage and end-chamber at Newgrange with the midwinter rising sun was a deliberate, highly meaningful act on the part of the designers and builders. Their ingenuity extended to installing a letter-box opening above the entrance doorway, to permit a narrow beam of sunlight to penetrate the monument to its innermost back wall and there illuminate its presumed contents for a few minutes each year.

This optical trick would work at no other time of the year but the winter solstice. It is as though the Sky God, represented by the sun and its beam of light, had mated with the Goddess, embodied in the tumulus. The letterbox opening and passage become vulva and vagina. The central end-chamber is the cavity that is the womb. The shaft of sunlight is the life-bearing semen. The whole is a vivid re-enactment of the Marriage of the Gods, and the spiral-covered entrance stone, K1, glorifies and tells the whole story in the medium of carving.

Newgrange is more than a passage-grave; it is a temple to the Goddess of a lost age. Moreover, being a solar-orientated device, it still works.

The carvings inside the tumulus reinforce the symbolism of the threshold stone. The triple spiral of the Goddess trinity appears again on a stone guarding the

The three-spiral engraving on stone C10 at Newgrange, the Goddess Stone, long since adopted as the logo of the Prehistoric Society of Britain.

entrance to the end-chamber, this time in an unusual double-lined form. The spirals cannot be reached by the rays of the winter sun, but could possibly have been feebly lit by reflected light from the end-chamber. About half-way along the passage, where it juts out slightly and catches the glancing rays of the midwinter rising sun, is a richly decorated stone, its upper areas covered with running zigzags which merge into a series of three spirals arranged around a single lozenge. The smallest is a solar right-handed spiral; the others, of the left-handed lunar type, may represent the lunar and terrestrial facets of the Great Goddess.

At the base of this stone are four further spirals, the lower pair being double, interconnecting returning spirals which are female and circulate in the opposite direction to those of kerbstone K67. They are set *into* the ground, highlighting their interdependence with Earth and showing that this part, at least, of the stone was planned and carved before being moved to the gallery. As paired Goddess

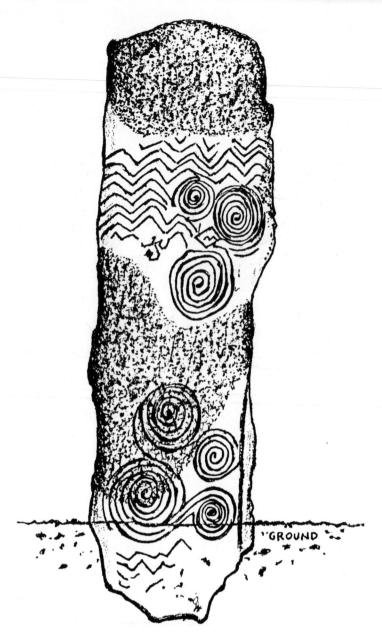

Stone L19 from the main passage at Newgrange.

spirals, the message seems to be the everlasting unity and continuity of the Goddess's lunar and terrestrial aspects.

There is a similar stone at the Temple Wood stone circle in Strathclyde, Scotland, where a left-handed spiral, associated with the Goddess, joins and mates with a half-buried right-handed spiral signifying a male divinity.

A further mystery lies at the very heart of Newgrange. As in the case of some round barrows, it contains a central turf core which had been transported some distance and then thinly covered with layers of snail-shells, pebbles and boulders.

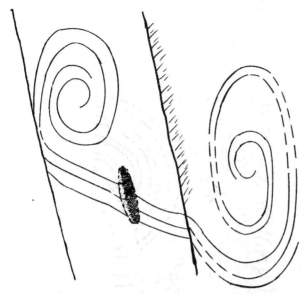

The coupled spirals of opposing type engraved on a northern megalith of the Temple Wood stone circle in Strathclyde, Scotland. Engraved on adjacent faces of this Goddess Stone, they meet across its north-eastern edge after crossing a stone-hole on their way.

Vortex-circle spirals must surely be the clue to the meaning of the sacred turf, as they are to so much archaic religious philosophy in Ireland and Britain.

Like Newgrange, the passage-grave of Dowth is orientated on the midwinter solstice, but Knowth's orientation is on the equinoxes, and its carvings are rich in symbols of the lunar calendar. Certain of its kerbstones have left-handed lunar spirals in which the outward flow gives birth to a crescent moon, and the wavy lines—known as *meanders*—on these and some other stones seem to be a form of counting method, as Martin Brennan has suggested. On one kerbstone (K4) the meander provides a count of 30, which may mean that the moon cycle recommences at the 30th day. On another (K51) the numbers seven and five appear, and also a small sun spiral. Taken together, it is not difficult to decipher the message: the moon cycle of growth and decay is repeated just over twelve times during a solar year, with seven cycles during the spring and summer period of agricultural growth and five in the late autumn and winter period of decay and death.

One of the most beautiful carvings, first deciphered by Martin Brennan, seems to show a complete lunar calendar, with the moon illustrated in 29 stages of waxing and waning and the last three crescent moons obscured by a lunar spiral corresponding to the three days and nights during which the moon's phases are invisible. On the basis of spiral imagery the myth expressed is quite clear. The Great Goddess gives birth to the crescent moon or Moon Goddess following three days of obscurity; and later, after her journey around the heavens, the Moon Goddess returns to the womb of the Great Goddess to undergo renewed incubation and rebirth. A central meandering strip extends the calendar by counting time in terms

Decipherment of the kerbstones from Knowth, which have left-handed spirals. *Top:* On K38 outward spiral flow gives birth to the young crescent moon. Being a left-handed spiral it is normal that such birth should be in the domain of the Great Goddess and that the moon-birth results from *outward* flow, as it does here. *Centre:* On K4 the crescent moon is shown at the extreme of its waning, after which it 'dies' for three days before its rebirth. In the left-handed coils of the Great Goddess it is caught in the death winding of inward flow and is carried to the spiral centre where a new moon is born (indicated by the open circle at the centre). The full lunar cycle is counted by each turn of the meander incised along the top of the pictogram. *Bottom:* Stone K51 with its left-handed lunar/Goddess spiral from which the lesser solar spiral (right-handed) draws crescents. The upper meander at the right may denote the seven agricultural or lunar months of spring and summer, while the lower meander counts the five 'dead' months of late autumn and winter.

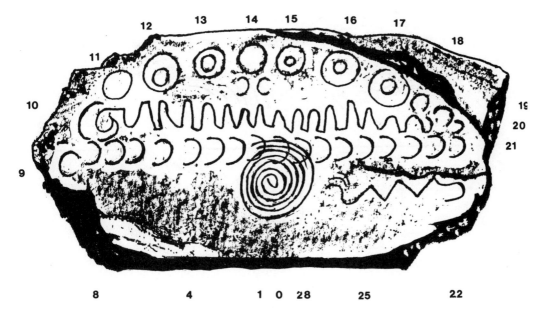

The calendar stone K52. For three days of the lunar cycle the moon is obscured, during which time it undergoes rebirth. This part of the calendar is depicted by 'concealing' the minuscule crescents within the windings of the Goddess spiral, and are designated, from right to left, by the lunar-cycle numbers 28, 0, 1 respectively. The moon is born on the 29th day denoted by zero; the remaining moon engravings designate the moon at its various phases, numbered from 1 to 28 going round the circuit. Full circles, numbered 11 to 17, denote the seven nights of brightest moon. The full moon, numbered 14, is shown as a circle with opposed crescents beneath it as a means of emphasising the transition from waxing to waning. As Martin Brennan first indicated, the five-pointed zigzag, bottom right, is a count of five which may indicate five solar years. The long solar central meander, reading from left to right, is a count of 31, which makes 62 for a complete cycle. This could reasonably refer to 62 lunations because a cycle of 62 lunations equals five solar years, after which lunar and solar rhythms harmonise exactly.

of months, each turn of the loop representing one day so that the whole is a count up to 31, or 62 for a complete cycle.

Several stones seem to suggest that the people of Atlantic Europe in the fourth millennium were aware that the lunar and solar divinities come together, as in marriage, to generate the entire moon cycle. One bears a right-handed sun spiral on either side of which are big moon crescents, one of which is shown coupled to the spiral. Another has lunar and solar divinities, pictured as spirals. They revolve and unite to produce horizontal and vertical sets of arcs increasing in size, which stand for the intensifying and weakening facets of sun and moon during seasonal and monthly cycles.

Sacred Marriage at Knowth. Kerbstone K5 bears a central right-handed solar spiral with lunar crescents on either side. One of the crescents is coupled to the sun, signifying a Cosmic Marriage between sun and moon. Photographed 1987 with the permission of Professor George Eogan who was present.

Just as at Newgrange there is a midwinter Sacred Marriage in which cosmic union is achieved through the intervention of a megalith's shadow, so at Knowth an equinoctial marriage is implied by the dual nature of the east–west galleries arranged in combination with the eastern-sunrise shadow cast by a phallic megalith a few metres to the east. The entire tomb and its east-facing passage (or womb-opening) act as though they *are* the womb, vagina and vulva of the Goddess who awaits consummation by the intervention of the shadow of the pointed megalith at the equinoctial spring festival. The great tumulus of Knowth, like Newgrange, was a temple of the Goddess.

Kerbstone K65 with another allusion to the Sacred Marriage. Right-handed and left-handed solar and lunar spirals revolve and unite to produce arcs of varying size which stand for the intensifying and weakening facets of sun and moon during their annual and monthly cosmic cycles.

9

Symbols of Divinity

Because Newgrange has one of the oldest stone circles yet dated, and the tumuli of Newgrange and Knowth both have unusual cores of ritually-deposited turf, it might be wondered whether the Boyne Valley was the centre from which the practice of spiral-worship spread to Scotland, Wales and England. There is evidence, however, that the symbolism of the spiral was already widespread in Britain by the Mid-Neolithic period. The unique achievement of the Neolithic Irish lay in the flowering and refinement of the megalithic art form.

From Ireland there seems to have been a spread of engraved spiral symbols eastwards to Scotland, Anglesey and northern England, but almost nowhere else. Where they are found, they are usually on burial or religious monuments, but they have also been found on exposed rocky slabs or outcrops, along with other inscribed symbols, chiefly cup-shaped depressions. Through these carvings, the stones come alive, for the cryptic engravings speak of gods and goddesses from a long-lost age in a world of peace.

Across the sea from the Irish Boyne Valley lies the island of Anglesey. Here there are passage-graves not unlike some of the Irish ones, and two possess stylised carvings with features reminiscent of the Irish technique. The first of these, Barclodiad Y Gawres, is a large round cairn built upon a turf core, with a passage and chamber containing five decorated stones.

Two Goddess Stones. *Left:* Barclodiad Y Gawres, where the tri-function Great Goddess is depicted through the six-turn left-handed spiral (possibly the Lunar Goddess) and the two lozenges which stand for the Earth Goddess and the Goddess of the Waters. The latter appear as birth-giving vulvas enveloped by the passage of fertilising waters or streams (the meanders) brought on by the rain (the upper zigzags). *Right:* Clear Island, at the extreme south of Ireland. This stone bears the characteristic divine spiral trinity, emblematic of the tri-function Great Goddess, with life-bearing water zigzags at the top which transform into downward flowing meanders.

14. Cup-marks with concentric rings on a nearly horizontal rock surface at Achnabreck in the Argyll region of Strathclyde, Scotland. The sixth ring of the nearer cup-and-ring system encloses two single cups which never acquired rings.

15. Natural quintuplet circles at Exton, Hampshire, June 1990, formed by linked whirling vortices. The large satellite circles are close to the central primary one.

16. *Top left:* The Corn Maiden as made in modern Wiltshire by Gill Henley. Fabricated from the last straws of the harvest, it was buried at the spring sowing to restore the fecundity of the earth. The practice appears to be a Goddess-religion survival which was tolerated by the Church, possibly because it did not fully recognise it for what it was.

17. *Top right:* 'Corn dolly' formed at the centre of a crop circle by a spiralling vortex at Beckhampton, 1990. One standing clump of corn, a metre high, resembles the traditional Corn Maiden. On this occasion neighbouring crop circles were united by a curving path in the manner of the returning spirals of megalithic carvings. *Photograph by Peter D. Rendall*

18. *Below:* This ancient example of the traditional Cretan labyrinth is engraved on a rock face at Rocky Valley, near Tintagel, Cornwall. *Photograph by Keith O. Mortimore*

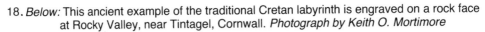

One of these has been so richly engraved with symbolic forms suggestive of the Great Goddess in her regenerative capacities, that it deserves the title of the Goddess Stone. At its top a lunar spiral stands for the Goddess's birth-giving aspect; zigzags signify her role in controlling lightning and hence the upper realms which bring the rain-bearing clouds, and these zigzags progressively transform into wavy lines or flowing streams on the lower part of the stone. The Goddess rules the rainwater and the springs, and the rain nourishes the 'sown' fields symbolised by earth-bound, square-shaped double lozenges on the central area of the stone. The double lozenge, of course, also represents the birth-giving vulvar lozenge which is the fecund Earth Mother herself, so that the whole stone portrays in symbolic form a trinity of goddesses and hence the Great Goddess. The carvings are the prayers of an agrarian people that their guardian Goddess will protect and nourish their crops and bring them abundant harvests.

A similarly-cut stone was found on Clear Island in southern Ireland, and a similar idea may have inspired the spiralled threshold stone and passage stone L19 at Newgrange. In fact the symbolism of the fertilising waters is apparent not only in all the principal Irish passage-graves, but also in Orkney, France, Portugal and Spain. On many stones the design is incised horizontally above head level, as on lintels to the entrances of galleries or cells, and sometimes running zigzags have been brought together in exact opposition, so that goddess lozenges magically appear, underlining the affinity of the deity with the fertilising waters.

Another carved stone inside Barclodian Y Gawres (see p. 130) displays the Goddess triad with a notable variation. Where the Newgrange artist portrayed the tri-function Great Goddess as three spirals, the Welsh stone has a group of two spirals and a fully-pecked lozenge with outer right-angled lines, of which one is joined to the larger of the two left-handed spirals (most probably the lunar one). Since the two spirals are images of the celestial Goddess, it follows that the Earth Goddess is here stylised as a lozenge-cut womb-opening.

This carving therefore provides important confirmation that the lozenge, here symbolising the Earth Goddess aspect of the Great Goddess, has equal rank with the lunar spiral (signifying the Moon Goddess) not only throughout the British Isles and Ireland, but in the Mediterranean as well. The veil of outward abstraction can be lifted further to enable us to interpret still more designs. At Seefin, County Wicklow, for instance, the megalith of a cairn is engraved with three double or triple lozenges (see p. 131), juxtaposed much as the spirals on the famous three-spiral stone at Newgrange. Knowing that the lozenge is the fertile Goddess, we can promote an apparently meaningless geometrical design to its true status—a trinity of goddesses, and so the Great Goddess herself.

A third important megalith at Barclodiad Y Gawres has four spirals, two feminine, two masculine. The two opposed spirals on the right are twinned and

 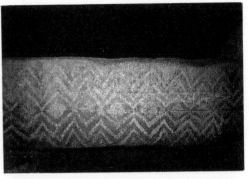

Zigzag decorations on lintels at Fourknocks, a splendid tumulus sited between Dublin and the Boyne Valley, hint at Goddess worship via the life-bearing properties of water. *Left:* A boldly-stated plain version. *Right:* Engraved out of phase, the running zigzags combine to produce a row of potent Goddess lozenges above the entrance to the cells.

Another Goddess trinity from Barclodian Y Gawres. This pattern on stone C1 consists primarily of two left-handed Goddess spirals and a set of nested Goddess lozenges.

Left: The Goddess Stone at Seefin, County Wicklow, south of Dublin. The three sets of lozenges signify the Goddess trinity.

Right: The Marriage of the Gods on stone C3 at Barclodiad Y Gawres. The spiral pair on the left constitute goddess and male divinities shown separately before matrimony. On the right the spirals have been coupled as in marriage.

depict an absolute unification of moon and sun, or Goddess and God, in a sensitive alliance of opposites. The design has every appearance of representing, once again, the cosmological or Sacred Marriage.

This circular passage-grave seems in sympathy with those of the Irish Boyne Valley, although of a rather later date. It adds to the mounting evidence that the religion of the Great Goddess spread right across Europe, using the symbolism of lozenges, squares or triangles for the Earth Mother and fertile Goddess, and zigzags of lightning and rain for the fertilising waters, if not, at times, for the seminal fluid of the Sky God. Many other symbols were widely used, not least the spirals of solar and lunar symbolism and the figurative phallic and vulvar archetypes, all of which played crucial roles in the religious world of early agrarian communities.

Bryn Celli Dhu is the second of the Anglesey passage-graves which contain spiral carvings. The main spiral is engraved on an unusual stone called the 'pattern stone'. On one vertical face a right-handed spiral opens into a winding line and wanders over the top surface to link with wavy lines on the reverse face. Because these unusual undulating lines issue from a rebirth spiral which has been given the right-handed or masculine direction, they may be intended to represent the outflow of life-forces, or male virility.

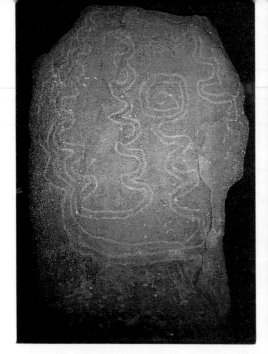

Left: The 'pattern stone' from Bryn Celli Dhu, Anglesey, now in the Welsh National Museum at Cardiff. The right-handed spiral issues streams of flowing male 'energy' which continue round to the rear of the stone. The temple is the Goddess herself, and she is supported by a fertilising father figure.

Right: The beautiful 'pillar stone' in the central chamber at Bryn Celli Dhu. The stone does not reach to the roof. Similar stones are known in some of Brittany's chambered megalithic barrows. They are probably all Goddess stones.

If so, this is one of two probable fertility stones in the tumulus. Standing high and erect in the main chamber, but not reaching to the roof, is a splendid, dressed stone known as the 'pillar stone'. In the religion of some primitive societies this might have corresponded to a local 'Centre of the World', but others might see it as a phallic symbol similar to those found in the Neolithic monuments of Malta and the Middle East, although none has been found inside Irish and British tombs of the period. Because of this, I rather think it is a second Goddess stone, responsible for the visible, generative life-force.

This is not the only unusual feature of Bryn Celli Dhu. It appears to have been built over an earlier passage-grave with a kerb which was concealed beneath the rising mound, and the builders seem to have deliberately incorporated two turns of 'a gigantic spiral' into the ground design of the underlying stonework. According to the excavator, a spiral route was marked out by the stone course-work using two hidden 'circles' in conjunction with the visible walls of the antechamber. The diameters of the two spiral loops are about 25 metres and, oddly enough, one stone bears an engraving of a spiral which is virtually a mirror image of the hidden ground-plan.

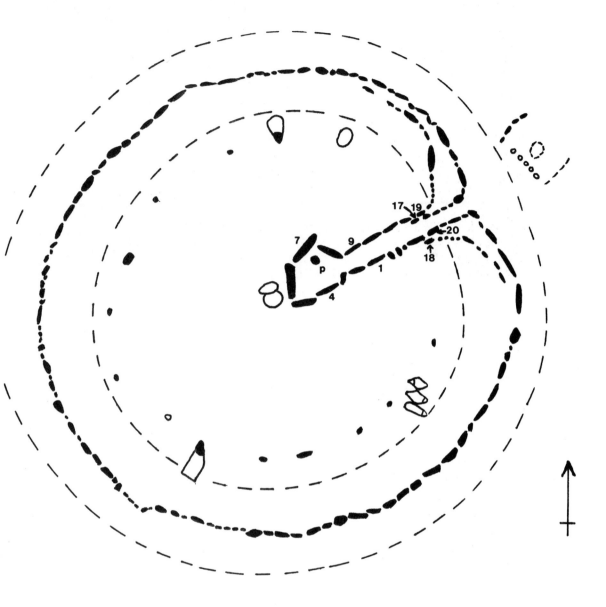

Plan of the Goddess temple of Bryn Celli Dhu, showing concealed details. The main passage is orientated approximately on midsummer sunrise. There are two hidden stone circles, the outer ring set in a still more ancient ditch whose boundaries are indicated by the pecked lines. The subterranean stone called the 'pattern stone' was formerly hidden at the centre of the monument. The cylindrical 'pillar stone' (p) stands freely in the chamber at the end of the passage. Note additionally the three recumbent stones lying together on the south-eastern side of the tumulus, their shapes suggestive of the triple Goddess and their position indicative of a foundation rite. Also note the bull burial located beyond the ditch in the direction of midsummer sunrise. The spiral route, as suggested by W. J. Hemp, begins at stone 18 and circles clockwise around the entire kerb to arrive at stone 19, where it loops along the sides of the passage and chamber to exit via stone 20. At this point it follows the larger kerb circle until it arrives at stone 17 where a clay-set wall takes it inwards to finish at stone 19. On the spiral theory such an outward clockwise spiral would symbolise the path of life and rebirth; its reversal as an inward anticlockwise spiral would correspond to the path of death. Both are the domain of the Great Goddess.

The entire tumulus was apparently planned as a temple incorporating male and female characteristics. The spiral shrine construction, standing for the Goddess's womb, would make it an appropriate abode for the rebirth of the dead, with the pillar stone greatly enhancing her customary powers. Positioned as it is in the chamber, the pillar stone stands within the symbolic womb and vaginal passage, the latter facing the midsummer sunrise. Another vertical but smaller stone, which may have been incorporated as a further fertility symbol, was sealed into the structure at the time of its ritual consecration. It stands hidden in a pit at the foot of a stone of the inner circle.

The body of a whole bull or ox had been buried in a pit beneath the entrance to the tomb, and in a metre-deep pit at the foot of a stone of the inner circle, in the heart of the mound, had been concealed a single bone—a human ear-bone or cochlea, the smallest bone in the human body! Its position in the inner zone of the tumulus, beyond the point where the passage above ground ends, suggests that those who put it there understood its normal function.

Bryn Celli Dhu seems less like a tomb than a place of communication between fearful mortals and their fertility and life-restoring gods. As an underground temple it symbolised the body of the Earth Mother. At the godhead was the Great Goddess herself, aided by a fertilising Father Figure in the shape of the sacrificed bull and the pattern stone.

And the ear-bone was there to assist with the dialogue.

*   *   *

Spiral carvings can be seen to this day in many parts of Scotland, on rock slabs on turf-free outcrops in fields and hills, and a few on stone-circle megaliths as well. At least a couple of dozen sites are known from southern Scotland and northern England where spiral motifs have been executed in the style of the passage-graves, but without any of the preconceived planning so often found at Knowth and Newgrange.

Few Scottish stone age tombs had spiral carvings. A ruined cairn on the Orkney island of Eday had a stone bearing a returning spiral pair representing the solar-lunar divine union. It may have been a lintel for a cell within the chambered cairn which was destroyed around 1821, and its message, as before, is that the society which built the cairn believed in the myth of the Marriage of the Gods—the union of solar-god and lunar-goddess, or of Sky God and Great Goddess.

Lozenges are found on stones from Orkney to south-western Scotland, and on an English chalk sculpture taken from a ditch of the causewayed enclosure at Windmill Hill, Wiltshire. The chalk plaque, now broken, had been cut to the shape of a lozenge, and off-centre a conical pit had been drilled or scraped into the

Spiral-engraved stones from the Orkneys. *Above:* From Eday Manse, a possible lintel which depicts the union of spirals of opposing sense. *Below:* A magnificent array of spiral pairs accompanied by big circles or spirals with infill lozenges, from a wrecked structure at Pierowall Quarry on the island of Westray.

obverse of the plaque which also bore scratched grooves, the deepest of which led to the 'hole'.

Six spiral-engraved megaliths, the Calderstones, now in Liverpool Museum, must originally have formed part of a Neolithic burial chamber and have, besides single spirals, rare foot-print carvings. The foot symbol carries the plain message of departure—the spirit of the deceased is being helped to go.

These stones, and the many other carved stones to be found in northern England, Scotland and Wales, are holy stones, once revered for their sacred imagery. We must cherish them and respect them, for we are their inheritors.

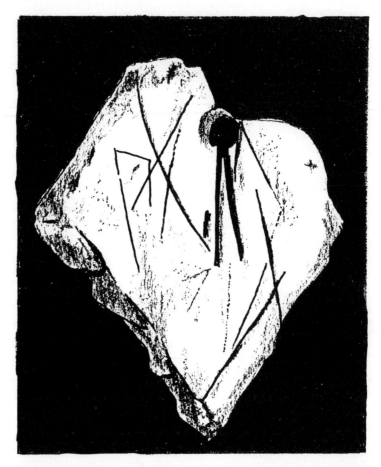

A piece of chalk, now broken, cut into the shape of a sacred lozenge and bearing a drilled pit and grooves (natural size). This obvious Goddess artefact was recovered when excavating the fourth-millennium causewayed enclosure at Windmill Hill, Wiltshire, and predates by hundreds of years the building of Silbury Hill and the Avebury circles.

10

Symbolic Ornaments

From the very dawn of prehistory people must have cherished a deep faith centred on the spiral symbol, for it has been found in some of the most ancient sites in Europe. Carvings of spirals on mammoth ivory were found by the Russian geologist M. M. Gerasimov at Mal'ta, a hunting encampment site on the River Byelaya near Lake Baikal, 90 kilometres north-west of Irkutsk. Dating from the Siberian Palaeolithic period (the Upper Aurignacian), the burials and their goods were varied and elaborate. As well as about fourteen ceremonial burials of animals, complete or partial, there were nineteen ivory statuettes representing the naked female form and one of a woman clothed in the skin of a cave-lion. Also in mammoth ivory were six birds (geese or ducks), carved as if in flight, a seventh carved as if swimming, an ivory baton (possibly a shaman's implement), and a fish with a spiral pecked on one of its sides.

This spiral was not an isolated find. There were others associated with the burial of a four-year-old child who had suffered from rickets and whose interment was accompanied by an opulent array of grave goods. The child had been laid on its back in a crouched position with the head turned to the east, the direction of the rising sun. A huge mammoth tusk curved across the body, and the child had worn a forehead band or crown of ivory, an ivory bracelet, and a necklace of 126 ivory beads with a bird-like pendant. There was another flying bird pendant nearby, and

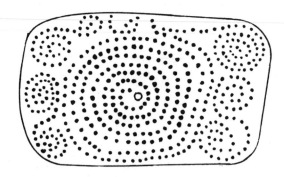

The oldest-known handmade spirals, found at Mal'ta in Siberia, date from about 16000 BC, in the Upper Palaeolithic. On this ivory medallion with pierced centre is one large spiral, a small spiral and three pairs of returning spirals, all made by drilling. The reverse bears three serpents.

two medallions, one of which had three cobra-like wavy serpents incised on one side, and on the reverse a left-handed spiral of seven turns enclosed by three spiralling S-shapes.

These remarkable discoveries suggest a surprisingly advanced set of beliefs concerning life and death. The goddess statuettes indicate spirituality, the serpent stands for eternal life, the cosmic fish symbolises the formal physical universe (possibly as the messenger or 'bird' of the nether regions), while the birds would bear away the soul after death. The various themes of rebirth are there, too: the foetal position of the body, the head turned to watch for the rebirth of the sun and the symbolism inherent in the spiral motifs combined with the presence of the Great Goddess. All this, many thousands of years before the written records of the later mythologies from Middle Eastern Neolithic cults of the fertility/vegetation Goddesses such as Aphrodite and Ishtar, which in turn embraced the symbolism of serpent, fish, bird and spiral.

In contrast to the variety and exotic richness of the spiral-painted and carved figurines and pottery vessels of Neolithic Eastern Europe and the Mediterranean, however, idols are virtually non-existent in Atlantic Europe, and much Neolithic pottery seems plain and unimaginative. The same can be said of the pottery of Beaker and Bronze Age Britain and Ireland; although it is of a higher quality and at times fine and beautiful in form, especially the funerary Beaker ware, it never carries human representations or obvious anthropomorphic images. Instead, plain designs and patterns are used, which seem visually uninteresting until the symbolism is understood; then the hidden beauty of the images is revealed and the funerary pots burst into life, pregnant with meaning.

The reason why representational art failed to develop was probably due to the strong artistic tradition whose high degree of conservatism suppressed most attempts at originality and ensured the continuance of conventionalised styles. It is probable, too, that numerous carvings were executed in wood, although not to a

Parts of spiral designs from broken pots which were probably sacred vessels, found at the Neolithic settlement of Skara Brae in the Orkneys.

great extent otherwise there would surely have been more durable interpretations in stone and bone as well. Among the few carved figurines which survive are three chalk drum-shaped 'idols' from Folkton in Yorkshire, a broken chalk carving from Windmill Hill and another from Neolithic Maiden Castle, and of course the Grimes Graves Goddess.

It is odd that, outside Scotland and Ireland, so few carvings of symbols and images were made on walls, stones and outcrops in megalithic England and Wales. On the other hand, there can have been little travelling between communities in those times, as distinct from flight and emigration, and the itinerant traders who did get about would hardly have been permitted to look at private tribal carvings inside the ancestral tomb-temples of others. Some traditions would have been closely guarded secrets, spreading only slowly between neighbours through alliances and marriages. Whatever the reasons, the Boyne Valley culture did not extend its artistic influences into England and Wales beyond the extreme west and north. Nevertheless, a certain dissemination of ideas took place, in tandem with the slow spread of technological and agricultural advances. Certainly, during the Neolithic and Early Bronze Ages (say, 4600–1500 BC) the basic religious beliefs seem to have been broadly similar across the whole of Britain and Atlantic Europe—but of course steadily diversifying and diverging as time went on.

So in Britain, spiral images on pottery and other articles which unquestionably date from the Neolithic era are few. Two pieces of pottery have been found at Skara Brae in the Orkneys—one a fragment with a three-turn left-handed spiral; the other a sherd large enough to reveal parts of two spirals (one sufficiently complete to show it to be left-handed, of the lunar-female goddess type) together with two nested lozenges enclosing a design of dots. These symbols resemble those used elsewhere in connection with the fertility-goddess.

In England, pottery with spiral decoration has been found in the Stonehenge area. Four late-Neolithic vessels were found at Durrington Walls, decorated with crude spirals or concentric circle patterns, and a more impressive 117-millimetre sherd from the rim of a vessel has a finger-drawn spiral and the clear beginning of another one beside it. This sherd, part of a large pot that would have been about 350 millimetres in diameter when complete, came from the soil around a post-hole of the southern timber circle which has been dated to about 2600 BC. A pit at Wyke Down Henge, close to but later than the Dorset Cursus, has yielded a well-decorated but badly-damaged vessel with three or more horizontal bands of sloping lines and at least two sets of rings which could be parts of large-diameter spirals.

It seems as if the few vessels sporting spirals or other finely-incised decorative motifs were used for ritual purposes at sacred functions, whereas the plainer pots served for everyday use. The finding of smashed holy vessels in post-holes, or in prepared pits, happens often enough to suggest that they were broken and deposited there in deliberate ceremonial acts forming part of a cult practice.

All this decorated pottery is of a type known as Grooved Ware or Rinyo-Clacton Ware (from the sites in Orkney and Essex where it was first found). We know little about the people who made it, but evidence of their cult and remains of their pottery appeared in scattered sites throughout Britain during the third millennium BC. Where design can be studied, the typical but monotonous styles are reminiscent of what is known from the Boyne Valley culture. Aubrey Burl comments that 'the fact that grooved ware has been recovered from some early stone circles and henges supports the idea that the vessels were elements of a new ritual that was rapidly adopted'. That new ritual is exactly what this book is about—*the cult of the spiral and vortex circle*. Spirals are found again on much later pottery of quite different types in the British Bronze and Iron Ages, but only spasmodically. A late example is a spiral-patterned pot-base from Winklebury Hill Fort.

Spiral decorations may also have been used on clothing, although naturally such perishable articles have not survived. As in Neolithic societies in other continents, garments were probably embroidered or knitted, dyed or painted. An idea of what may have been lost can be gained from a reddish-brown pottery statuette from the Romanian Bronze Age, which shows a fully-dressed figure wearing an embroidered skirt similar to clothes worn in the same part of the Balkans to this day. Numerous interconnecting spirals have been deftly woven into the pattern of a finely-worked dress, giving a dense display of symbolism which suggests it was worn by a priestess.

Facial and body tattooing is another means by which spirals and other symbols could have been displayed, at least by part of the population. It is known from the human bodies preserved by the permafrost of Siberia that tattooing was already practised in Palaeolithic times, and the art of tattooing as a spiritual and ritual

Pottery statuette recovered from a Bronze Age cremation site at Cirna in Romania. The spiral motifs, including the Sacred Marriage theme, which appear on the robe were probably embroidered.

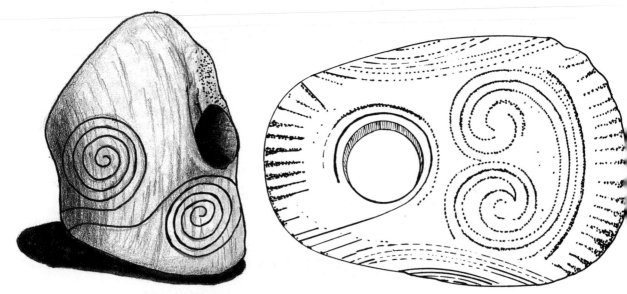

Carved maceheads. *Left:* Antler bone bearing four-turn spirals which wind in opposite senses, preserved by the mud of the Little Ouse at Garboldisham, Norfolk, for more than 4,500 years. *Right:* One face of the exquisitely tooled macehead found at Knowth. Made from hard flint, it plainly displays the theme of the Sacred Marriage via its returning spirals.

activity has continued through to the present day in many parts of the world.

Spirals were used as decoration on ceremonial axeheads, maces and the like, and on charms, amulets and jewellery. In 1964 a fine macehead of antler bone was found one-and-a-half metres beneath the bed of the Little Ouse at Garboldisham in Norfolk. It had been beautifully incised with one single and one pair of returning spirals. A carved flint macehead of exceptional artistic merit and craftsmanship was buried beneath a cover of shale in a pit within the Boyne Valley passage-grave of Knowth. It had a complex design of single and double spirals, together with narrow-faceted lozenges, images usually associated with the Goddess. The decoration had not been engraved; despite the hardness and brittleness of the material, the artist-sculptor had gone to the enormous effort of creating designs in relief. This excellent piece of early Irish workmanship must have been executed before the final sealing of the tumulus, about 4,500–5,000 years ago.

Each single-spiral design on the macehead relates to the handle-hole. The tails of the outward-turning spirals wind back around the hole as though the intention is to transfer to the handle and its priestly bearer the powers thought to penetrate the hole and flow along the spirals. It recalls the enigmatic *bâtons de commandement* of the French and British Palaeolithic era and their authoritative role in the hands of spiritual and clan leaders. Some of the French *bâtons* are also exquisitely carved in flowing spirals. The Knowth macehead has a splendid double spiral turning in opposite senses, to symbolise the Sacred Marriage.

The most perfect and extraordinary objects in carved chalk to have been found

One of three finely-carved chalk objects, diameter 122 mm, discovered in a child's Bronze Age grave at Folkton, Yorkshire.

in Britain are certainly the drums found in the grave of a child in a Yorkshire round barrow at Folkton. These objects are no toys. The rich decoration, incorporating the chief symbolic elements of the time—lozenges, chevrons, triangles, spirals, and others—is skilfully integrated into unified patterns which fill the available space to give pleasing aesthetic fields. One might expect such objects to be part of the magical equipment of a religious leader, and the fact that they were buried with the corpse of a child plainly indicates the importance of the child to the mourners. One of the chalk cylinders had been placed behind the child's head; the others were behind the hips. One drum carries a Goddess lozenge and a primitive rendering of the Sacred Marriage theme with the connecting spirals.

Among the heavily-decorated objects so far found, the most puzzling are the stone balls. Discs protrude from the surfaces of many of them, and it is on these that the artisan has toiled so lovingly. The finesse of the craftsmanship is amazing for such a difficult medium; some of the balls are made of hard granite or greenstone, and one is made from white quartzite, although most of those with spiral decoration are fashioned from the more easily worked and aptly named serpentine.

About fifty engraved stone balls and 360 ungraved ones are known from Scotland, and spiral designs feature on fourteen of them. Three of those without knobs have had the whole ball carved into a spiral, but the majority have from three to nine knobs and 66 examples have ten to 160 knobs.

The use to which such balls were put is unknown, but the care and effort that went into them indicates that they must have been prestige objects conveying authority or religious significance. They seem to have been made to be held or

Three stone balls from Buchan and Alford, northern Scotland, two of them wholly carved as running spirals (after Dorothy Marshall).

A selection of stone balls, some with knobs or lobes. Centre right is one from the Isle of Lewis; the others are from Skara Brae.

passed around. The majority are about 70 millimetres in diameter but a few are bigger, the twelve largest being between 90 and 114 millimetres in diameter.

I have noticed a similarity between lobed or knobbly stone balls and giant hailstones, which are surprisingly alike in size and shape. Large-diameter hailstones are often non-spherical, and diameters up to 75 millimetres or so occur occasionally in Britain, with larger ones more rarely. I believe that the balls were carved as permanent replicas, admittedly sometimes stylised, to preserve a record of the fall of giant hailstones at the time of ferocious summer storms. As objects that dropped from the sky, hailstones shared in the sanctity of celestial space. They came from the godhead at the time of fierce thunderstorms and were viewed as precious instruments or divine gifts, albeit with a brief life on earth. Replicas gave the bearers the authority of the Great Goddess and her Sky God: because the stones bore lasting and tangible witness to the severity of past storms, they also commemorated past visitations from the Sky God. They may therefore have been part of the mystical equipment of the tribal priestess or priest.

In contrast to such fine works of art the Neolithic balls of chalk or stone from eastern and southern England are crude and appear hurriedly made—such as those from the Grimes Graves votive group—and their purpose is likely to have been quite different from that of the Scottish balls. Chalk balls were found at Mount Pleasant in Dorset, and these are more carefully rounded and smoothed, but their discovery with phalluses, as at Grimes Graves, hints at fertility or superstitious use. Excavations at Windmill Hill in the 1930s turned up 30 chalk balls in all, their diameters ranging from 37 to 74 millimetres (fourteen within the 50–60 millimetre range). Two limestone balls were also found in the plough-soil in front of Stoney Littleton long barrow in southern England, probably due to careless dumping of the contents of the barrow when the rubble infill was cleared away in the nineteenth century. These various stone carvings are often found in pairs, and sometimes with phalluses. They must surely have been used as part of a fertility rite.

The first engraved metal objects date from the Continental copper period of the Neolithic era. In parts of Central and North Central Europe engraved copper objects even became quite numerous, to judge by the finds among grave goods. Spirals were commonly used in finger rings, arm and leg rings and bracelets, and in hair ornaments, necklaces and ear-rings.

Returning spirals, or 'spectacle spirals', have been found, made into brooches by hammering flat a thin copper rod into the form of two coils in opposition. They symbolised the dual nature of life and death, both mortal and seasonal, but especially the cosmic solar-lunar duality or Sacred Marriage, and in the age of the Goddess must have rendered powerful service as an elegant and effective 'good luck' charm.

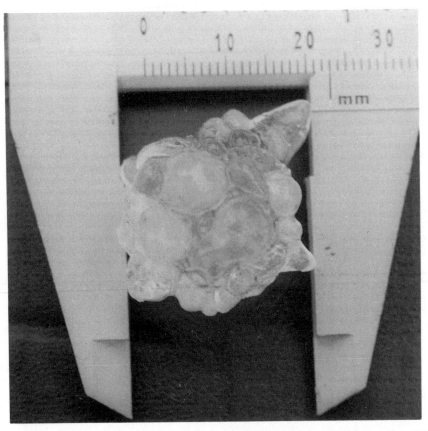

A heavily-knobbed hailstone photographed by David C. Smith at Carmarthen in 1974.
Hailstones exceeding 75–80 mm are known to occur in Britain.

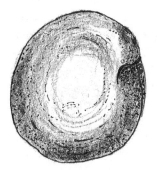 

Objects of chalk from the famous Neolithic causewayed enclosure on Windmill Hill
overlooking Avebury. Chalk balls and occasionally vertebral discs are often found in pairs
at Neolithic sites.

Twin-coiled spirals of copper used for adornment because of their talismanic value. Called 'spectacle spirals' by some archaeologists, they have been recovered in hundreds from graves across the northern continent of Europe. These are from Poland (Brzesc Kujawski).

Neolithic men, women and children were often buried wearing bracelets or anklets of spiral rings or cylindrical beads, and around their necks necklaces of cylindrical or tubular copper, and pendants of round, triangular or double-spiral form. This suggests that not only the spiral but also copper, being an imperishable self-coloured metal, had already acquired some mystical quality in the beliefs of the wearers, just as it did later with the Bronze Age Torque people and numerous other Goddess and post-Goddess societies. This mystical aura has survived in a degenerate way to our own day, among those people who choose to wear copper bracelets for 'medicinal or curative' purposes (as an aid to cure or ease rheumatism).

In ancient times copper was associated with the dawn sky and the planet Venus (the Morning Star). It resembled the coppery sky that presages dawn and, like the opening of a womb, the birth of a new day; it therefore symbolised the birth of the world at the dawn of time and with it aspirations of the attainment of paradise. This link is reinforced by the twisting spiral copper cylinders which have been found around bird bones. Birds were seen as messengers of the gods, occupying the zone between heaven and earth. They heralded the approaching storm, itself a manifestation of the Sky Divinity, and gave warning of the change of seasons by their migratory patterns. Hence they symbolised the souls of ancestors passing in flight, and it was thought advantageous to have the souls of birds to accompany those of mortals to the other world. Spiral cylinders have also been found twisted around amber, the fossil resin found on Baltic shores. Amber stood for immortality and was thought to speed the souls of the dead on their final journey.

The use of the spiral in jewellery may have been related in some degree to the symbolism of the torc (or torque), a twisted rod turned back to form a gapped or incomplete circle. In ancient times it was commonly worn as an arm or neck ornament, and was probably related to the mystic spiral and the Goddess religion.

An immense technological advance came with the discovery of bronze, by which the physical properties of pure copper were immeasurably improved by combining them with the metal tin. The result was an alloy that was malleable, ductile, and of low melting point, giving an easily-worked and durable material.

As the fruits of this discovery were steadily disseminated across the Continent to Britain, the age of metals began. This was the start of the so-called Bronze Age, in which bronze was used for tools, ornaments, weapons and shields, and within which we find the first sacred engravings on bronze metal objects. Very quickly, precision and high quality were achieved.

Spiral ornamentation was practised widely and reached a peak of development in Scandinavia, at a time which corresponds with the Middle Bronze Age in Britain and the Tumulus Culture in central Europe. A bronze disc-headed pin, 140 millimetres in length, decorated with a spiral, was found in a round barrow at Shrewton, not far north-west of Stonehenge, and suggests a use which brings further involvement with the spiral. Pins of this type, whether of metal or bone, may have been used for fastening hair buns, which are in fact tightly coiled spirals, or for securing double-spiral coils of hair around the head as seen on East Balkan miniature sculptures of the fifth millennium BC. In cremation graves of the British Neolithic and Bronze Ages long bone pins are often found, sometimes partly burnt, sometimes not. Stonehenge, too, has produced bone pins, and the spiral-bun fashion was clearly a Goddess-religion concept. A spiral-coiled hair-style is found later in Hindu religion, where the deities Rudra and Pushan wore their hair spiralling upwards as in a shell. Rudra was an Indo–European Storm God who rode the whirlwind and set the primordial waters in motion. It is possible that the purpose of the unexplained funerary cups found beneath British Bronze Age barrows was to hold the deceased's tightly-coiled bun of hair which had been cut off before cremation. At funerary rituals in Malaysia it was the belief that the soul departed for heaven via the spiralled hair bun, and this would explain the ritual deposits containing bone pins, as in the Irish Neolithic pits at Knowth, where long pins of antler bone were found in deposits only a little later than the spiral macehead. The offering may have been spiral-coiled hair held together by the pins, bearing the message of hope for immortality. In past ages societies associated hair with virility, which is held to be a reason for the use of wigs in Egypt, for instance, so the idea of virility may have arisen in the context of the spirituality associated with spiral hair-buns. The bun was buried with the deceased because it was a vital force.

One of the earliest worked bronze objects known in Britain was found in a round barrow at Sewell in Bedfordshire. This was a bronze spiral-headed pin 72

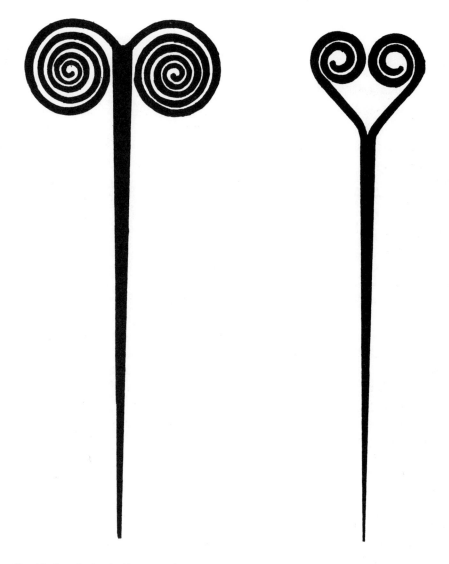

Double-headed spiral bronze pins. *Left:* A long pin from a round barrow at Sewell in Bedfordshire, dated to *c* 2300–2100 BC. The other is from St Albans, Hertfordshire—which borders Bedfordshire—and is dated to the fifth or sixth century AD.

millimetres long with a square-sectioned shaft. Joining the shaft at the head were two spirals, each of four-and-a-half turns, but one had been lost. The date would be about 2300–2100 BC. The object was in the grave near the deceased's left hand, and because a pair of opposed spirals would provide a veritable symbol of power through the Sacred Marriage concept, it may have been fastened to a wooden shaft in the manner of a bishop's crozier. The deceased may have been a medical or 'pharmaceutical' specialist if, even at this early date, the double-spiral emblem

Above: A Bronze Age jet necklace from Pitkennedy, Angus, Scotland, engraved with Goddess lozenge insignia. Many Bronze Age examples are known and all exhibit the finest craftsmanship in the drilling, the decoration and the finishing. *Below:* Gold lunula neck ornament from County Cavan, Ireland, bearing Goddess insignia and maintaining the familiar shape of the earlier jet and amber necklaces.

served a similar purpose to the spiralling snake or serpent on the staff of healers—like Hermes, the phallic wind-god who carried the souls of the dead to Paradise and led the Graces, bringers of agricultural fertility, from the underworld of winter.

A very similar double spiral-headed pin was found at St Albans, not far from the Sewell round barrow but dating from the fifth or sixth century AD. More than 2,500 years separate the two pins, yet the closeness of design suggests a common belief.

Another ornament laden with lunar-solar symbolism was the crescent-shaped necklet known as a lunula. Its earliest form was a necklace of beads, later of jet or amber, with connecting plates inscribed with familiar goddess and fertility symbols of lozenges and apex-meeting paired-triangles. In the Neolithic era even a single-string necklace was charged with power, not just because of the symbolic quality of the beads or charms but because the shape conformed to the circle of the heavens and the celestial deities. In the medium of gold lunulae retained their symbolic qualities but became ostentatious status symbols as well. The use of gold was an Irish idea, and the few examples found elsewhere in Britain are thought to be exports. Gold lunulae are believed to have come into fashion about the middle of the Bronze Age, when the divine status of the sun was beginning to supplant the pre-eminence of the Goddess moon. For people wealthy enough to afford it this was reflected, literally, in the change of material from the night-black of jet to the gold of the sun.

11

Nature's Spirals

The inhabitants of Neolithic Britain were aware of the sacred spirals all around them—not only the deeply significant spiral-circles which appeared so dramatically in crops and grass, or the whirlwinds with their alarming message, but the whirlpools they saw in the rivers and seas and the spiral forms in flowers and animal life, including the ammonites they found magically trapped and preserved in solid rock. They were signs of the Goddess, to be treasured and revered, or copied in clay and stone. Spirals found in Nature became an inspiration in their art, and the most obvious and prevalent model was the familiar snail-shell.

Spiral shells embody a compact and impressive two-fold symbolism. Viewed on the snail's back the shell projects a right-handed, clockwise outward-flowing pattern, indicative of the imagery of birth, rebirth, masculinity, creativity and the solar cycle. Looked at the other way, as the snail withdraws into the shell, the right-handed pattern flows inwards, standing for the opposing images of death and decay, and hence spiritualisation. Nonetheless, the closest affinities lie with women, the moon, and the Goddess, which gave the mollusc value as a talisman associated with birth. This is because, in addition to the symbolism of the shell, the most powerful symbolic images result from the dynamic movement of the living tissue. When the creature comes out of its shell the symbolism is that of life itself (as with the mystical interpretation of the spiral ground-traces formed in crops and grasses), together with the imagery for the direction of outward spiral flow. By contrast, when the snail retreats from view beneath its tomb-like cover, the meaning takes on that of inward spiral flow which is that of death and dematerialisation.

This ability to alternate between appearance and disappearance is the pre-eminent attribute of the moon, which in itself provides a persuasive reason for regarding the snail as primarily a lunar object. But the moon is a manifestation of the Great Goddess, and like the snail has horns. In folklore the bulhorn snail was highly regarded, and this tradition was alive until quite recently. Nineteenth-century Cornish miners, upon meeting a bulhorn on their way to work, would propitiate the snail, to avoid ill-luck, by giving it a particle of food, or some tallow from their lanthorns. This peculiar custom must be a relic of the pre-Christian era when the snail was revered as the symbol, companion or attendant, or even manifestation, of the Goddess. The miner fears danger or death when at work in the bowels or womb of the Goddess. He wishes to come back out, as the snail comes back out of its shell. The food offering is to encourage the snail to stay out, and not to withdraw into darkness; and the tallow symbolises the need for illumination. It is probably the same association of ideas which has led to snails being accredited with the power of healing. European folklore steadfastly regards snails as the bearers of good luck, above all the dark-banded variety whose divine statement is proclaimed plainly by the alternating black-and-yellow spirals.

This belief reveals unwitting insight on the part of ancient man, because the snail is an hermaphrodite—possessing dual sexuality. Its spiral shell therefore truly symbolises the universe in miniature. It embodies facets of the male and female deities, of the sun and the moon, of life and death; it represents mankind's eternal hope of salvation and immortality. What is more, the ease with which the creature glides from its shell is the gift most desired by woman at the moment of child-birth.

All this amply explains why Neolithic people maintained such a strong fetish for the shells of molluscs whether from land or fresh water, as well as spiraliform sea-shells and fossil spiral types. It solves a number of mysteries which have puzzled archaeologists for some time, particularly the superabundance of snail-shells at some sites in unexpected places and on a global scale. Large quantities of shells were found in the ruins of Pompeii, and in a crypt in a Mayan pyramid in Yucatán. The 8,000 shells from Grimaldi were obviously a collection for religious and decorative purposes, not the result of some collecting pastime. Surprising quantities of water snail-shells were found in Neolithic post-holes at the Sanctuary near Avebury, and in the core mound beneath Silbury Hill, suggesting some occult ritual involving the snails rather than the accidental result of reed-gathering in the case of the Sanctuary or water sprinkling in the case of Silbury.

An unusual number of snail-shells was found at Stonehenge, at the bases of trilithon stones and in the great ditch, and in some of the ritual Aubrey holes, which may mean that they had been deposited there deliberately. On the other hand, it is probable that snails swarmed over the area during a time when it was temporarily abandoned as a sacred site. At any rate, the possibility remains that Neolithic and Bronze Age tribes, at least on some occasions, gathered snails from farther afield in order to provide material for a ceremonial scattering of spiral-shaped shells in sanctified areas. Dr John Thurnam, who excavated a number of barrows in the nineteenth century, stated that:

> shells of the terrestrial mollusca occur sometimes in the Wiltshire tumuli. In the barrow on Roundway Hill (near Devizes) numerous shells of *Helix nemoralis* were met with at between two and four feet down into the grave. These snails at the present day abound in the brushwood on the sides of the hill, but not on the down where the barrow is situated; and it was inferred by Mr W. Cunnington that they had been brought to the spot where they were found for use as food; whilst Mr J. W. Flower gives reason for thinking they had been deposited in the grave from 'some strange superstition'.

Then there is Alexander Keiller's discovery of the infant burial in a ditch at Windmill Hill, with its evidence of ritual deposits. He found that the corpse had been placed on its right side, with the head facing east, as was common in interments of the Neolithic period. Unfortunately, so many of the bones had been damaged or dislodged by burrowing animals that it was impossible to tell whether the body had originally been curled up like an unborn child, although this seems likely. What was most significant was that, as Isobel Smith recorded in her book *Windmill Hill and Avebury*, 'snail shells and fragments of charcoal were distributed among the bones that were still in place, and animal bones lay in close proximity'.

Further examples are plentiful. It seems that the people of those times, if obsessed by the strength and fear of a spiral-based religion, may have gathered snail-shells for ritual scattering upon funeral deposits, or over sacred areas, just as quartz, coloured pebbles and other stones are known to have been collected and sprinkled in this way.

Snail collections were being assembled as late as the British Iron Age or Late Bronze Age. In Oxfordshire at Rainsborough Hillfort a pit was found to contain a collection of 922 large snail-shells. All but about fifty were either single-banded or five-banded. Almost all the shells were whole, so if the snails had been gathered as food they must have been boiled to remove the contents. But was food the primary or even secondary objective?

The respect shown for snail-shells was already ancient by the beginning of the Neolithic era—4500 BC. The antiquity of such practices dates back at least to the Magdalenian era of the Upper Palaeolithic, some 10,000–20,000 years earlier than the British Neolithic. In the Grotte des Hôteaux, Departement d'Ain, France, were found seven skulls separated from the bodies for burial, two skull tops shaped into bowls, and a woman's skull surrounded with snail-shells many of which had been perforated. It is probable that in these remote times the snail was revered for some essential quality other than that of its whorled coils, and the symbolism of birth seems the most likely. Thus when the shell acquired value as a talisman, the spiral of the whorl became its symbol; and in the course of time the concept was widened to include other natural spiral images such as the spiralling whirlwind (although the whirlwind's symbolism may have had a different origin as we have seen).

A final point may be significant. The snail is related to the marine shell not only by its shape, but also by the hum which sounds inside its windings when it is held against the ear. This adds to the symbolism of birth and rebirth if the noise is thought to be linked to the sound of the 'creative breath'.

Despite their hardness the shells of land snails are thin and brittle, making them useless for personal adornment, but their marine cousins have strong, thick shells, adapted to withstand the action of fierce coastal waves. Freshwater snail-shells are also tougher than the land species, which may help explain why water snails are often found among grave goods or as ritual deposits at prehistoric ceremonial sites.

Perforated sea-shells have been found at many Neolithic and Bronze Age sites in Britain, as well as at more ancient Palaeolithic sites. They were used chiefly as necklaces, perhaps more rarely as brooches. The dog-whelk shells found at the Severn–Cotswold chambered long barrows of West Kennet and Nympsfield, including *Nucella lapillis* and *Nassarius reticulatus*, have conical spirals emblematic of the common whirlwind, and would have made splendid devotional brooches or pendants. Their shapes are reminiscent of the conch which resembles the cornucopia, both traditional instruments of the wind and of fertility. Perforated shells were also found at the West Kennet barrow. Besides *Nucella lapillis* and the whorled whelk, *Nassarius reticulatus*, there was a spiral bead or pendant made from the whorl of a periwinkle, *Littorina littorea*, and a twice-perforated cowrie, *Cypraea*.

In the National Museum of Wales in Cardiff is a Palaeolithic marine-shell necklace, the sole accompaniment of a skeleton whose bones were stained red with blood-coloured ochre. The corpse had been buried in a cave at Paviland on the West Glamorgan coast more than 20,000 years ago. This find not only proves the antiquity of the necklace in northern Europe, but hints at the long history of

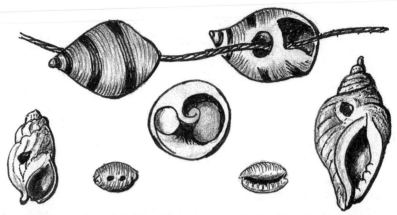

Spiral symbolism in pierced shells, which were used in Neolithic Britain as talismans and amulets. Shown threaded is a Nucella shell (both sides) from Nympsfield chambered long barrow in the Cotswolds. The others are from West Kennet long barrow. On the left is another Nucella, on the right a Nassarius, and in the centre a spiral bead or pendant fabricated by cutting a whorl from a shell. Finally, both sides of a cowrie are shown, pierced with two holes for a string.

spiral symbolism. Naturally-occurring spiral-shaped objects were used in this way, but more surprisingly, beautiful images of spirals were incised on bone surfaces—even at this early date! An understanding of spiral imagery seems to have preoccupied prehistoric peoples for at least this same grand span of time.

The shells of cowries, *Cypraea*, are particularly important in prehistoric symbolism. Found everywhere, their shape resembles the female vulva, and therefore represents fertility. They are easily fashioned into beads and necklaces, and perforated specimens have been found from all periods throughout the world. In Britain cowries were discovered in the Neolithic chambered barrow of West Kennet, a Bronze Age barrow at Langton, East Yorkshire, and a barrow near Dorchester, Dorset. Marine shells of other types have been found in the Stonehenge region, at Winterbourne Stoke and near Woodhenge, and there was a cowrie in the Neolithic tumulus Bryn yr Hen Bobl on Anglesey. This tomb, heavily laden with symbolism, contained a megalith inscribed with a triangle and had about a dozen conical limpet shells carefully arranged on stones projecting from the bottom of a wall of the chambered cairn. It dates from around 5,000 years ago.

Limpet shells were used symbolically over a long period in many areas. On the island of Malta a limpet pierced for use as a pendant reveals a deep concern for the symbolism of the triangle and cone at an early date in the fifth millennium BC—a concern which relates mystically with the Feminine through the triangle, and hence Goddess belief in rebirth. The perforated limpet shell from the long barrow at West Kennet, and those from barrows at other inland sites, may have a similar meaning. Limpet shells with their tops removed were found in a Neolithic site at Isbister, Orkney, where a collection of 21 truncated limpets had been grouped together, separately from another group of uncut ones. The excavator, John Hedges, was of the opinion that 'the former were not deposited as shellfish, as such, but as specially collected shells.' Two more lay with the human remains. The special attention reserved for the decapitated cones suggests that some further symbolism may have been involved: perhaps the feminine, Goddess imagery of the solid conical triangle was enhanced to include 'earth' symbolism, in which the ritual indicated an appeal for life-after-death rather than the more prosaic idea of a simple 'food-offering'.

If the early peoples revered natural spiral shells, how much more must they have been in awe of the fossil shells they found in stone. Petrified spirals would share in the imagery and sacred values associated with stone—its durability and ageless-ness which symbolised undying strength in a world of transience and decay. Fossils certainly seem to have been treasured, and there is evidence of a legacy of ideas based on prehistoric beliefs surviving into modern times.

The molluscan shells, whether fossils or finds from the recent ocean, most favoured by Palaeolithic people were the gastropod or univalve shells, especially the pointed spiral forms and cowries. These included limpets, whelks and snails. Bivalve shells (such as oysters, mussels, cockles) were chosen much less often for jewellery, and their occasional inclusion may have been to add variety to a necklace. Fossil and recent shells are found at both inland and coastal settlement sites. The choice may have depended on nothing more than local availability, but certainly there is ample evidence of shells and fossils being traded over great distances. Much effort would have been required to extract fossils neatly from their rocky bed, and one can imagine the prestige gained by the person who wore the graded fossil-bead necklace found with a Neolithic burial in Dorset.

The conical spiral of the tertiary gastropod *Sipho menapiae* was discovered deep in a Lascaux cave in a Palaeolithic deposit from the Magdalenian period. As a Pliocene fossil it is known only from the Pliocene beds of Wexford (Ireland) and the Isle of Man, so it must have been brought to France by traders. This find was one of only four portable items of culture unearthed in the painted caves of Lascaux and its presence indicates that it was treasured in Magdalenian belief.

Certain proof of archaic reverence for spiral fossils has been found on the islands of Malta and Gozo, in Neolithic temples which themselves are rich in spiral decoration. Not only Miocene gastropod shells, but also carved *imitations* in limestone were found, and replicas made from baked clay. Such laborious copying suggests a devotion due to more than symbolic awareness and a desire for ornamentation—nothing less than true iconography, one might think.

Many other fossil types have been uncovered by archaeologists in Palaeolithic, Mesolithic, Neolithic and Bronze Age sites on the Continent of Europe. In Britain Bronze Age sites have yielded the long, narrow cone-shaped *Dentalium* and the

Limestone carving of a fossil gastropod from the renowned Neolithic temple of Gigantija on Gozo in the Maltese islands. Replicas in clay were also modelled and baked.

bead-like *Porosphaera globularis*. It is the spiral fossils, however, which are particularly important, and the best representatives are undoubtedly the ammonites.

These molluscs with their whorled chambered shells belonged to an extinct order of cephalopods, a class featuring a distinct head or tentacles and including the cuttle-fish and the nautilus. The word 'ammonite' derives from the Latin *Cornu Ammonis*, and the name Ammon's horn is occasionally found in British folklore. Ammon was the Egyptian Ram God and sported tightly spiralling horns. A Bronze Age round barrow at Garton Slack in North Yorkshire had a large piece of ammonite among the grave goods, but the Neolithic long barrow at Stoney Littleton, near Bath, has the most important evidence of fossil use. One large fossil, 32 centimetres in diameter, is situated on the entrance door-jamb. There is another at the entrance to the first chamber on the right. The fossil-bearing Jurassic stone slabs were clearly chosen specifically for their fossil content. This sets an early date for the use of the spiral coil in southern England because the barrow dates from the early fourth millennium BC. I have found that the gallery is aligned to correspond with the point of the rising sun on midwinter's day, so it seems the barrow was more than just a place for the dead; it was a temple and shrine for the living, built as the womb-tomb of the Great Goddess who awaited the annual return of the sun, as at Newgrange and Knowth.

Another English folklore name for ammonite is snake-stone. This stems from its resemblance to a coiled snake, because both land and water varieties of snake wind themselves in spirals. The Liassic ammonites of Whitby in north-east England have long been looked upon as snakes; they are said to have been petrified by the prayers of St Hilda at the founding of the convent there, and decapitated by the curse of St Cuthbert. In *The Natural History of Selborne*, Gilbert White uses the name Ammon's Horns, and tells a fable of St Keyna, of Keynsham, a town on the Liassic fossil-bearing limestone of the Mendip Hills. The saint's prayers are said to have converted the snakes in the wood where she lived into (headless) snake-stones.

The most ancient evidence of the reverence for ammonite fossils comes from the Upper Palaeolithic period in Central France. A set of six Liassic ammonites, and a bigger seventh one, perforated for use as jewellery, were found at the Fourneau du Diable, Bourdeilles. The site dated from between 25000 and 20000 BC. Even in these ancient times the spiral had acquired a well-developed significance whose meaning could be passed to others, and to the divine. It was a sacred symbol, immediately recognisable and as pregnant with meanings as the Cross to the Christian, the Mandala to the Hindu, or the Yang-Yin to the Chinese. The gastropod shell, snail, marine or fossil, took the place of the man-made spiral— until one finds the appearance of spirals on Mesolithic and Neolithic rock art in south-eastern Spain, in Irish passage-grave art, in the Neolithic ceramic and mural art of the emerging city-states of the Near and Middle East and Mediterranean, and the Neolithic imitation conical-spiral gastropods of the Island of Gozo.

There are many other spiral forms in Nature which would have had meaning for prehistoric people but which, if they were used in rituals, would leave little or no permanent trace. The pod-bearing climbing plants would have been revered for their ability to wind about other plants or trees in a spiralling formation, either clockwise or anticlockwise. The honeysuckle or woodbine is one of many other climbing plants that do the same. The growing stems follow a spiralling path, the three-dimensional curve obtained by encircling a cylinder, very similar to the aerial course of birds soaring in the rising air of a hot-air thermal on a summer's day. There is also the mistletoe, so beloved of the Celts and the Druids, the plant which lives in the sky and the trees above one's head. Those Iron Age worshippers very likely received their mistletoe mythologies from practices established in Bronze Age and Neolithic times. Mistletoe is said to have been deposited at the centre of Silbury Hill and in a round barrow.

Another common European climbing plant is the convolvulus or bindweed, a large genus of the Morning Glory family with 150 species. Its very name betrays its coiling, encircling character, and it is known to have been used in Ancient Egypt. Spiralling plant types appear carved on stones and frequently on Grecian and Cretan painted pottery. Spiralling forms bearing the message of the tree of life were painted on ceilings in the Neolithic Maltese hypogeum at Hal Saflieni (early-mid third millennium BC), and survive to this day as a puzzle for interpretation.

Not surprisingly, the spider's web is loaded with meaning in primitive and classical mythology. The spiral web combines a mystic Centre with an obvious

Whirlpools in streams, rivers and springs would have intensified the identification of these watery places with the Great Goddess. This photograph was taken in the river at Bradford-on-Avon in Wiltshire.

spirit of creation, overlaid and enforced with the rays of the sun. At the same time it expresses a deadly contrast, for the web is a spiral-net converging to a point where death and dissolution await—just like the destructive aspect of the spiralling tornado, and like Medusa, the snake-haired Gorgon, who waits at the centre of her inward-turning mosaic.

Snakes, too, when coiled in sleep, can be seen as spirals, and in motion, the opened, unrolled spiral becomes the meander symbol, the shape of the uncoiled snake. Spiral-centred crop circles have been called 'snig's nests' in northern England, from the name given to the young eel; and there must have been occasions in ancient as in modern times when a farmer chanced upon eels or snakes lying in a 'cup-shaped' spiral-circle in his crop and associated the two as cause and effect.

Spiral-shapes sometimes occur in clouds, especially wispy cirrus and mountain lee-wave clouds, which doubtless at times were taken to be portents of the celestial deities; and the whirlpool eddies which occasionally appear in streams and springs were surely a sign of the Goddess. Water, always revered by ancient peoples on account of its indispensability, was the oldest of the Divine Powers and regarded as the source of all life. As the sacred emblem of the Great Goddess, it formed part of a Goddess–moon–waters–earth complex. In the whirlpool, as in the water-spout, could be seen the cycle of life that recreates, rejuvenates and returns refreshed. Conversely, it is also the cycle that destroys. Pools and streams that regularly furnished whirlpools would therefore be centres of propitiation and magical rites.

The followers of the cult of the Great Goddess worshipped every manifestation of the spiral—her epitome—in Nature and art. In their need to express their devotion they were even willing to move mountains. This was their purpose in building Silbury Hill, the greatest artificial mound of prehistoric times, raised by a devout population to the glory of spirality and the Goddess of the Waters, the Earth and the Moon.

12

The Secrets of Silbury Hill

It is best to approach Silbury Hill by the ancient pathway south from Avebury's henge and circles. The footpath follows the Winterbourne stream of the immature Kennet. Waden Hill, scene of Early Neolithic occupation, is on the left and the later chambered long barrow of West Kennet refashions the skyline ahead. On nearing Silbury the path swings suddenly west to avoid a lesser winter-stream, and the dead rings of the Sanctuary on Overton Hill to the south-east come into view.

Eternally serene, Silbury would still occupy a sea of tranquillity on Wessex's green and open downs were it not for the main road so unhappily close beneath it. No more than a truncated cone, the hill's plain exterior conceals an extravagance of planning and effort beneath its grassy slopes. Yet in remaining unweathered and undefiled since it was laboriously raised 4,600 years ago, Silbury has defied the attentions of antiquarians and archaeologists who sought to uncover its message. Like its much later, inverse counterpart, the Wilsford shaft near Stonehenge, this extraordinary monument looms from prehistory as a seemingly pointless exercise in human endeavour. Why was it there, and why so big? That it could guard the secrets of its origins for so long is due entirely to the loss of all understanding of the essence of British Neolithic and Bronze Age religion. The crucial factors underlying this ancient cult, which I have tried to explain in this book, may help to open our eyes to the vision and purpose which inspired Silbury's builders.

Silbury Hill was built in the Late Neolithic period, in the twenty-seventh century BC, at a time when circular monuments, especially the earlier henges and stone circles, were becoming familiar to more and more communities. The hill rose on ancient pastureland, on the land of the peoples we know as belonging to the Windmill Hill culture. The nearest long barrows at South Street, Horslip, Longstones, Beckhampton Road, West Kennet and East Kennet had been founded hundreds of years earlier, and were still in use as tomb-shrines at the time that Silbury was being arduously engineered one kilometre south of the future henge and megalithic circles of Avebury. Not far distant, to the east, a small circular structure of timber posts (which may have been roofed) had been in use on Overton Hill for a couple of centuries. This was the Sanctuary, phases I and II. The tribal society which raised Silbury and the Sanctuary was also to build Avebury, its coves and its avenues. William Stukeley wrote in 1743 that 'Silbury indeed is a most astonishing collection of earth, artificially rais'd, worthy of Abury'.

The excavations of Richard Atkinson in 1968–9 proved that the hill was built without major interruptions or delays. Except perhaps for occasional hold-ups due to bad weather and wintry conditions, the work seems to have been pursued relentlessly until it was completed. Chalk was prised and scraped from encircling quarries using deer-antler picks and wooden shovels and perhaps scoops made from the shoulder-bones of oxen. Keeping to a careful design, meticulously planned to guarantee stability, millions of baskets were filled and emptied until, when a height of 40 metres (130 feet) had been reached, almost half a million tonnes of chalk had been shifted. Silbury's diameter then measured 160 metres (522 feet) at the base, and the monument covered 2.2 hectares (five-and-a-half acres). The builders were not to know it, but they had constructed what was to endure for thousands of years as the highest artificial mound in prehistoric Europe. This was the era, in northern Africa, of Egypt's fourth dynasty, in the twenty-seventh century BC, when the earlier pyramids were being built. The achievement of Silbury came about a hundred years before the Great Pyramid of Cheops at Giza, and despite a lack of communication between Egypt and Britain it is likely that some of the immediate social and economic effects on the societies involved were not dissimilar.

Silbury's external appearance is that of a flat-topped cone, not unlike a decapitated limpet. The internal structure comprised several sections which Richard Atkinson named Silbury I, II, and III. What we look at today is Silbury III. Atkinson gave the name Silbury IV to the shallow quarry extension to the west. Building materials consisted of chalk rubble and chalk blocks which were used to make uncemented internal walls. Only in the innermost mound, Silbury I, were materials other than chalk found. Chief among these was a circular stack of

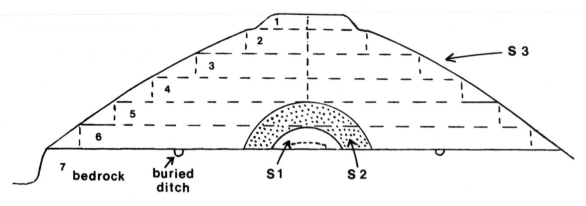

Diagrammatic view of the interior of Silbury looking westwards. S1 is the primary core standing on the ancient surface, and S2 a chalk mound surrounded by a buried circular ditch. S3 is the Silbury we know today. It is a six-tiered stable structure wholly covering S1 and S2 with an outer ditch on its south side crossed by two causeways (not shown) of uncut chalk rock of differing widths and heights.

turf. It is understandable that the importance of this turf-stack should have been overlooked by early excavators who felt deceived in finding no rich burial, but there can be no doubt that the turf was hallowed in the eyes of the people who took such pains to select and consecrate it. In a world dominated by magic and religion the turf was infused with their spiritual adoration, and this profoundly holy respect elevated the dark inner core to the status of priceless treasure.

Silbury I lies at the heart of the hill as a complex, layered mound, overlying a small core, five metres in diameter and 0.8 metres high, made of clay mixed with a liberal supply of flints.

From this centre, reposing on the ancient ground surface, there radiated lengths of twisted string. Lengths of this string had been noticed in 1849 when a tunnel was driven to the centre of the hill. In the words of the supervisor, John Merewether, 'on the surface of the original hill were found fragments of a sort of string, of two strands, each twisted, composed of (as it seemed) grass, and about the size of whipcord'. Richard Atkinson found samples, too, but he reckoned it more probable that they were made from 'twisted fibrous plant stem, mainly of nettle'.

A low wattle fence had next been constructed, 20 metres in diameter, supported by widely spaced wooden stakes to form a broad circle around the clay centre. Then the entire land surface inside the circle had been stacked over with piles of turves and soil to shape a low mound with a height of 3.5 metres. This in turn, together with the enclosing fence, had been completely concealed by four successive conical layers of chalk gravel and topsoil, each layer half-a-metre deep, until the primary mound of Silbury I attained a height of five-and-a-half metres and a diameter of 36.5 metres. Reclining on the sloping sides of the circular mound were several sarsen stones, scattered with fragments of

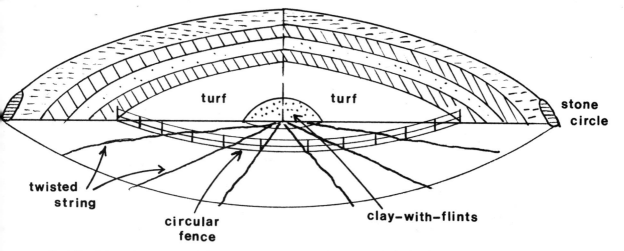

turf　　　turf

stone circle

twisted string

circular fence

clay—with—flints

Details of the primary mound S1 (after R.J.C. Atkinson). A tiny core of clay-with-flints was covered by a circular heap of turf inside a wattle fence. Water snails and land snails were liberally sprinkled on the surface of the mound, which in turn was enclosed by four successive layers of material consisting of chalk, soil and river gravel. On this rested a ring of sarsen stones. A deposit reported by John Merewether as coming from close to the centre comprised a large tooth and caudal vertebrae from, most likely, a bull.

bone and twigs, which seem to indicate a ritual of some kind.

The next stage was the piling up of the chalk structure of Silbury II, 73 metres in diameter, using chalk rubble hewn from an encircling ditch, whose average inside diameter was 116 metres (380 feet). The width of the ditch, discovered by Atkinson, was 20 metres and its depth much the same except for a conspicuous step towards the outer edge; there were plentiful signs that work on the ditch had never been completed.

The appearance of Silbury at this stage was that of a broad domed cone about ten metres high and separated from the deep ditch by a circular strip of land about 21 metres wide. At this stage of construction it could have resembled, in shape and scale, the Neolithic bermed mound adjacent to Knowlton henge in Dorset.

The builders of Silbury now changed their plan. The unweathered vertical sides of the ditch and its unfinished state prove that, without any obvious delay, the ditch was refilled, and work proceeded on transforming this modest hill into the massive monument that we know as Silbury. But before its infilling began, ample care was first taken to strengthen the ditch with a number of radial and cross-radial walls composed of large chalk blocks. The intention was certainly to guard against the risk of future subsidence and to guarantee the longevity of the mound.

A new ditch was begun, its inside diameter 160 metres as against 116 metres for the abandoned one. From the new ditch were prised blocks of chalk to be used in providing an array of stepped walls within a drumlike pattern as a stable basis for infilling with chalk rubble. Six tiers of drums were raised, one above the other, with diminishing radius but each having a similar depth of about five metres.

As the ditch deepened, the natural terrace upon which Silbury I had been set became isolated and the sides of the developing knoll increasingly accentuated so

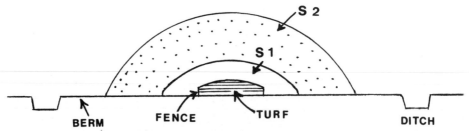

Cutaway view of Silbury to show how it looked as originally planned—an oversized round barrow with concentric berm and ditch.

that it too became somewhat drum-shaped, apart from two causeways retained on the southern side. A wholly complete circular moat could never have been intended because part of the plan was evidently to preserve the causeway entrances, to allow regular access to the slopes and summit—in flat contrast to the requirements of round barrows which were not built with the intention that people should climb over them! The reason for the quarry extension which bulges to the west of the moat is puzzling, unless it was merely the incidental consequence of extending the search for good-sized building blocks of chalk and the extra rubble required to complete the infilling of the rising tiers. The suggestion of Michael Dames, that the water-filled quarry was engineered as a deliberate part of the symbolism of the monument, is highly doubtful.

At this stage of its construction the mound was a gleaming white stepped cone with a broad flat top, surrounded by a ditch nearly ten metres deep spanned by two chalk causeways. Much of this ditch is now largely filled with water-borne sediments caused by the annual flooding of the neighbouring stream.

The platform perimeters of all the tiers except the highest were filled with chalk rubble to produce the outline familiar to us today—a flat-topped cone with a single terrace five metres below the summit. The mound was raised with such precision that the centre of the flat summit lies vertically above the centre of the deeply-buried primary mound with its clay core. What is more, by virtue of the high-level terrace, otherwise difficult to understand, the shape of the summit echoes the size and circular shape of the primary mound hidden far below. The ambition of the builders appears to have been to create a platform off the ground which was strictly above the carefully prepared internal one.

It is likely that the final stage in the building of Silbury was the laborious act of turfing over the entire monument. Considered in conjunction with the obsession for considerable stability of construction, it is evident that what the turfing meant was this:

Silbury was built to be climbed.

Left to itself, hundreds of years would have passed before the powdery chalk-rubble grassed over naturally, during which time it would have been difficult to climb, and impossible in rainy weather. Furthermore, because the hill was provided with entrance and exit causeways, the goal was plainly to use them. Silbury may therefore have been completed with a spiral pathway to the summit as well.

There is no doubt about the time of year when the building of Silbury commenced: the probability is extremely high that it happened either in July or the first week of August. It is at this time of year on the Wiltshire Downs that ants develop wings and embark on their brief mating flights, and Silbury's inner turf mound disclosed the presence of large numbers of winged ants. In 1985 I was on the Chalk Plain on 3 August when the mating flight began, and in 1990 I was at Silbury Hill itself when, again on 3 August, the ants flew. As the British climate was generally drier and warmer at the time when Silbury was being constructed, it is likely that the ants flew in July then, rather than in early August or late July as they do now. Why should a needy farming community disrupt its summer schedule of hard labour prior to harvesting in order to commence the arduous toil of monument building? Such an operation would make no sense unless there had occurred some highly propitious event which directed the minds of the community leaders away from the usual worries about the harvest to matters of religion—above all, some event which reawakened their highest ambitions, their hope of recompense for life's hardships: the dream of immortality which we know, from the written pre-Christian records of the Middle East, can be traced back to Gilgamesh and beyond.

The idea that the hill was built as a sepulchral barrow, to house the remains of a powerful chieftain, used to be favoured by the few archaeologists or antiquarians who would commit themselves to an opinion. That Silbury was never intended to be a burial mound has been established beyond doubt by the excavators who reached the heart of the inner mound and were met with a complete lack of human bones or human memorial. Far from being constructed to house the dead, I believe that it was built to benefit the living.

It has been suggested that Silbury was used as an astronomical observatory, but what advantage could there have been in selecting a site on a valley floor for a platform which would require four million man-hours of labour? Any number of broad hill-tops were available nearby. Moreover, from low-lying Silbury there are no distant landmarks suitable for use as solar or lunar alignments, although relatively small displacements of the site could easily have ensured alignments with the rising or setting sun or moon over pre-existing earthen or chambered long barrows, or with Windmill Hill or the Sanctuary. The archaeologist Aubrey Burl, among others, proposes that the site could have been chosen *because* it was low-lying, and not far from water, and 'Silbury . . . raised just because it was so novel to the natives of the Marlborough Downs, suggesting a new cult structure by people from the east who were becoming dominant in this part of the downs.' While it is true that working together on such a project would have the socially desirable effect of uniting a scattered community under a single administration, (as with the Egyptian pyramids), it would not succeed unless the leaders could draw on a compelling spiritual motive.

Religious inspiration is what Michael Dames strove to find in Silbury Hill. He proposed that the surrounding quarry was dug and deepened to ensure that it would flood and create a semi-permanent water-filled moat. His vision of the archaic mythological concept of the 'White Mountain in the primordial water', combined with the primitive idea of the Cosmic Egg, has appealed to some theorists, and it is conceivable that there are shades of truth in these ideas. Most of the other suggestions spelled out so eloquently in his book *The Silbury Treasure*, however, are rather too fanciful—apart from his important general assumption that the Great Goddess is deeply involved, possibly in a seated or throned capacity. That this must be so is self-evident because the religion of the epoch was undeniably centred on the concept of the Great Goddess; but that the Hill-Moat combination was an architectural rendering in landscape art of the recumbent pregnant Goddess looks to be a fantasy that could only occur to peoples familiar with the figurines and painted art of Eastern and Mediterranean Neolithic Europe.

Michael Dames' suggestion that water played a part in the original concept fails at the outset, for no better reason than that the third-millennium water-table at Silbury was at least ten metres lower than it is today, meaning that the ditch, like round barrow ditches, was dry practically all the year round. The digging of the great ditch could never have been completed in the presence of the water that is there now in the late winter months. But the quarry's great breadth and width do have the majestic effect of augmenting the apparent height of the artificial hill, and that could be reason enough for the westerly extension.

The grass of Silbury's hidden core is amazingly well-preserved. John Merewether noted that the mound which had been laid on the former grass surface, the latter compressed into a thin line of clay, comprised 'a black peaty substance, composed of sods of turf piled together, containing great quantities of moss still in a state of comparative freshness'. This moss, he wrote, retained 'its colour and texture'. One hundred and twenty years later Richard Atkinson commented: 'Some of the grass and moss here is still green, and the remains of ants and insects are so well preserved that an expert can tell that the turf must have been cut and stacked in the late summer, because it is only then that the insects would have reached the state of development observed.'

While it is not so surprising that beetle cases and land-shells should be well preserved, the conservation of the softer tissues of ants and flying-ant wings was a biological delight. We do not know whether any specimens of the invertebrate spiral-web weaver were detected, but the twisted nettle-fibres may have been laid in imitation of a spider's web, or as part of a spinning or spiral ritual. Merewether suggested that mistletoe may also have been present.

Samples of the turves were passed to D. Williams of the Environmental

Archaeology Unit of the University of York for botanical analysis. He reported that they

> . . . had not been derived from the land surface under the mound, which had a soil of a brown earth type, developed in a local patch of clay-with-flints. This is a calcareous soil typical of periglacial deposits commonly found elsewhere on the chalk of Wiltshire, so it is not unreasonable to suppose that the turves had been cut in the neighbourhood and carried no great distance to their chosen resting site. John Evans notes such deposits from the base of slopes in valleys and coombes.

Why were the turves cut elsewhere, not close by, to avoid carrying them any distance at all? What was so special about the grassland valley from which they were taken?

Williams went on to analyse the mosses which had been growing in the turves and which remained so firmly attached to them. The majority were species of mature grasslands, mainly *Pseudoscleropodium purum*, with *Rhytidiadelphus squarrosus* and *Acrocladium cuspidatum*, their known habitat preferences suggesting that the turves may have originated from a north-facing slope. Because neither tall herbaceous vegetation nor short turf is favourable for moss growth, Williams concluded that moderately-grazed mature chalkland existed in the vicinity of Silbury Hill when the mound was built. The most likely height of the grass would have been in the region of 15 to 30 centimetres. Confirmation that the landscape in the proximity of Silbury Hill was open grassland came from a study of Silbury's land-snails by John Evans, the conchological archaeologist. He concluded that their types and numbers indicated 'an environment of very dry open grassland' at the time of construction.

What motivated our British forebears to select this particular site for their colossus? Why did the primary mound consist of turf cut and carried from grassy slopes where the landscape was dry and open, rather than from a nearby area? Why were these labours begun, compulsively it would appear, in July or at the start of August when the work of farming and stock-raising would be at its peak? And why was the mound overlaid with layers of river gravels 'saturated' with aquatic snail-shells? The answers lie in the ancient beliefs enshrined in the magical turf, because the turf *was* the Silbury treasure—the *raison d'être* of the hill itself.

No amount of logic can ever explain to nonbelievers the actions of the pious in pursuance of their religion. Silbury was raised at a time in the prehistory of religious thought when people worshipped a female deity—the Great Goddess— who in conjunction with some lesser Sky God embraced all life on earth and in the heavens. She was Earth Mother, Lunar Goddess, Goddess of the Waters, all in one.

The attainment of a blissful afterlife, then as now, was seen as the due reward for submitting to the daily rigours of a harsh environment. The spiral-circles formed in fields, as I have proposed, were believed to be the vulva of the Goddess releasing subterranean spirits on their journey to paradise, and whereas some of the circles were used as a means of communicating with the dead through the construction of henges and stone rings, others became sites for round barrows as a route to everlasting life. Now, here, in the land of the Windmill Hill people, another idea was born. A temple-shrine was built to facilitate communication with the Goddess, a shrine that in its completed form would have no equal, before or after, in the prehistoric world of the North Europeans.

From the available facts I have tried to piece together what may have happened.

On a bright summer's day or at night, in July or about the start of August, an atmospheric vortex laid flat a circular area, some 20 metres in diameter, in the long grass of sloping pastureland beneath a north-facing ridge or escarpment, of which there are several in the district. It was a place where the chalky soil was quite different from the soil at Silbury. Whether or not the vortex was seen in action we cannot tell, but the prevailing religious beliefs insured that the turf of the spiral-circle was regarded as sacred.

The reason for choosing the Silbury site is another matter. Was it the result of a logical decision, as has been supposed by antiquarians in the past? Or was it—for this has to be considered—the place marked out by divine intervention?

If the former, the low-lying site seems hardly to have been the proper choice, since altitude would have added to the eminence and prestige (although a steeply-sloping site would have created practical engineering problems). Moreover, to the observer, the site of Silbury is so low-lying that the surrounding streams must have restricted access in the wet months of winter and limited the opportunities for ceremonial activities—unless of course water was an essential part of the concept. However, I suspect that the presence of water was incidental to the choice of location. The people were living nearby because of the water, and where they lived was where they worked and then built, as called for, their ceremonial precincts.

I suggest that matters could have developed following the sighting of a visual, divinely interpreted phenomenon—a vortex-forming spiral-circle—at the Silbury site itself, and that it was there, at the place of the supposedly spiritual visitation, that an initial plain ring was marked on the grass. Five metres is a typical diameter for a small spiral-circle, and five metres was the diameter of the inner core of clay which could have served to preserve the spiral pattern beneath it. But instead of raising a small uncomplicated round barrow, as became the standard funerary

This spiral-centred circle, diameter 15 metres, formed overnight in a green wheatfield near Silbury in June 1989.

custom in later years, it was decided to carry to the site the sacred turf from another larger, more distant grass circle which had appeared at about the same time, in order to augment the intensity of the magic in the spiral-blessed turf that was to become the heart of the structure.

This explanation meets all the difficulties previously encountered in the Silbury problem because it is more natural to suppose that site selections, like celestial and atmospheric phenomena, should lie in the province of Divine Will. That spiral-centred crop circles are fairly common in the region is known to the farmers of today, and many small and large single circles and multiple circles are detailed for the Silbury region in the archive of CERES from 1986 onwards. Indeed, a spectacular set of circles appeared close to Silbury Hill each summer of 1988–90.

The site of Silbury, whether humanly selected or divinely inspired, was a grassy terrace-like spur close to a pathway leading in one direction to the Sanctuary on Overton Hill and the chambered barrows of West and East Kennet, and in the opposite direction to South Street long barrow and Windmill Hill. Before the sacred turf was stacked within its circular wattle fence—indeed one must presume before the clay core was laid—strands of twisted 'nettle-string' were ranged on the old land surface, radiating outwards in star-like fashion. Some vortex-circles have radial patterning like this; one was found in Hampshire in August 1987.

On the other hand, a pattern more like a spiral-star may have been intended, in the manner of some observed crop circles—for example, at Beckhampton and Bratton (Wiltshire), Headbourne Worthy (Hampshire), and Oadby (Leicester). The 'slow' spiral or the spiral-star is already familiar to archaeologists and ecclesiastics in the form of the Celtic whirligig.

Close observation of natural spiral-circles often reveals twisting and inter-weaving of the stalks of long grasses, corn or weeds, and this could have been interpreted as the wholly natural art of a spinning and weaving Great Goddess. In many archaic religions this divinity is envisaged as the Great Spinstress who weaves the web of life and spins the threads of fate. Such metaphors have had a universal appeal since Neolithic times when these crafts first appeared. Life is woven, as is fabric, by the crossing of threads which is the symbol of sexual union and a normal part of the world of woman—and so of the Great Goddess. The local spiritual leader who wrought this handiwork at the base of Silbury can have been no mere shaman but surely a priest or priestess, of considerable knowledge and standing. The twisted string bears its own message, imitating the twisted grasses in the natural vortex circles, while the internal clay core might have served to unite and retain the inner ends of the strings at the centre of the mountain.

The four coverings of chalk-river gravels and topsoil layers worked into the central core indicate the importance of soil and water fertility for the shrine. Certainly, the inclusion of the many hundreds of water snail-shells cannot be dismissed as an incidental result of gravel collection from the river-bed: the gravel was probably dredged not only for its own sake but because the spiral snail-shells were necessarily gathered in too. A similar reason could explain the discovery of vast quantities of water snail-shells in the post-holes at the Sanctuary, a kilometre to the east. Until now it has been ingeniously suggested that this must indicate long periods when water-reeds were used for thatching, but the deliberate seeking of spiral-shells seems more likely. As Merewether wrote when discussing the inner turf stack with its moss, 'the freshwater shells which were interspersed on its surface are still preserved in most remarkable freshness and transparency'. This

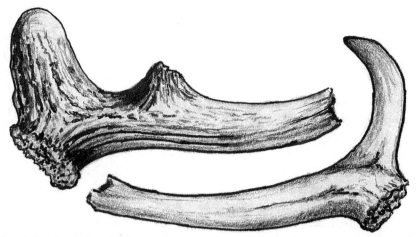

Antler picks of red deer found in 1849 in the turf core of Silbury (S1). They were clearly part of a foundation offering because, although no chalk had been cut at that stage (only turf and clay), the picks were worn with use.

can only mean that the water-snails were placed there deliberately, as if poured from water jars.

Sarsen stones were spread about the exterior of the primary mound forming a stone circle, 'some of them placed with their concave surface downwards, favouring the line of the heap, as is frequently seen in small barrows, and casing, as it were, the mound'. The stones probably served in their usual role as guardians or keepers of spirits, perhaps in a similar way to the familiar guardian megaliths standing at West Kennet, Wayland's Smithy, Cashtal yn Ard (Isle of Man), Cairnholy (Kirkcudbrightshire), and many other long barrows in Britain and Brittany.

Commenting on the sarsens Merewether wrote:

On top of some of these were observed fragments of bone, and small sticks, as of bushes, and, as I am strongly disposed to think, of mistletoe . . . and two or three pieces of the ribs of either the ox or red deer, in a sound and unusually compact state, and also the tine of a stag's antler in the same condition. This being the second instance in which this portion of the stag's horn has been found in these operations, it is not improbable that it may have been specially regarded.

This was evidently an act of ritual consecration, which would also account for the other animal bones and small bushes placed within the mound. Even the red-deer antler picks, although worn and no longer fit for use, must have been deliberately added to the core, for they were hardly likely to have been worn out after cutting the turf. As gifts from the gods and the tools of diggers, the antlers, always symbolic of fertility because of their spring shedding and rapid regeneration, were offered back to the Goddess at the end of their use, as tokens in support of verbal prayers for regrowth and further supplies.

Another of Merewether's discoveries from the inner mound, the 'caudal vertebrae of the ox, or perhaps the red deer, and a very large tooth of the same animal', may be open to the same interpretation as male fertility symbols. Similar comments were made by the archaeologist Stuart Piggott on finding two ox-vertebrae in a long barrow on Thickthorn Down, Dorset—a barrow which had already yielded a carved chalk phallus.

The next step in the building of Silbury was the excavation of a grand circular ditch 116 metres in diameter. This provided the innermost mound with a protective covering of broken chalk and also surrounded the hill of Silbury II with a defensive circular barrier. As with the ditches of henges, the aim was to demarcate the sacred area from the profane. But if Silbury had been intended to be nothing more than a shrine to be visited rather than walked upon, like the majority of shrines, it would have been built as a simple mound. We know, however, from the subterranean explorations of Richard Atkinson, that even diminutive Silbury II was very strongly built with a chalk-wall system. For such a low mound, only ten metres high, the requirement for abnormally good stability is unexpected *unless it is accepted that even Silbury II was meant to be stood upon*. It follows that the intention must have been to hold ceremonies at its summit, in a place directly over the magic turf with its hidden spirals—the womb-opening of the Great Goddess—through which spirits had already passed.

Unfortunately, as Silbury II neared its moment of triumphant completion, it was decided that the height of the Hill was insufficient. Situated so low in the landscape, the size of the 'cosmic' hill did inadequate justice to the grandeur of the conception. The circular ditch had to be filled in and the White Mountain heightened. The planners then embarked upon the construction which ended with Silbury as we know it today.

The labour required to create Silbury III and IV by quarrying the chalk blocks and rubble from the deepening ditch and the western quarry extension was a hundred times greater than what had gone before. The enormity of the project would not have been realised when the primary hillock, Silbury I, was commenced, for the evidence of a change of plan is quite clear. The labour spent was realistically estimated by D. W. A. Startin as four million man-hours. The final apparent volume was 350,000 cubic metres, of which 250,000 cubic metres were moved by hand, the volume difference arising from the use of the cut-off spur of natural chalk. If 400 people had toiled ten hours a day, it would have taken ten years to complete. Such sustained effort is inconceivable. The farming, herding and hunting requirements of the regional community could not have been totally neglected for years at a time. But if each able-bodied person contributed three months of work annually to the project, and supposing some 400 such people could be organised in this way, then 40 years might elapse between foundation and completion.

Silbury was endowed with two causeways, and because needless luxuries were few or absent in those times, some good reason must have necessitated two causeways rather than one. Besides this, there was the platform summit and the prominent terrace a few metres below the top. Because of the precision of the builders, it was possible to hold ceremonies on the flat summit in the knowledge that they were taking place exactly above the sacred spiral turf which the participants knew to have been blessed and consecrated by the ascension or resurrection of ancient spirits. It could be said that the worshippers stood at the Centre of the World on the *axis mundi*—an idea which is popular in innumerable stone-age theologies.

By means of their laboriously-planned edifice the believers were able to place themselves literally on the pathway to the celestial gods. For the first time in the world, humans, by the efforts of their own hands and the logic of reasoning, had raised themselves beyond earthbound limits. They had moved nearer to the celestial vault, setting themselves on the path taken by subterranean spirits when they ascend 'on the whirlwind' to heaven. They were in the perfect position to call upon the spirits from the deep and converse with celestial deities. Sorcerer or sorceress, shaman or divine arbiter, priest or priestess—whoever it was, he or she took centre stage upon this spiral mountain in the light of the rising moon or the rising sun.

Something of the ancient concept of the White Mountain rising from the primordial waters may have entered these beliefs as well. Silbury may have had a spiritual resemblance with the fourth-millennium Sumerian ziggurat, a four-sided pointed hill of mud-bricks with a sanctuary on top, whose cosmic symbolism was centred at the holy circle of space where earthly and celestial powers met in harmony and could be joined in ritual marriage. Whatever events may have taken place at Silbury, we may be sure that the sacred hill was the practising centre of a very complex mythology involving the Great Goddess.

The conical exterior of the hill lends itself, more efficiently and impressively than any other contour, to a dignified ceremonial climbing march. This would justify the two puzzling causeways and explain why the western causeway is broader and higher than the other. It must have been the point of entry on to a spiral path up the hill, and by following a double spiral course, hundreds of people could have spiralled up the hill in a long procession to arrive at the magical centre of the summit platform, and subsequently spiralled down again to leave by the narrower causeway without the descending worshippers crossing or interfering with those still going up. That processional marching was beloved by these ancient peoples is suggested by the later construction a short distance away of the great megalithic avenues of West Kennet and Beckhampton which are centred on the Avebury circles.

The route of the spiritual march is clockwise inwards to the centre, which symbolises the path of death, and then anticlockwise back again, which symbolises the concept and hope of rebirth. The double causeway system suggests that this must be so, with the superior height and breadth of the left-hand causeway encouraging entry to the left-hand side of the hill and subsequent left-handed spiralling. As we already know, throughout the age of Newgrange and Stonehenge the left-handed spiral was the Goddess Spiral, standing as both image and symbol of the Great Goddess herself, so it follows that Silbury was the Goddess. This theory agrees with Michael Dames on this point, but for quite different reasons.

Silbury became famous because of its immensity. Yet there are sister hills, smaller and now damaged or obliterated, certainly of considerable importance in their time, which are hardly known or visited by non-antiquarians. Yet the raising of these small hills exacted prodigious feats of labour in their time.

TABLE II
Locations and sizes of prehistoric mounds in Britain

Name	County	Diam	Present Height	Volume	Ditch diam
Silbury III/IV	Wiltshire	160m	40m	*250,000m³	160m
Silbury II	Wiltshire	73m	10m	c1,500	116m
Clifford Hill	Northants	115m	26m	c100,000	not known
Marlborough	Wiltshire	c100m	20m	50,000	not known
Hatfield Barrow (in Marden henge)	Mid-Wilts.	25m	10m	10,000	25m
Silk Hill	S. Wilts.	42m	6m		42m?
Knowlton (by henge)	N. Dorset	40m	c8m	[2,500]	c40m (inner) c100m (outer)
Gib Hill (by Arbor Low circle-henge)	Derbyshire	c25m	6m		not known
Dove Holes (by henge)	Derbyshire	20–22m			

* 350,000 cubic metres including the natural spur beneath.

Few of these artificial mounds have been excavated, none by acceptable modern methods. The biggest is Marlborough Mount in the grounds of the public school. Quantities of antler picks have been taken from this abused hill whose steep sides

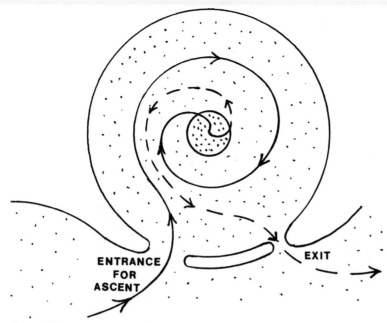

ENTRANCE
FOR
ASCENT

EXIT

This plan of Silbury may explain why the holy hill was given *two* causeways. The route demonstrates how the causeways, the slopes of the hill, and the flat summit could be used to support the continuous ascent and descent of a long spiral procession. The idea follows that of the ancient spiral dance (including the Cornish Creep), the Delian dance and maze processions.

and conical shape nevertheless indicate an inbuilt stability comparable with that of Silbury Hill eight kilometres to the west. Most known prehistoric mounds, perhaps significantly, lie close to henges, the conventional centres for sacred and probably secular activities of the local society. A hill without a henge suggests the possibility of a lost henge or stone circle, and in the case of Marlborough Mount this could have been obliterated by the nearby western end of Marlborough High Street and the adjacent church.

Knowlton Mound is of interest for its double concentric ditches, both long since filled in by mediaeval and recent farming but recognisable today on aerial photographs. The inner ditch is peripheral to the mound, though a former berm seems probable, so the ditch may have served a similar purpose to that intended for Silbury II—to emphasise the mound's height. Knowlton Mound was once bigger than it is now: its size above the natural land surface was reduced at the time when the ditches were filled in, particularly the inner one.

Gib Hill and Hatfield Barrow suffered from reckless excavation in the nineteenth century. The latter, which formerly stood inside Marden henge (Wiltshire) was so much disturbed in 1821 by William Cunnington and Richard Colt Hoare that the farmer took the opportunity of pushing what remained of it into its own encircling ditch and the henge ditch, and the mound is no more. But at least the excavators proved that Hatfield Barrow was not a burial place. Among the material collected were fragments of wood, and animal bones including the antlers of red deer. Hoare wisely decided that 'it may have been devoted to religious as

The artificial mound known as Gib Hill, as seen from the henge of Arbor Low in Derbyshire. Several Neolithic sacred hills survive to this day, not all of which have been recognised for what they are.

well as civic purposes . . . either a Hill-Altar, or a *locus consecratus*'.

Thomas Bateman demonstrated that Gib Hill in Derbyshire was a complex mound with clay in its base besides 'numerous pieces of calcined flint . . . brought from a considerable distance . . . because pure flint is not indigenous to Derbyshire'. The presence of hazel twigs, animal bones, charcoal, burnt flints, and layers of vegetable matter lend support to the idea that Gib Hill was another ritually-consecrated shrine or 'hill-altar'. In fact, the barrow had been built to cover four small clay mounds containing these deposits. The four-mound idea suggests the possibility of complex crop-circle formation by multiple natural vortices.

There are likely to be other Neolithic artificial mounds awaiting discovery, mounds put to other uses in later times and eventually incorporated into castles and public buildings but whose prehistoric origins have yet to be investigated. These may include the high artificial mound at Windsor Castle upon which the keep is built, and the mounds at Oxford Castle and Totnes in Devon.

The concept of a round hill with clay core and/or turf centre has undoubted affinities with the earlier, seemingly oversize, round barrow traditions of north-eastern England—notably Yorkshire. Prominent in that county for their size are the earthen round tumuli of Duggleby Howe (volume 3,200 cubic metres), Wold Newton (750 cubic metres), and Willy Howe; the second and third of these have no burials, yet this part of Britain was the birthplace of the idea of individual inhumation beneath round barrows. The practice seems to have spread down the east of England, and one of the earliest-known round barrows in the south began as a mortuary structure within a circular ring-ditch at Whiteleaf Hill in the Chilterns. It could be said that its position placed it on the road to Wessex and the west.

When Silbury Hill was built, the region's chambered long barrows were in their twilight years of up to a thousand years' existence. The radiocarbon dating evidence from West Kennet long barrow shows that the twenty-seventh century BC, when Silbury Hill was built, was perhaps only a century before the famous long barrow was sealed up. Spiral shells were worn as jewellery by the last users of the tomb (whorled periwinkle shells and dog-whelk, and a perforated cowrie amulet), all of which encapsulated the usual birth symbolism. The Late Neolithic pottery found at West Kennet and at the nearby Sanctuary on Overton Down had clear links with vessel types originating in eastern England. It may be that the newest ideas prevalent in this part of the Late Neolithic era filtered into North Wiltshire from the east by following the Thames Valley, before spreading outwards across the fertile plains. The new styles of pottery came this way, as did the idea of round barrow burial and round hill-altars. Now it seems that with Silbury (and Marlborough and Marden-Hatfield) this new concept was being expanded about a framework in which the religious view of spiral-centred crop circles was treated as if bearing spirits or emissaries from the womb of the Great Goddess.

To come back to Silbury, I believe that the Goddess is to be found in the hill's construction, although not as envisaged by Michael Dames. The inner mound has to be recognised in its role as the Goddess's womb, partly from its position, partly from what it contains—chiefly its entrail-like pile of spiral-wound turves cut by devout witnesses from the spiralling turf. The twisted string spreading radially outwards in the manner of a star (or spiral-star) carries with it the traditional symbolism of the vulva, as does the spinning wheel.

Silbury therefore embodies the vision of the Goddess partly-buried and rising from the ground. Her womb is in the earth; her head reaches for the sky, like the early Goddess figurines from the pre-Mycenean era of Old Europe, which had the lower part 'undifferentiated like a bell or platform'. Erich Neumann writes of them that the symbolism 'reminds us of Gaea, the earth Mother, whose womb coincides with the earth, the lower territory of fertility. The same is true of the Indian "busts" of the Great Goddess, the lower part of whose body is in the earth.' In contemporary mythology Silbury would have been revered for its divine revelation. At certain times, for certain festivals, the mound would have become the Goddess or Earth Mother in a purely spiritual sense. It was at such moments, when the seasons and the sacred or secular forces demanded it, that a procession of ardent believers, itself a sacred winding line of motion, would have spiralled round the personification of her body to a meeting with the Goddess, and possibly with tribal ancestors, at the summit.

Mythical imagery like this is truly ancient. It is inherited from the Palaeolithic era, and appears variously in myths ranging from Siberia to ancient Egypt and to Stone Age Australia. Everywhere we find that death is symbolised by a mounting of steps, or a stairway, or a ladder: the souls of the dead climb the ladder or mountain pathway to get to heaven. But first there may have been a descent into the depths of the earth or Hell, which the round barrow funerary practices of the Late Neolithic and the Bronge Age seem to suggest. The Egyptian *Book of the Dead*, in referring to Re says, 'the gods make him a ladder, so that, by making use of it, he may go up to Heaven.' Initiation ceremonies may have played a part, too, because they involved a symbolic death and resurrection or a descent into the underworld followed by ascension. Just as the temples of the Greeks were so grandly located on hill-tops, the summit altar was sited to be nearer to heaven—if not precisely at that very place where Heaven and Earth are presumed to meet.

By being poised at the point of communication between Heaven, Earth and the Underworld, the summit of Silbury was a sacrosanct precinct focused on the internal mound of spirit-turf and eminently suitable as a meeting-place with ancestral spirits and for ceremonies involving communication with the gods. These could have included initiation ceremonies, funerary rituals, auguries, worship and priestly enthronement. Silbury must have been a sanctified Centre, a local Centre of the World, with a purpose-built cosmic ladder connecting the three cosmic zones—the Underworld or Hell beneath the spiral turf centre which was its gateway to the Goddess's womb; Earth or Goddess represented by the internal womb and triangular/conical form of the Hill; and Heaven, symbolised by the summit, where the Goddess Hill contacts the Sky.

13

Gods, Goddesses and Spirits

From time to time in this book reference has been made to the Sky God, bridegroom of the Great Goddess, who manifested himself in the form of thunderstorms and tornadoes and played a vital role in awakening new life in the Earth. His lesser cult within the Neolithic was perhaps as ancient as that of the Goddess herself, and belief in the Divine Pair seems to have been brought to the British Isles by the first colonisers who arrived after the retreat of the polar ice. With the coming of the Neolithic settlers and the new pattern of life based on farming, the influence of both Sky God and Great Goddess grew and widened, becoming more complex. We know this from the history of other stone age religions and from the archaeological evidence of the British and Irish Neolithic period.

Grave goods and ritual offerings can tell us much about the beliefs of the age. Horns and skulls of oxen, bulls or stags are common in Neolithic ditches and ring-pits. Even the complete skeleton of an ox or bull has been found in what was evidently a foundation offering at the Welsh passage-grave of Bryn Celli Dhu. This surely points to the British Neolithic equivalent of the Mediterranean practice of bull-worship, the bull's roar resembling thunder and its strength the power of atmospheric forces. In the Cretan and Mycenean religions the bull, as the sacred beast of the Sky God, was sacrificed and buried in his name. The Goddess-worshipping Cretans saw the bull as the supreme agent of masculine fertility. They believed that his vital forces were concentrated in the horns, probably because of their rapidity of growth, so in their rites they offered the horned head to the Sky God and the blood to the Goddess. In Britain so many picks of antler bone have been recovered from ditches that they must have been deposited deliberately as a tribute and offering to the Goddess, for some were quite new and had possibly never been used. In some ditches they appear to have been arranged with great care, spaced out regularly and with precision.

Bull-worship continued in Britain right through to the round barrow burials of the Bronze Age. At Irthlingborough, Northamptonshire, a Bronze Age barrow had its primary Beaker burial enriched by the addition of at least a hundred ox skulls, in the same sacrificial way described by Homer a thousand years later. Many burials were accompanied by antler-horn deposits, particularly of the red deer. It may seem paradoxical that 'fertility' symbols should lie in graves, but they carried with them the symbol of rebirth as well. In a Wiltshire round barrow near Everley Richard Colt Hoare reported a cremation deposit 'surrounded by a circular wreath of horns of the red deer'. In another were stag's horns at the head and feet of a skeleton with bronze weapons and a drinking cup or beaker. Similar lavish use of stag's horns has been found elsewhere in England, including a large round barrow near Mildenhall, Suffolk, where the skeleton of a young woman was protected by a pile of eighteen horns. Roe deer horns have also been found in barrow excavations as carefully-placed deposits.

The cursuses of the fourth millennium, the most mysterious monuments of the age, continued in use long after 3000 BC and provide another clue to the strength of belief in a Sky God and his intimate association with the Earth manifestation of the Goddess. Moreover, in the construction of both cursuses and contemporary long barrows, there were ritual links with bulls or oxen and their heads and horns.

From 3200 BC onwards, when the cult of the circle began to make its mark on the buildings and monuments of Britain, henges, earthen circles, and stone circles became the places of worship. They embodied the spiritual power of the spiral-centred crop circle—the spinning movement frozen into the stones and stored by means of sometimes extraordinary peripheral shapes (flattened circles, ellipses, egg-shapes) so that even with the passage of time the secrets of their origin can be unlocked again.

The glory of the megalithic era and its culture peaked between 2500 and 1500 BC. Throughout this time the stones must have been venerated—even idolised—partly because of the spirits which were thought to animate them, but perhaps also because of the belief that they had come from some special place. An old name for the sarsen sandstones found lying about on the chalk downs of Wiltshire is bridestone. This may refer to the British Goddess Bride (or Brigit, Bridget, etc.)

which suggests that it was believed the stones had been provided by the Goddess for use as standing stones.

Stones, whatever their size and location, have a hardness, an immutability, which contrasts totally with the uncertainty and fragility of human life. At one extreme are the naturally-lying gigantic boulders or rocky outcrops; at the other are small portable stones or pebbles carried about as talismans or for religious purposes; and in between are loose but heavy stones of immense proportions, which were erected as standing stones at places of sanctity.

A great many stones were, to a greater or lesser degree, thought to be inhabited by ancestral spirits, somehow locked into the stone, whether by a ritual ceremony or by a natural occurrence. Prayers and offerings were used to persuade the entrapped spirits to intercede for the community—for assistance in the fertilisation of fields, animal stock and, not least, women. Some of the empowered stones were identifiable by their shape or origin; others were recognised by the symbol that sanctified them. Special regard must have been paid to menhirs upon which were carved spirals or other designs and into which were scoured the ubiquitous cup-depressions. A good many of these were certainly Stones of the Goddess.

When gigantic stones were raised at West Kennet, Wayland's Smithy and elsewhere in the British Isles and France to seal the tombs, they were surely intended to function as sepulchre guards by dint of their holiness and inviolability, and menhirs, too, served as protection against thieves and evil spirits. In Brittany and Britain a stone may stand beside the burial inside, or outside the tomb, or vertically above it. The Wiltshire long barrow Warminster 1, which overlooks Upton Scudamore, has a pillar-like menhir concealed inside it; under these circumstances, out of sight in a chamberless tomb, any phallic symbolism (which is usually linked with male fertility, divinity and strength) seems improbable. What is more likely is an alternative wisdom arising from the immutability of stone by which the souls of the dead were able to maintain a peaceful presence, while the stone acted as a means of communication between the living and the dead. In one way or the other, the stone functioned as an everlasting representative of the immanent Goddess.

The magical fertilising property associated with certain stones was thought to emanate from the ancestors acting through them; it is therefore amazing that the physical rituals necessary to secure fertility should have survived (at least in principle) for thousands of years, long after the underlying religious beliefs had been superseded and forgotten. Even into recent times in twentieth-century Europe, women in some country areas believed that they could become fertile by rubbing or sliding their bodies against a rock or megalith. There is no question that these ideas originated in the remote past, and from the early years of Christianity

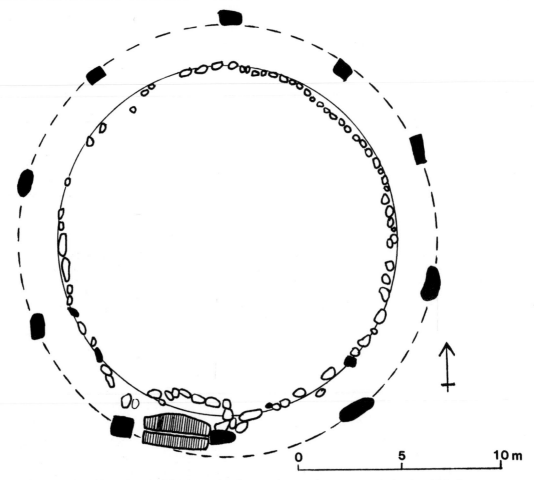

A plan of Loanhead of Daviot, one of several recumbent stone circles in which the principal megalith lies prone or recumbent between standing flankers (after Alexander Thom). The diameters are 20.4 and 16.6 metres. The circle dates from the middle of the third millennium BC.

right through the Middle Ages, the Church made vigorous attempts to suppress what was obviously a pagan, Goddess activity.

In its purest form the ritual stems from the belief that, especially by contact with the bare belly, the essential life-giving force will pass from ancestral stone to womb, completing the process begun by husband and wife. Hundreds of stories have been collected, showing the strength and persistence of the cult, but it was to the Goddess believers of megalithic times that these concepts were of the greatest moment. They help to explain other puzzling aspects of the period, including the recumbent stones of stone circles and the use to which 'holed' or perforated stones were put, and they shed light on the strange cup-marks and cup-and-ring marks found on so many megaliths.

Recumbent stone circles are a mainly Scottish tradition in stone circle building. What distinguishes them is that one stone in the circle is lying down—usually the most massive and attractive of all—and if one stands at the centre of some of the

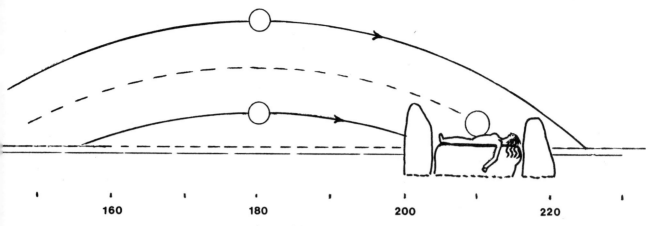

160	180	200	220

The recumbent stone in a stone circle may be the local Goddess Stone and the flankers the Goddess's attendants. At some circles the recumbent forms the true horizon as seen from the centre; this would apply to more circles if a priestess, say, lay upon it as part of a ritual drama. The sketch is for moonset at Old Keig, to the west of Aberdeen, for which the recumbent is centred on 210 degrees. Celestial paths are indicated for various southerly courses of the moon.

circles when the moon is following its most southerly course in the night sky, the moon appears either to rise or set in the direction of the recumbent stone. At several of the stone circles (Loanhead of Daviot, Cothiemuir Wood, Old Keig and Easter Aquorthies included) the mighty recumbent stone plays the role of a near-horizon. Three circles have their recumbent stone planted in the direction of the most northerly moonset, and according to Aubrey Burl as many as 45 lie in the narrow arc of sky between south-south-east and south-south-west, either at or between which the moon rises and sets. In other words, where a recumbent stone was not aligned to moonrises or moonsets the circle builders had set it on an axis to correspond with the moon when it had risen into the sky.

The intention may have been to saturate the horizontal megalith with the spiritual light of the full or waxing moon, symbol from earliest times of woman's menstrual cycle and pregnancy. In some traditions the moon was also the resting place of the ancestors; the Egyptians and Greeks saw it as the abode of the dead (at least, for the people who had been 'good' on earth), while other cultures believed that it had the power to regenerate the souls of the dead. This makes the horizontal stone eminently suited to lunar-orientated sliding and rubbing rites with the object of reabsorbing the 'moon-power' or 'ancestor-spirits' from the stone. The reclining stone therefore emerges as a female, moon-worshipped or Goddess Stone, bearing life-giving powers which would also respond to the rituals used to promote fertility in the soil and in animals. At times of high ceremonial a priestess may have lain on the recumbent stone, her body the new horizon against which the moon would set at many of the recumbent stone circles.

At Kintraw in Strathclyde there is a variant on the recumbent stone idea. Here the horizontal stone lies beyond the kerb-ring in front of the blind entrance to the cairn. Once more, it seems to serve as the local Moon-Stone or Goddess Stone.

The stones near Madron, Cornwall, called Men an Tol. There is a tradition that sufferers of disease can be cured if they pass through the holed stone. This and similar aspirations held to apply to other megaliths in the world seem to be folklore remnants from the days of Goddess belief. *Photograph by Keith O. Mortimore.*

Perforated stones, known also as ring stones or holed stones, appear to have properties similar to those of fertility megaliths. Sometimes the holes are natural, but many are man-made. In William Stukeley's day there was a ring stone at Avebury positioned between the south circle and the southern main entrance to the great circle. Local customs and folklore surrounding perforated stones retain no more than a trace of the former beliefs attached to them, but the traditions that endure are invariably linked with fertility, rebirth, health and magic.

At Fouvent-le-Haut in France newborn babes were passed through the hole to ensure their happiness and freedom from spells, and in the district of Amance money was thrown through the hole-stone while prayers were said for the health of the children. In Paphos (Greece) and in England are perforated stones through which sterile women or sick people used to climb. The curing of sickness was allied to the notion of rebirth, and, even if this was not the original intention of the hole-cutters, the idea is certainly very old. Until quite recently the Cornish Tolven Stone and Men an Tol were both used to cure sick children, and the former also bestowed fertility on the supplicant who passed through it nude. At Men an Tol people with ague would crawl through nine times against the sun. In India, where the hole-stone was an emblem of the vulva, the rebirth concept was altogether more complex, for the passage through the hole, besides representing rebirth via the female principle, also conveyed solar symbolism linked to 'the gate of deliverance' and liberty from the world order.

One of the most puzzling symbols of the megalithic age is the cup-mark, a cup-like depression hollowed into the hard surface of rock by rotating a hardstone tool to form a regular, circular pit. They are usually about ten centimetres in diameter and a few centimetres deep, but all sizes down to a couple of centimetres in diameter have been found. They first began to appear in the fourth millennium, and then more widely throughout Northern, Western and Central Europe during the Bronze Age and even into the Iron Age.

These strange symbols are found on natural rocky outcrops, on standing stones including the megaliths of stone circles, and on slabs or smaller stones forming parts of burial places, particularly the capstones or side slabs of cists. An early example is a cup-marked slab from beneath the Scottish long barrow at Dalladies (Kincardineshire), dating from the early fourth millennium BC. At the other extreme, examples have been cited as late as AD 100.

In the Late Neolithic and Bronze Ages cup-marks became common, particularly in connection with the stone circles and Clava cairns of north-east Scotland and on megaliths, cists and rocky outcrops elsewhere in Scotland and northern England. The custom seems to have reached its peak around 2000–1600 BC, but it barely reached to the south of England, although cup-marks have been found in cists and cairns beneath round barrows in Cornwall, Avon County, and Dorset. At Hendraburnick in Cornwall the upper surface of a stone displays 17 cups. Elsewhere in Northern, Western and Central Europe cup symbols have been found here and there but nowhere better than in Galicia where there are strong similarities with the later development, so frequent in northern Britain, of cups with rings and tails.

What meaning is intended by cup-marks? So far no satisfactory solution has been found, but I believe that the ancient cult of spiral-circle symbolism may provide the key to the mystery.

The peoples of Neolithic and Bronze Age Britain regarded spiral-centred crop circles as evidence of the passage of spirits—released from the womb of the Earth Goddess through her vulva, the cup-shaped depression formed by the whirling vortex. This symbolism is echoed in the carved chalk cups found as dedicatory offerings, and might it not also have been expressed in the cup-marks bored into stone which was the resting-place or refuge of the ancestral spirits and the temporary abode of deities? They were intended to allow spirits, whether ancestral or divine, to pass in and out of the sacred stones, and to achieve communication between the living and the dead. By the same token, cups or

The megaliths surrounding the altar at the temple of Mnajdra in Malta are densely drilled with small holes. This has the undoubted effect of heightening the sense of spirituality in the precinct. The same was done in other Maltese temples.

natural depressions in rock surfaces may have served 'summoning-up' and oracular functions as well, as possibly at Stoney Littleton where a cup on a stone at the end of the gallery is illuminated by the midwinter sunrise. At Kintraw there is a kerbstone which has cups engraved near its base *below ground level*, perhaps to provide access for subterranean spirits directly into the stone from the earth.

Despite some evidence of the rough-working of apparently unfinished cups, the majority are smooth. There may be further symbolism in the rotary movement of the hand which, as it rubs and deepens the cup, imitates the turning motion of the universe. The action is circular, coiling and spiralling, which results in a cupped or drilled hole bearing within itself the philosophy of both circle and spiral. The drilled decoration of the Neolithic temples of Malta, where the deep, narrow holes cover the entire surfaces of sacred stone slabs, creates an intensely powerful effect which must have been awe-inspiring to those who understood its significance.

The idea of the hole as a spiritual doorway may already have been ancient in Neolithic times if it could be proved that the hole in the Palaeolithic *bâtons de commandement* (referred to in Chapter 10) was used for summoning up spirits.

Cup-marks and cup-and-ring engravings at Whitehill on the north-western outskirts of Glasgow.

The same principle could apply to the Neolithic ceremonial maces. Can it, however, explain the related engravings known as cup-and-ring marks, which are found chiefly on open rocky outcrops? Often these are clustered in vast numbers—there are hundreds on just one slab at Achnabreck in Strathclyde, together with more conventional, plain cup-marks. Rocks like these were cut over long periods of time, by different people, possibly over several centuries. Some cup-and-ring systems appear to have grown in diameter as outer rings were added, occasionally causing an overlapping of adjoining cups-and-rings. There seems to be more here than simply calling up the spirit from the stone.

In early societies it was believed that the union of a man and a woman was not enough to produce a child. Special precautions were necessary to provide it with a soul, and this was where a stone or rock made its indispensable contribution: *it bore the spirit that would vitalise the baby*. It therefore seems likely that the purpose of cutting a circular cup in the surface of a rocky outcrop was to liberate a spirit and so ensure a complete and successful child-birth, almost certainly with the help of ancestors if not the Goddess herself. At some later date a ring would be

Cup-and-ring markings at Old Bewick, Northumberland, in northern England (G. Tate 1864). There are cases of overlap, radial grooves and interlinked grooving.

circumscribed about the cup to guarantee a second child, and in this way, as the years passed, the ring systems built up. At Achnabreck the biggest number of rings around a cup-mark is eight, which suggests a nine-child family. Cups-with-nine-rings are known from Greenland, Bowling in Strathclyde.

In short, these rings are family rings. When there is a radial line extending from the central cup it may indicate the directional movement of the phallus, or perhaps the umbilical cord, the life-supporting link between stone and outside world. And where long lines interlink the centre of one cup with that of another we may have evidence of inter-family bonds and relationships.

Cup-and-ring marks in the southern half of Scotland are rarely found on rocks sloping at angles greater than 30 degrees—indeed, most are horizontal or nearly so—and, according to Ronald Morris, 'where there is a tail or radial groove from near the middle of a cup-and-ring, seven times out of eight, where there is any slope, the tail runs downhill.' This may mean that part of the ritual involved the woman actually sitting on the rock, bare-bottomed, and aligning herself with the cup-mark to allow the fertilising spirit to pass from the rock into her womb. Perhaps it was even believed that the spirit of a former ancestor could be retrieved from a particular rock in which it had been stored or 'trapped' while awaiting rebirth in a new foetus.

Hence that which is in preparation in the womb is dependent upon the success of the sympathetic magic outside. The mother's womb and vulva are as the Goddess's womb and womb-opening, whether cupped spirally in the field or cupped into the rock. Both are outward-flowing spirals of generation; for the spiraliform character of the womb is plainly stated by the gyrations of the foetus and the inevitability of the twisted umbilical cord.

A regional census of cup-and-ring marks might well provide information about childbirth frequencies in different areas. I did a pilot test on the rocks of Rombalds Moor in West Yorkshire, and found that, compared with well over a thousand

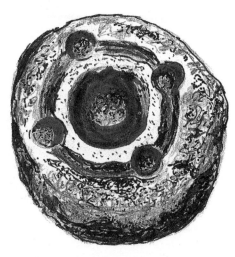

Portable cup-marked lumps of stone. *Left:* Made of Oolitic limestone and found at Nottingham Hill in the Cotswolds. Note the ring and groove and the secondary cup. *Right:* An unusual stone from Ayrshire, Scotland. Cupped circle systems reminiscent of this have been found in English wheatfields in recent years, as quintuplet crop circles.

plain cups, the numbers of differently-ringed cups are as follows: one ring, 214; two rings, 27; three rings, 9; four rings, 3; five rings, 1. On the rocks which I was able to study at Achnabreck in Scotland the totals work out as follows: plain cups 276; one ring, 43; two rings, 29; three rings, 24; four rings, 16; five rings, 9; six rings, 6; seven rings, 4; eight rings, 1.

It is impossible to tell who carved the rings—the women, the men, or a priestess or priest—but there are some portable cup-marks which could have been part of a specialist's magical paraphernalia, such as the cup-marked stone found in the Iron Age hillfort of Nottingham Hill, at Gotherington in Gloucestershire. The carved stone, 30 × 30 × 11 centimetres, is thought to be of Bronze Age or Neolithic date and consists of soft, fairly porous local Oolitic limestone. In the store of the Dick Institute in Kilmarnock, Strathclyde, is an amazing piece of gritstone. Measuring 25 × 25 × 10 centimetres, it has an 18-centimetre ring cut into one face, with a central cup and four equally spaced smaller cups inside the ring. Had the carver of this item a memory of observing crop-markings of similar shapes, rather like the crop-mark type illustrated in picture no. 15 of the colour plates.

Plain cup-marks on vertical (standing) stones are found at some open-air sites engraved on south-facing sides, although by no means invariably, so there may be a link between the cup's spirit- or soul-releasing aspect and its female symbolism: the sun's rays will ritually fertilise the vulvar cup. Perhaps in this case, because the cup-marks are on the vertical faces of standing stones, a kind of Sacred Marriage was intended, in which the sun or Sky God fertilised a manifestation of the Earth Mother in a Goddess Stone. We may never know for sure.

In the Inner Hebrides, at Kilchoman on the island of Islay, an extraordinary tradition continues to this day, which is obviously a survival from prehistoric practice. In the churchyard there is an early Christian cross for which a prehistoric cup-marked stone serves as pedestal. Using a pestle provided by the church-warden, people can make a wish while turning it three times in one of the cup-marks in the direction of the sun; they then drop silver into another cup-mark for the benefit of the church. If the wish concerns fertility, it is said to come true. It is clear that at the time when the stone was 'Christianised' by the addition of the cross the churchmen understood its hidden symbolism.

The pestle-and-mortar is a well-known and ancient fertility symbol; it has an obvious connection with corn-grinding and an inbuilt sexual symbolism. It is then but a short step to extend the principle to that of the mace with its handle–hole relationship.

Only a few cup-marks are to be found on any of the carved stones at Newgrange in Ireland, but there is a large number on K52, the kerbstone aligned on the midsummer sunset. Some of the cups have been fashioned from natural hollows by deepening and smoothing, but several others may be entirely artificial; all of them have been skilfully incorporated into the overall design by the master carvers. As with K1, the kerbstone of the midwinter sunrise discussed in Chapter 8, the symbolism largely concerns divine fertility.

Stone K52 is divided by a vertical channel, just like K1 at Newgrange and the two entrance stones at Knowth. It is orientated on the main passage of the tumulus but on the opposite side of the mound where there is no entrance for mere mortals. It is likely that here, too, a megalith from the great encircling ring or an earlier stout post formerly cast a shadow towards the vertical marker.

The left-hand (eastern) panel displays fourteen goddess lozenges combined with upward-turned triangles in the bottom row and downward-turned triangles in the top row, all fully picked out to leave edges in relief. Symbolically, the pattern is the familiar one in which opposed triangles unite to produce lozenges so that the upturned triangles, standing on the ground, represent the earthly domain of the Goddess while the hanging triangles symbolise her celestial qualities. By contrast, on the right-hand panel triangles appear within multiple arcs in a way suggestive of the rising, generative forces of Goddess vulvar symbolism.

Above the triangles on the left-hand panel of K52 are two right-handed spirals which mirror, perhaps deliberately, the right-handed spirals on the right-hand (eastern) panel of threshold stone K1. These are solar spirals, which may have been traversed by the shadow of a megalith of the great circle as the sun moved westward and set on midsummer's eve. Beside the two right-handed spirals is a left-handed spiral in the position which on K1 is occupied by the nested lozenges. This reinforces my belief that the lozenge represents the Goddess.

In place of the left-handed three-spiral system symbolising the goddess trinity, that appears on the left-hand (western) side of K1, the mirrored (western) panel of

East West

Kerbstone K52 (upper drawing), the magnificent engraved megalith which faces the midsummer sunset at Newgrange. The principal compositions on this stone bear direct comparison—east with east, west with west—with those on the entrance stone K1 placed on the opposite side of the monument to await the midwinter sunrise. To facilitate the comparison K1 is shown inverted beneath K52.

K52 has three oval cartouches, each containing a row of three cup-marks. These also stand for the Goddess trinity, and the double and triple rings of the enclosing cartouches were added to enhance the powers of the deities. In these cup-symbols the meaning of the complex spiral is reduced to its simplest form. Through their vulvar capacities, their feminine energies, these triple Goddess cups are receptive to the last rays of the summer sun as night approaches. They symbolise the penetration of the stone—and hence the wall of the tumulus—by the solar energy. Behind K52 there is no door and no gallery for mortals to pass; but the cups receive the sun and let through its powers. Here was built an entrance to the tomb that was intended as a passage only for spirits or the fertilising powers of the sun.

Again we are in the realm of the Sacred Marriage, by which people sought to harmonise and regulate the universe. If there was once a standing stone or stout post to the north-west of K52, its shadow at midsummer would have moved across the stone, and upon reaching the vertical line would have achieved union between its halves. The symbolism might correspond with what happens on the other side of the great mound, at stone K1, six months later on midwinter's morning, when again we have the Marriage of the Gods.

The ornamentation on K52 is a prayer for life, fertility and the renewal of life. It was a beautiful, fully-planned scriptural composition, incorporating in symbolic form the contemporary beliefs of the Irish Neolithic era. The immediate aim was the fertility of the farms and the women through divine intervention and favour. This was the ambition of Neolithic farmers worldwide but rarely was it so ornately and poetically expressed in stone as here. The ultimate aim, as ever, was that other birth wish: the renewal of life after death.

At Newgrange, as at Knowth and many other Neolithic sites of similar age in Ireland and Britain, the primary symbolic elements—the spiral, the circle, the cup, the lozenge, the triangle and the zigzag—all bore meanings well understood at the time of their carving. Arranged together in a pleasing artistic design, they are thought by many people to have been planned for aesthetic and visual appeal alone. But as Ralph W. Emerson said, 'we are symbols and inhabit symbols', and should not be misled by the classical works of Greece and Rome to believe that representational art alone was fired by mortal realism. Abstract forms of art define and camouflage intense human and spiritual meanings as well, and it is only by objective analytical reasoning that the logic behind some of them can ever be uncovered.

The abstract decoration on the principal stones was subtly planned using conventional symbolism either to carry a spiritual message or to meet a religious purpose. The geometrical elements were combined to produce ideograms in which the joint symbolism conveyed the sense and the story on a level the worshippers of the age could understand. So potent was their effect that they stood the test of time, surviving until the arrival of the Christians who absorbed them into their own religious imagery.

*   *   *

Circle and spiral symbolism may have been at the root of the astounding Neolithic practice of circular trepanning, too. Trepanning, or trephining, is the surgical art of cutting out from the human skull a round piece of bone, usually more than 50 millimetres in diameter. It is a delicate operation, tedious for the surgeon and dangerous for the live individual, yet it dates from antiquity, and was, quite surprisingly, still being performed in various parts of the world until recent times.

The practice was common throughout prehistoric Europe, the most ancient datable examples being from the Neolithic and Bronze Ages. Neither the ancient Egyptians nor the Sumerians carried out trepanation, but the methods were

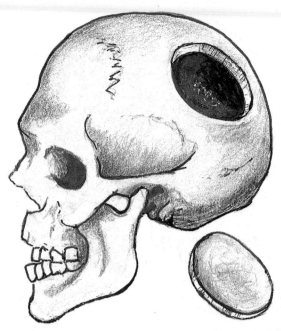

The mystery of trepanning, the removal of a round piece of the human skull from a living patient. This skull of the British Beaker Period (late third millennium BC) was found in a barrow on Crichel Down, Dorset, together with the excised section.

known to Iron Age Europeans, the Romans, the Arabs, the Irish of the Dark Ages and, besides others from antiquity, a number of races of later times. Some at least of the patients survived these assaults by the stone chisel and graver, for several cases are known where fusion of the replaced cranial disc was successful, or, if it had not been replaced, where bone had regrown around the hole. What can be the meaning behind this astonishing and apparently pointless practice?

A study of trepanning throughout Europe was made by the archaeologist Stuart Piggott after he had excavated a trepanned skull from a chalk-cut grave beneath a Beaker round barrow on Crichel Down in Dorset. This was a late Neolithic burial and therefore much later than the construction of the Dorset Cursus to its north but approximately contemporary with the use of the henges on Wyke Down and at Knowlton.

The Crichel Down skeleton lay on its left side, with legs flexed, left arm extended, and right arm bent with hand on shoulder. The hole had been cut in the left parietal bone by bevelling a channel through the outer table of the skull using a sharp point, most likely of flint. The layer of spongy tissue between the tables was cut next, and grooving of the inner table commenced. This had some cracks in it, resulting from a levering manoeuvre intended to avoid damaging the brain and its blood vessels. At any rate, the patient seems to have died soon afterwards because no fusion had taken place between skull and excised disc. A skull from a long barrow at Bisley (Gloucestershire) had an unfinished trepanation. This may not have been the primary burial. Another trepanned skull came from a Beaker cemetery at Eynsham (Oxfordshire), and one from a ditch of the Earls Down Farm round barrow (Wiltshire) was of a 20 to 30-year-old male, the skeleton laid on its right side with its head to the east. On Snail Down, Everleigh, Wiltshire, in a pit beneath a saucer barrow site, the bones of a young adolescent were found. Although the corpse had been cremated we know the skull had been trepanned because the cranial disc, which was omitted from the cremation rites (perhaps because of its circular symbolism), had been returned and was carefully positioned at the base of the pile of bones. This was either a late Neolithic or an Early Bronze Age burial. The pit had been filled in with 'occupation earth', incorporating food refuse and broken domestic pottery.

From what we know about the passage of spirits through earth and stone, it is a logical step to extend these ideas to the human body. Circles in fields and the spirallings of the whirlwind vortex were both seen as evidence of spirits released from the earth through the earth. Just as with stones, where the wish was to extract support and benevolence from the spirits within, so with the brain there was an opposite intention: to liberate from the head supposedly malevolent spirits by opening a circular passage through the skullbone. One can only suppose that this drastic surgery was believed to cure the illnesses that we call insanity, epilepsy, cancer, Parkinson's disease, tumours and other cerebral conditions.

Because of the considerable skill required for the operation and the proof that many corpses were given dignified burials in late Neolithic or Bronze Age round barrows, the operation may have been the ultimate treatment practised on or reserved for prestigious sick members of society. That it was expected to stand any chance at all of success may be thanks to the strength of the spiritual powers associated with the mystic circle.

Both the circle and the spiral lie at the heart of that great Neolithic discovery the ceramic pot, the vessel created by the chemical magic of heat upon clay. While pots are obviously circular, it is not so clear that spirals lie at the very core of pottery techniques. In prehistoric times, indeed for thousands of years before pot-making moved on to the wheel, the clay was rolled into long narrow cylinders and coiled into spirals or rings in order to create the basic forms, especially for anything other than small pots. The clay was regarded as a material substance extracted from the Goddess's womb; it was rolled and coiled, chiefly by women, and pressed into shape before passing to the heat of the fire or the furnace. Only by coiling could medium-to-large pots be moulded to shape; only by firing could the clay achieve a permanent, durable shape and provide sound vessels for domestic and sacred use. This magical transformation may have been thought to stem from the special creative and life-bearing properties of the spiral coil.

The production of a pot was regarded as a spiritual as well as a manufacturing art. Every pot stored within itself the secret of generation and life; it was born of the earth, but without primordial coiling it would not attain the required perma-nence. Therefore, when men and women died, the coils and spirals of their pots

The bell beaker vessel from West Kennet long barrow, heavily decorated with Goddess and water symbolism. This was a precious vessel, sacred to the Great Goddess.

should die too. This can help explain the prehistoric conundrum of the ritual breaking of pots as a funerary rite. Sherd-filled deposits of 'occupation earth' were sometimes taken from settlement floors to form part of burial mounds, and ritual pits and graves were filled with offerings of what appeared to modern excavators to be no more than bizarre, sherd-filled domestic rubbish.

In the late third millennium a rather sudden change of funeral practice was adopted by the tribes we call the Beaker people. At the time of interring their dead a single fine unbroken pot was added to the grave as the chief or only durable item of grave-goods. It resembled the type of drinking vessel which today we call a beaker, and was decorated with an ordered design using geometrical markings, pitting, and other devices. For the first time in the British Isles a reverence was displayed for the unbroken funerary pot. What could this mean? Scholars have traditionally identified the typical 'vessel of containment' with basic concepts such as the Great Goddess, fertility, Nature's inexhaustible womb, or rain, and several have studied the various relationships in depth. Does the patterned decoration agree with such interpretations?

A splendid Beaker pot was recovered from the chambered barrow at West Kennet in the 1859 excavation. It is 200 millimetres tall and measures 195 millimetres across the lip. It is a truly holy vessel, rich in expressive ornament that displays in triplicate the Goddess symbolism of the Earth/Moon/Waters deity—the Triple Goddess of later Celtic art and literature.

The main element of the design, repeated in three broad running bands, is three-fold or four-fold lozenges-within-lozenges, symbolic of the fertility powers of the Goddess. Each Goddess band is associated with additional running bands. At the top are zigzag motifs which, by seeming to stand for lightning, relate to the moon. Neolithic people saw lightning as a manifestation of the power of the moon, both in its cold, bright light and in the fact that it heralds rain, which the moon controls. In the central band are sloping lines of rain with their seminal overtones indicative of fertilising waters, while the lower bands and the overall background of horizontal lines may refer to the lower regions of the waters—the springs, the streams and the lakes. The whole is a sacred vessel decorated to the glory of the chief divinity of the age—the fully fecund Great Goddess.

The sloping lines or zigzags indicative of 'rain' are motifs frequently used on early pots because the rain symbol also stands for 'life' and existence. As Juan Eduardo Cirlot wrote, 'Rain has a primary and obvious symbolism as a fertilising agent, and is related to the general symbolism of life and water . . . in many mythologies, rain is regarded as a symbol of the "spiritual influences" of heaven descending upon earth.'

Whereas the earlier Grooved Ware, which has been found in widely separated locations in Wiltshire, Oxfordshire, Yorkshire, Scotland and Orkney besides the Irish Boyne Valley, has plain patterns occasionally relieved with spirals or lozenges, Beaker Ware is free of obvious spirals. Bands of lozenges appear occasionally on British beakers but they are especially common on the early beakers of the Languedoc region of southern France. That some ritual element must have been involved is suggested by the widespread use for four hundred years, over a large part of western and Central Europe from Britain and Spain to Hungary and the Rhineland, of the singular technique known as 'corded' decoration.

In this, the design is projected on to the pot by impressing the surface with a twisted cord while the clay is soft. By the action of the cord the symbolism of the coiled spiral inherent in the pot itself (because pots are made by coiling clay) is impressed on its sides in a permanent and visible form. The era of the Beaker pot, which began with the all-over corded versions, was preceded by a late stage of Peterborough-ware with pots decorated with horizontal corded lines. Thus, through the symbolism of twisting cords, the spiral element was presented widely to the gaze of the Western Neolithic eye.

14

The Legacy of the Spiral

During the Iron Age of the first millennium BC the intensive use of spiral symbolism gradually diminished. The latest rich burials beneath round barrows had ended by 1500–1400 BC, about the time in the Bronze Age when the megalithic age, with its strong religious links with the spiral, was ending—just as, centuries earlier, the long barrow era had been phased out by the end of the Neolithic period. The age of the spirit whirlwind—and the dependent cult of the spiral—was drawing to a close.

Some customs continued. Burial in round barrows persisted for many centuries more, in fact intermittently through Romano-British and non-Christian Saxon times, but it seems to have survived more as a convenient tradition than as a religious acknowledgement of the atmospheric vortex as driving force. Early in the Iron Age a move away from round-house building back to rectangular construction commenced; the motivation for circular construction, the primitive concept of the Centre which had concentrated mystic thought for some two thousand years, was lost. Enclosures, too, became square or rectangular in shape after being mostly circular for thousands of years.

The end of the spiral-based religions with their reverence for the mystic Centre comes at about the time that Andrew Fleming has proposed for some cataclysmic catastrophe in Britain, such as the plague. It corresponds roughly with the transition from the Late Bronze Age to the Iron Age, a period marked by the building of great hillforts whose defensive features show, almost for the first time on British soil, a need for improved security. This could suggest settlement through conquest by an invading warrior race whose success was achieved by the use of iron weapons. The drive of religion is such an influential force on human behaviour, and so powerfully manipulated and maintained by an entrenched priestcraft, that only total conquest of a people possibly decimated by disease seems able to account for the social upheaval which accompanied the downfall of the megalithic age.

Some pots of the Iron Age and Romano-British period carry spirals, as do a few Romano-British mosaics, but in company with so many other motifs that one suspects the old meanings were no longer pre-eminent, if not partly lost, after degenerating with time. It therefore comes as a surprise to find spirals in use again in the early Christian Church, at a time when little effort could be spared for carrying out superfluous decoration for art's sake. Although the art of that period certainly had its finesse and beauty, we may be sure that all motifs and other design devices had symbolic intentions that were meaningful to artist and beholder alike.

The adoption of spirals by the Christian Church must be due to a continued understanding of its former symbolism. There survives in County Kildare an eighth-century granite cross, the High Cross of Moone. This slender stone, five-and-a-quarter metres tall, is a masterpiece of the sculptor's art with its well-organised panels of biblical scenes and symbolic shapes and figures.

On the west face of the cross the centre is occupied by a multi-armed spiral device sometimes known as a whirligig. It radiates outwards in an anticlockwise sense. The opposite face carries the body of Christ. Anticlockwise outward spiralling signifies resurrection—rebirth after death (the latter indicated by clockwise inward spiralling). Beneath the spiral another familiar symbol is boldly displayed—the lozenge! What is more, the lozenge encloses as many as four spiral-like motifs within its borders.

The lozenge is a recurrent feature in early Christian art and has been recognised as a Christian symbol, but Hilary Richardson, writing in 1984, says that we have yet to rediscover the meaning of its symbolism, suggesting that 'in some Carolingian manuscripts the shape indicates the cosmic and material worlds with Christ enthroned for the second coming. The Frontispiece to the Gospels in the Vivian Bible painted at Tours about 845 AD shows Christ in Majesty against this lozenge frame', while the Book of Kells contains many similar uses. 'The lozenge is nearly always located in a strategic, dominant point in the design.' This leads Hilary Richardson to believe that where it occurs alone it probably stands for Christ.

I have been fascinated by the importance assigned to the lozenge throughout antiquity, from the Neolithic and Bronze Age Mediterranean to the lozenge

The eighth-century AD Irish granite cross at Moone, County Kildare, which identifies the resurrection symbolism of the outflowing spiral with that of Christ.

engravings and lozenge-shaped megaliths of the British Isles and the lozenge designs on funerary Beaker pottery and Wessex bronze and goldwork. I have explained why I believe the lozenge at that time stood for the Great Goddess, and two or three thousand years later we find that the same shape has been appropriated by the Church because the old meaning, still then well understood, required 'Christianisation'. The symbol of the Great Goddess became that of the Father God of the Christians and that of Christ as well. Hilary Richardson writes: 'The subtle abstract decoration of the Celts, which remained the basis for the first Christian art in Ireland, was for hundreds of years constructed on established semi-geometric principles.' The spirals and lozenges in this Celtic symbolism are easily identifiable and traceable back to the Neolithic era, and with little change of meaning.

The number four, wrote Juan Eduardo Cirlot, is held to be 'symbolic of the earth, of terrestrial space, of the human situation . . . It is equated with the square and the cube, and the four-pointed cross represents the four seasons and the points of the compass.' This was so in the time of the Babylonian ziggurat, and the same

Spirals engraved on grave stones from Llangaffo *(left)* and Llangeinwen in Anglesey. They date from the ninth to eleventh centuries.

could be said of the Egyptian pyramids. The four slopes of these monuments face the four points of the compass, throughout the four seasons of the year, and the summit, the fifth point, reaches to the sky. Time and space are united, and are portrayed on that eighth-century cross of the early Church at Moone where an unknown sculptor encompassed the four everlasting spirals within the universal perimeter of the divine four-sided lozenge.

In the first millennium AD spirals were carved on many of the stone crosses of Ireland, while in Wales examples have been found on gravestones some of which later came to be incorporated into walls of churches or churchyards. A curious herringbone carving on a Christian stone at Llanafan also recalls the running chevron patterns of Neolithic 'fertility' times. Good examples of spirals from the ninth to eleventh centuries can be seen in the churchyard at Llangaffo and the church wall at Llangeinwen on Anglesey. The rebirth symbolism of the returning spirals must still have had some meaning, for otherwise such a motif, one of the most difficult to carve in stone, would hardly have been chosen merely to fill up space.

Spirals, or more often the simplified whirligig version, have appeared on Celtic crosses ever since, bearing as they do the evident connotation of resurrection and rebirth. The granite South Cross at Clonmacnoise, County Offaly, in Ireland, is perhaps a little later than the High Cross of Moone, and is in a village not more than 60 kilometres from it. On the east face there has been a notable transposition of the four lower spirals to the extremities of the cross. A thousand years later the same device is still sometimes adopted by stone-masons for stone or marble gravestones in Britain, the five bosses of the cross being infilled with spiral-whirligigs or Celtic knots. Four are positioned as if they were at the points of a compass with the intention of focusing symbolically all the 'terrestrial energies' at the fifth point, which is the spiral-centre where heaven and earth meet. Because of its related origins the Celtic knot is often substituted for spirals or whirligigs on Celtic crosses. The knot is studded with its own symbolic values which include directed whirling motion, because it is based on the still more ancient four-armed swastika.

Could the inspiration for the five-fold arrangement of spirals have come from seeing the five-spiral circle patterns in the fields of summer? Whatever the truth, it is certain that in the early Church there took place a renaissance of the primordial image of the spiral with its symbolic indications of everlasting life. The notion that outflowing spirals are symbols of life has survived in other ways. In the twelfth-century Abbey of Blanchelande in Lower Normandy the two spirals which decorate the chimneypiece of an early eighteenth-century extension are actually shown sprouting leaves and flowers.

Another early use to which the true spiral was put in the Christian Church appears on the outside of the seventh-century Bible of Athlone. It is faced with a bronze relief of Christ engraved with a multiplicity of spirals. The body has a panel of six spirals symbolising life and death, resurrection and rebirth, and above the head is a trinity of spirals, interlaced and mobile, representing without any doubt the Christian Trinity.

The purity and simplicity of this sublime vision are moving. In principle, the basis for this three-spiral symbolism is no different from that of the left-handed three-spiral ornamentation at Newgrange, but there is an interesting development. Three thousand years after Neolithic Ireland the gods have changed and the religion has become patriarchal. The spirals of the new trinity are right-handed and masculine, standing for the Father, the Son and the Holy Ghost. The artist obviously understood the significance of left-handed and right-handed spirals.

The same theme is seen on a brown glass stud with the spiral ornament set off in contrasting yellow, found at Westbury-on-Trym, Bristol. It may have served to adorn a crozier or a chalice. The spirals are again the right-handed spirals of a

A three-spiral design of Celtic type taken from an ecclesiastical glass stud found near Bristol, which is probably first millennium. The pattern is used as the logo of the Bristol and Avon Archaeological Group.

paternalistic religion, but in terminating with tails they provide a touch of the cosmic-unity symbolism of a much earlier period.

There may be a connection here with the 666 numeric-symbolism cited in Revelations 13, verse 18, and credited to the 'Beast'—meaning the Antichrist, Devil, or Beast of the Apocalypse. Perhaps the 666 devil-symbolism arose at a time and in a country where contact with triple-spiral images had diminished so far that the triple spiral came to be viewed as a pagan symbol and was given satanic status. It could be that '666' became numeric shorthand for what had been in earlier times the triple spiral of the Christian-displaced Goddess Trinity.

On a more homely level is the traditional corn dolly whose obscure origins reach back into the mists of time. These were made at the critical period of harvest and took many forms, the most common being the cigar-shaped dolly. Was it a three-dimensional rendering of the archaic, carved, returning spiral? If so, it combines within its windings a compact symbol of the hopes and desires of a people striving for the continuance of what they needed to sustain life—and hence life itself. Other dollies were more elaborate, sometimes of tripartite construction with left-handed or right-handed spiralling—perhaps originally intended to portray a trinity of pre-Christian deities. Some were more obviously representational, such as the Earth Mother, a rendering in straw of the prehistoric Corn Goddess, natural descendant of the Great Goddess, and the traditional Corn Maiden, made from the last corn to be cut at harvest-time, and stored over winter in the barn or house before burial in the field at sowing time. In this way the 'corn spirit' survived from one harvest to the next and ensured the fertility of the soil in the spring. The importance attached to the Corn Maiden over such a passage of time suggests that she may have been the Neolithic archetype of the Corn Goddess—the corn itself, every grain of which was the Goddess in microcosm; for like the cowrie shell and the grooves on a Grooved Ware pot, it signified by its vulvar shape the Goddess in person.

After the early period in which true spirals appeared in churches, a subtle

The traditional corn dolly whose three-dimensional spiral echoes the spinning of the spiralling whirlwind and the vortex which makes the Goddess circles in the cornfields. The idea for the triple corn dolly may have been born of the concept of the tri-function Great Goddess.

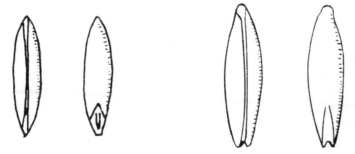

As with the cowrie, the grain of wheat exhibits through its shape the vulvar symbolism of the Goddess. This imagery was wholly appropriate at the dawn of agriculture when the power of the Goddess to produce food from planted seeds came to be recognised. On the left is a grain of emmer wheat (opposite sides shown) as compared with a modern variety.

change took place. The Church adopted a modification of the spiral theme—the Minoan labyrinth—and in some designs it came complete with Minotaur, the Bull of Minos!

The Cretan legend, dating from the second millennium BC, is that within a labyrinth which had been built by Daedalus for King Minos of Crete dwelt the Minotaur, half bull, half man. Theseus, son of the King of Athens, decided to slay the monstrous beast in order to put an end to the annual Athenian tribute of sacrificial youths and maidens. He succeeded thanks to the help of Minos's daughter, Ariadne, who gave him a bobbin of thread to guide him through the labyrinth. As he went in he unwound the thread behind him, and he wound it up again on his way out. Both Virgil and Ovid refer to the labyrinth as though it was an architectural construction, probably underground, although archaeology has failed to uncover any definite sign of such a work other than the lower parts of the Palace of Knossos itself.

The earliest form of the single-line labyrinthine pattern (as distinct from the plain spiral) is certainly Cretan. It appears on first-millennium coins of the town and Palace of Knossos in square and rounded versions and in countless artistic and symbolic depictions ever since. Plain spirals had long been widely known and used in the ancient Middle East and Eastern Mediterranean, and the Cretan variant may be seen as an extension of the idea intended to heighten its complexity. Thus a well-liked conventional design became established and, although it came to be re-used in numerous contexts by Greeks, Romans and others, it is odd that the Christian Church should have endorsed it as well. As a consequence, labyrinths of Cretan type became ecclesiastical images, and some remain to this day on the pavements, pillars, walls and furnishings of Italian and French churches—a few can still be seen in Britain.

Older than the labyrinth depicted in churches is the outdoor turf maze. Despite the metamorphosis that garden mazes have experienced in historical times, turf mazes may have their origins in British antiquity. The majority of these quaint, grassy constructions were circular in design, their patterns related to but more complex than the plain spiral. This form of the labyrinth, in which the windings are created by the spade cutting through short-cropped grassy turf, is largely peculiar to the British Isles, but the execution of mazes by the ordered patterning of stones or pebbles was a practice common to a number of societies in various parts of the world at different times. Both turf and stone mazes predated the topiary maze of clipped hedges which is familiar to most people today; the latter is chiefly a post-mediaeval variant in the history of maze development.

Turf mazes require continual and considerable dreary effort for their maintenance; within a few short years of neglect they are overgrown and gone for ever. Sadly they are even more vulnerable to the plough, so that, whereas fewer than a

Left: Plan of the Shepherd's Race, a spiral-circular grass maze, diameter 12 metres, formerly at Boughton Green in Northamptonshire. The maze is mentioned in a charter by King Edward III in 1353 as a feature of the three-day June fair; unhappily it was destroyed around 1916. Notice how easy it is for the pattern to transpose into a simple spiral by following the swirl out from the centre and sweeping straight through the windings. *Right:* A rare, elliptical spiral grass or turf maze, about 8 metres by 9 metres, called the Walls of Troy. It was on Rockcliffe Marsh, inland from the Solway Firth, Cumbria.

dozen turf mazes survive in England to this day, ancient records suggest that many hundreds, and probably thousands, once enriched the countryside and villages of Britain. Whatever their origins and uses may have been, by mediaeval times they were regarded as an agreeable part of country life. William Stukeley wrote that 'lovers of antiquity . . . always speak of 'em with great pleasure and as if there was something extraordinary in the thing, tho' they cannot tell what.' Fortunately, although so many turf mazes have vanished, drawings of some of the lost patterns remain.

In Northamptonshire a turf maze formerly existed at Boughton Green. Known as Shepherd's Race, it dates at least from 1353 when it was mentioned in a royal charter granted to the local June fair. A Yorkshire maze at Ripon was ploughed away in 1827. The diameters of these two mazes were respectively 12 and 20 metres. The single-line element underlying each is striking, incorporating a basic idea which we know to be primitive—a continuous convolution which can be reduced to a regular spiral without false ends—in other words a single spiral. Another spiral maze that we know of had an almost elliptical shape, about eight metres wide and nine metres in length. It was inland from the Solway Firth in Cumbria, until it was ploughed away a hundred years ago.

Some mazes can still be visited today, in remote parts of the country. One is north-west of the village of Breamore in Hampshire, close to the Wiltshire county border, south of Salisbury. The simplest way to reach it is to leave the main

Left: The turf maze on the flat top of St Catherine's Hill outside Winchester, Hampshire. It is in the heartland of the most prolific part of Hampshire's spiral-circle country which includes Cheesefoot. The maze is known to be several centuries old and to have been recut after periods of neglect. This explains why the turf windings are where the chalk walls should be, and why it is the only square turf maze known. The plan is that of Edward Trollope, published 1858, and differs in minor respects from the current one.
Right: The former maze at Sneinton in Nottinghamshire went under the names Robin Hood's Race and Shepherd's Race. Its four-fold symmetry with corner circles may be related to the occurrence of five-circle vortex patterns in cropfields.

Salisbury–Ringwood road and travel a kilometre to Breamore House, then continue along a public right-of-way for a further two kilometres, through a wood on the Breamore Estate and out on to Breamore Down, where the maze is in a small copse, some four kilometres from the road. This splendidly maintained maze lies close to a Bronze Age round barrow and not more than 300 metres north-east of Giant's Grave long barrow. It shares some of the characteristics of a barrow in that the word 'barrow' really means low hill, and the maze centre is in fact a low hill half-a-metre high and two to three metres across, with the windings inclined about ten degrees to the horizontal. No houses or settlements have been near it in historic times.

There are other mazes, also remote from any settlement, which are adjacent to round barrows; one is at Wing, near Oakham, Leicestershire. St Catherine's turf maze in Hampshire has a further peculiarity: besides its proximity to the nearest town of Winchester it is placed on the flat top of a high hill which was reshaped in Iron Age times as the local hillfort. Did the Britons respect a pre-existing maze when building the fort, or was the maze a later introduction? This maze is curious for its rectangular shape, at present about 28 metres × 28 metres. Records and tradition hold that it was recut several times following periods of neglect, so it is probable that on one of these occasions it was replanned to conform to the shape of the available or assigned space. The squareness does not modify the essential

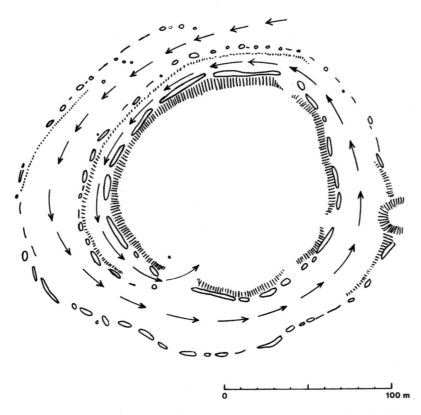

The spiral ditch system of the Neolithic causewayed enclosure at the Trundle, Goodwood, Sussex, which dates from the fourth millennium BC (after E.C. Curwen). One kilometre long, it is Britain's biggest ancient spiral, but at one time it was still longer because its outer parts, probably a whole loop, were destroyed in the Iron Age by the building of a fort. The causeways were positioned to oblige a ceremonial procession to follow the spiral route indicated by the arrows, in the way suggested for Silbury Hill.

concept: as elsewhere, the convolutions remain unicursal and are reducible to the simple spiral.

I believe that the prototypes of the spiral-patterned turf mazes were naturally-formed spiral-circles, just as in earlier ages they were likely to be the origin of the first round barrows, stone circles and henges. This may hold true for the apparently complex maze patterns, too, such as the former Robin Hood's Race or Shepherd's Race on a hill at Sneinton in Nottinghamshire, and the existing one at Saffron Walden in Suffolk. These have a four-corner symmetry incorporated into the edges of the central design and the whole is suggestive of the quintuplet spiral circles known from crop circle surveys.

A forerunner of the field-spiral idea may be the Neolithic camp at the Trundle, above Goodwood on the Sussex Downs, which has boundary ditches deeply incised into the chalk. This interrupted enclosure, which is certainly more than five thousand years old, has the distinction of being Europe's oldest surviving landscape spiral, as well as the largest. The excavation by E. C. Curwen in 1928 revealed that the ditches follow two-and-a-half turns of a right-handed spiral for a distance of nearly a kilometre. This is the anticlockwise, inward direction, as in a tornado-type whirlwind.

The Neolithic causewayed camp on a hill a few kilometres north-west of Stonehenge is of interest for its name, Robin Hood's Ball, which is clearly mediaeval. The name may have been applied to the nearby wood initially, if a spiral turf maze once existed there, like Robin Hood's Race at Sneinton. Other names formerly given to turf mazes, and still associated with some of them, are Mizmaze, Troy Town, Walls of Troy, Julian's Bower, Shepherd's Ring, Shepherd's Race, Shepherd's Labyrinth, Shepherd's Crook, and Caerdroia (the City of Troy, in Welsh).

The Cretan labyrinth is probably a descendant of the plain spiral versions. It dates at least from late Minoan times (the middle of the second millennium BC). Other labyrinthine variants are of similar antiquity but the Minoan pattern, together with the Minotaur–Theseus tale, acquired a remarkable continuity of use which transcended age and empire. Perhaps the philosophy which led the early Church to adopt it is related to that which carried the true spiral into early Christian symbolism.

Maze historians like W. H. Matthews have made a case for regarding the British turf maze as of Roman origin, but he puzzles over the remarkable survival of a maze-related 'child's game' through subsequent centuries. How could such a custom persist after the recall of the Romans and in the face of waves of subsequent invaders—Saxons, Danes and Norsemen—when turf mazes need constant maintenance? Could the invading newcomers also have known of the labyrinth idea, and carried the custom to these islands where it was anyway already prevalent? That they knew of it in later centuries is undoubted. Interesting pebble and stone mazes survive in Scandinavia to this day, and many examples have been described in all four Scandinavian countries, the oldest publication being that of O. Rudbeck in 1695. In the same century John Aubrey wrote: 'we received these Mazes from our Danish ancestors'.

Spiral symbolism is certainly ancient and widespread. Spirals are found throughout the world, and in every society the symbolic meaning is traditional and its beginnings undatable. In later times spirals range from the art and magic of aboriginal Australasia and the Pacific Islands to Africa, Asia, and the pictograms and sand drawings of the North American Indians, like the coiled snake quintuplet of the Navajo medicine man.

Spiral-dancing is another form of the maze idea, known throughout recorded history from the ancient Delian Dance to the Cornish Snail Creep. The latter persisted as a Cornish tradition right into this century, in a simple but obviously

Left: A stone maze on Wier Island in the Gulf of Finland, after the sketch by E. von Baer in 1838. Notice that by shifting the stones marked in black to adjoining gaps a perfect spiral appears. *Right:* Sand drawing of a quintuplet spiral system composed of coiled snakes, made by the Navajo Indians of America as part of a healing rite. The similarity of the pattern to the quintuplet vortex circles in cropfields is uncanny.

degenerate form of what may once have been a fertility rite. A musical band led the spiral dance whose circular inturning progressively tightened until the band reached a centre, a situation which would have provoked chaos (equivalent to destruction and death) but for a sudden reversal of direction which unwound the spiral as effectively as it had been made (equivalent to rebirth and resurrection). Ad de Vries suggests that there may be a connection with the threshing-floor dances of the spring festivals. 'It represents the Conquest of death by Resurrection; the labyrinth then represents the universe, with the Moon-sickle in the centre, the upperworld reflecting the underworld.'

W. H. Matthews came close to the truth as regards the antiquity of mazes:

. . . nobody . . . can avoid the conclusion that at any rate there must have existed in very early—possibly Neolithic—times an extremely widespread and important ceremonial, generally of the sacrificial type, in connection with the spring awakening. So deeply seated was this ancient tradition that traces of it have persisted, with various local modifications, right down to the present day.

A. B. Cook says, 'It can hardly be a coincidence that the distribution of mazes and labyrinths corresponds so closely with that of the megalith monuments of Europe. This suggests that the original maze-makers were akin to, or even identical with, the unknown builders of cromlechs, menhirs and avenues.'

The spiral is the embodiment of these ideas: the inflowing spiral is an indicator of death—for men and women, for nature and the seasons. The outflowing spiral symbolises the birth of new life in all forms animal and vegetable, and the rebirth of the dead; so, too, it signals the rebirth of the year and the return of spring.

These aims, these hopes, were enshrined in the pervasive spiral symbolism of the Neolithic age, and encapsulated by the harvest corn dolly whose origins may lie just as far back. And so was the naturally-laid grass spiral. Not only was the grass or crop spiral the Mother of the ritual circle and the round barrow in the British Neolithic and Bronze Ages, but it gave birth to the elementary spiral labyrinth in the form of the turf maze, in which myth was combined with rite for the intended participation of the believers. And it is the repeated return of the grass and crop spiral every year in Britain's fields that ensures the perpetuity of spiral and maze patterns in the face of repeated invasions and the passage of four millennia.

In 1858 W. H. Mounsey described an ancient custom, still then performed by Cumbrian shepherds, of cutting on the turf pasture a labyrinthine figure which they called the Walls of Troy. 'They cut the figure as they had seen it cut by others, when tired of lying on their backs, merely because they had nothing else to do, and named it as they had heard it named without knowing or caring what it meant.' A similar tradition was formerly known to have prevailed among Welsh shepherds but was reported to have long since fallen into disuse.

Why should humble shepherds bother at all, if they were so lazy as implied by Mounsey, since the cutting of a turf maze was a laborious and skilful process? And why are so many ancient mazes set deep in the country? Why, to cap it all, should a Shepherd's Crook appear at Stonehenge in the year 1851, and disappear not long afterwards? In Bell's *Life in London* an anonymous person wrote, '. . . and, as we gazed upon the Shepherd's Crook, deeply carved upon the virgin turf, we thought of the many generations of those who had watched their fleecy care beneath the shadows of this mighty pile.'

The pattern for the children's game of spiral hopscotch, which the author recently drew in the sand in the same way that he was taught by older children when he was young.

Stonehenge is about as remote a place as any to pursue an ancient turf-cutting tradition. What better motive could a shepherd at Stonehenge, or anywhere else in the British Isles, have for a sudden burst of enthusiasm for landscape gardening than one precipitated by the witnessing of a whirling spiral image formed in the grassy turf, perhaps before his very eyes? The turf maze is only a little less impermanent than the vortex-made spiral, so it is easy to understand how the frequent appearance of the ethereal spiral crop circle enabled the tradition to survive for so many thousands of years.

Erratic, uncommon, unpredictable but immediately recognisable, the spirals reappear, sometimes with attendant vortex, sometimes not. A shepherd acquainted with ancient folklore might prepare on the spot a Shepherd's Crook, his own Walls of Troy. In recent centuries he was presumably doing this more to pass the time, though with a certain respect for ancient customs. By following the traditions he was maintaining an archaic art-form without comprehending the symbolic spiritual values which it had held centuries and millennia earlier as part of an extinct pre-Christian religion.

Although we do not know what pattern was chosen by the Stonehenge shepherd, we know that it could have been a plain spiral, clockwise or anticlockwise, or some traditional elaboration on the spiral theme, as for instance the Cretan labyrinth. The Stonehenge maze would not have remained there long; without re-cutting weeds would soon have overwhelmed it. None of the nineteenth-century antiquarians reported the maze so it was probably no more than a few months old when it was seen on 18 March, 1851 and, although 'deeply carved upon the virgin turf', it quickly lost its distinctive appearance.

The ideas decadent, the old meanings lost, the attraction for the spiral maze nevertheless persisted. The shepherd cut his maze as children today mark out the pavement or sandy beach for spiral hopscotch, neither shepherd nor child knowing the underlying reason why. Much the same applies to those who preserve spring customs by dancing around the painted maypole with its upward spiral twist.

Nature's spiral has taken us full circle. As an image in megalithic art, the spiral was never a meaningless motif. Although one of the hardest geometric curves to draw well, it attracted more attention than any other and mothered a deep spiritual philosophy consistent with the yearnings of early farming societies. The megalithic age saw the development of a new cult centred on the peaceful Goddess religion. The spiral was its image—and the circle, the cup and the lozenge its emblematic companions.

Of the many meanings stored within the spiral symbol the images of birth and rebirth were paramount because they signified fertility and immortality, and stone circles and round barrows were erected with these concepts in view. The Goddess of Nature and the Universe was idolised as the Goddess of the Stones. In a precarious world the people sought guidance and succour, of which She was Provider throughout the immense period of time which was the Neolithic and Bronze Ages, an era which for Britain, Ireland and Brittany was largely a time of tranquillity. She ruled over a classless, balanced society, until the convulsions of the Iron Age brought widespread fortification of hilltops following invasions by male-ruling, God-dominated warrior groups—the so-called 'heroic' societies.

Thus ended the serenity of the Age of the Goddess. So began the Age of Wars which has lasted to this day.

Bibliography

This select bibliography lists the most useful works on archaeology, ancient religion, symbolism, megalithic science and crop-circle science in which the reader can find further details of the basic material discussed in the text.

Archaeology

ASHBEE, Paul (1960). *The Bronze Age Round Barrow in Britain*. Dent, London.

ASHBEE, Paul (1978). *The Ancient British*. Geo Books, Norwich.

BRADLEY, Richard (1984). *The Social Foundations of Prehistoric Britain*. Longman, London.

BURL, Aubrey (1976). *The Stone Circles of the British Isles*. Yale University Press, New Haven and London.

BURL, Aubrey (1979). *Rings of Stone*. Frances Lincoln, London.

BURL, Aubrey (1979). *Prehistoric Avebury*. Yale University Press, New Haven and London.

BURL, Aubrey (1987). *The Stonehenge People*. Dent, London.

BURGESS, Colin (1980). *The Age of Stonehenge*. Dent, London.

CLARKE, D. V., COWIE, T. G. and FOXON, Andrew (1985). *Symbols of Power at the Time of Stonehenge*. H.M.S.O., Edinburgh.

EHRENBERG, Margaret (1989). *Women in Prehistory*. British Museum Publications, London.

GIMBUTAS, Marija (1982). *The Goddesses and Gods of Old Europe: 6500–3500 BC Myths and Cult Images*. 2nd edn. Thames and Hudson, London.

GIMBUTAS, Marija (1989). *The Language of the Goddess*. Harper and Row, San Francisco; Thames and Hudson, London.

MEADEN, G. T. (forthcoming 1991). *The Stonehenge Solution*. Souvenir Press, London.

PIGGOTT, S. (1954). *Neolithic Cultures of the British Isles*. Cambridge University Press, Cambridge.

SMITH, Isobel F. (1965). *Windmill Hill and Avebury: Excavations by Alexander Keiller 1925–1939*. Oxford University Press, Oxford.

WAINWRIGHT, Geoffrey (1990). *The Henge Monuments*. Thames and Hudson, London.

Goddess Religions, Comparative Religion, Symbolism

CHETWYND, T. (1982). *A Dictionary of Symbols*. Mandala/Unwin, London.

CHETWYND, T. (1986). *A Dictionary of Sacred Myth*. Mandala/Unwin, London.

CIRLOT, J. E. (1971). *A Dictionary of Symbols*. 2nd edn. Routledge and Kegan Paul, London.

DE VRIES, Ad (1974). *Dictionary of Symbols and Imagery*. North-Holland, London.

EISLER, Riane (1987). *The Chalice and the Blade*. Harper and Row, San Francisco.

ELIADE, Mircea (1957). *The Sacred and the Profane. The Nature of Religion*. Rowohlt, Hamburg. (1959) Harcourt Brace Jovanovich, Florida.

ELIADE, Mircea (1958). *Patterns in Comparative Religion*. Sheed and Ward, London.

ELIADE, Mircea (1978). *A History of Religious Ideas: Volume 1. From the Stone Age to the Eleusinian Mysteries*. Univ. of Chicago Press, Chicago.

GADON, Elinor W. (1989). *The Once and Future Goddess*. Harper and Row, San Francisco.

GIMBUTAS, Marija (1982 and 1989). See her two books referenced under Archaeology.

NEUMANN, Erich (1963). *The Great Mother: An Analysis of the Archetype*. 2nd ed. Princeton University Press, New Jersey.

SJOO, M. and MOR, Barbara (1987). *The Great Cosmic Mother*. Harper and Row, San Francisco.

WALKER, Barbara G. (1988). *The Woman's Dictionary of Symbols and Sacred Objects*. Harper and Row, San Francisco.

Megalithic Science including Stone Circle Analysis

HEGGIE, Douglas C. (1981). *Megalithic Science: Ancient Mathematics and Astronomy in North-west Europe*. Thames and Hudson, London.

THOM, Alexander (1967). *Megalithic Sites in Britain*. Clarendon Press. Oxford.

THOM, A. and THOM, A. S. (1982). *Megalithic Remains in Britain and Brittany*. Oxford University Press, Oxford.

THOM, Alexander, THOM, Archibald S. and BURL, A. (1980). *Megalithic Rings*. British Archaeological Reports no. 81, Oxford.

Crop Circle Science

MEADEN, G. T. (1989). *The Circles Effect and its Mysteries*. Artetech, Frome Road, Bradford-on-Avon, Wilts. 2nd edn. 1990.

MEADEN, G. T. (Ed) (1991). *Circles from the Sky*. Souvenir Press, London.

RANDALLS, J. and FULLER, P. (1990). *Crop Circles*. Robert Hale, London.

OTHER REFERENCES

The works cited are listed under the first chapter to which they are appropriate although some appertain to more than one chapter.

Chapter 1. Stone Age Mysteries

BARNATT, J. and MOIR, G. (1984). Stone Circles and Megalithic Mathematics. *Proc. Prehistoric Society*, Vol. 50, 197–216.

BURL, A. (1969). Henges: Internal Features and Regional Groupings. *Arch. J.*, Vol. 126, 1–28.

BURL, A. (1987). *The Stonehenge People*. Chapter 7, 129, 134–5.

CLARE, T. (1986). Towards a Reappraisal of Henge Monuments. *Proc. Prehistoric Soc.*, Vol. 52, 281–316.

COWAN, T. M. (1969). Megalithic Rings: Their Design and Construction. *Science*, Vol. 168, 321–5.

FLEMING, A. (1972). Vision and Design. Pp. 59–60 in *Man*, Vol. 7, 57–73.

HADINGHAM, Evan (1974). *Ancient Carvings in Britain*. Garnstone Press, London.

HARDING, A. F. and LEE, G. E. (1987). Henge Monuments and Ritual Sites. *British Archaeological Report* no. 175, Oxford.

SMITH, I. F. (1971). Causewayed Camps: in *Economy and Settlement in Neolithic and Bronze Age Europe*, ed. D. D. A. Simpson, Leicester, pp. 89–112.

STARTIN, D. W. A. (1982). Prehistoric Earthmoving. Pp. 153–6, in *Settlement Patterns in the Oxford Region*. CBA Research report no. 44.

STUKELEY, W. (1743). *Abury*.

THOM, Alexander (1955). A Statistical Examination of the Megalithic Sites in Britain. *J. Roy. Statist. Soc.*, A Vol. 118, 275–295.

THOM, A. (1971). *Megalithic Lunar Observatories*. Clarendon Press, Oxford.

THOM, A. and THOM, A. S. (1978). *Megalithic Remains in Britain and Brittany*. Clarendon Press, Oxford.

WOOD, J. E. (1980). *Sun, Moon and Standing Stones*, p. 56, Oxford University Press, Oxford.

Chapter 2. The Spiralling Whirlwind

ANON. *Notes and Queries* (1897). 8th Series. XI, p. 47.

CABLE, Mildred. *The Gobi Desert*, quoted by P. R. Scott in The Gobi Desert. *Weather*, Vol. 9, 355–6, 1954.

CAFFYN, T. Whirlwind in Sussex. Letter to *The Times*, London, 11 August 1938.

COOK, A. B. (1912). *Zeus*, pp. 162–165.

FRASER, J. Gordon (1911). *The Golden Bough, Vol. 1, The Magic Art*, 329–31.

IDSO, S. B. (1974). Tornado or dust-devil: The enigma of desert whirlwinds. *Amer. Scientist*, Vol. 62, p. 532 of 530–41.

MEADEN, G. T. (1985). The Classification of Whirlwind Types and a Discussion of their Physical Origins. *J. Meteorology*, Vol. 10, 194–202.

MEADEN, G. T. (1985). *Tornadoes in Britain*. 130 pp. Report for H.M. Nuclear Installations Inspectorate, Bootle, Lancs.

PEARSON, J. F. (1990). Whirlwind Circles. *J. Meteorology*. Vol. 15, 219.

PEDOE, D. T. (1958). Whirlwind at Flatford Mill, Suffolk. *Weather*, Vol. 13, 50–3.

RENDALL, P. D. Circles made by a Whirlwind, Avon County, 5 August 1989. *J. Meteorology*, Vol. 14, 414–15.

Chapter 3. The Circles Effect

BENNETT, M. (1990). The Mechanics of Crop Circle Formation. *Weather*, Vol. 45, 456.

CINDEREY, M. J. (1988). Stationary Wind-Devils in the January Snow in North Yorkshire. *J. Meteorology*, Vol. 10, 339.

JUNG, Carl (1959). *Flying Saucers: A Modern Myth of Things Seen in the Skies*. London and New York.

KIKUCHI, T., SNOW, J. and MEADEN, G. T. (1991). Nanoburst, the Microburst by Spiral Vortex Suggests the Origin of Circular Crop Damage (offered to *Nature*).

MEADEN, G. T. (1985). Advances in the Understanding of Whirlwind Spiral Patterns in Cereal Fields. *J. Meteorology*, Vol. 10, 73–80.

MEADEN, G. T. (1987). An Anticlockwise Spiral-Circle in a Cereal Crop: Part 1. *J. Meteorology*, Vol. 12, 44–9.

MEADEN, G. T. (1988). The Vortices of Vapour seen near Avebury, Wiltshire, above a Wheatfield on 16 June, 1988. *J. Meteorology*, Vol. 13, 305–311.

MEADEN, G. T. (1990). An Eye-witness Account of Crop-Circle Formation. *Weather*, Vol. 45, 273–4.

MEADEN, G. T. (1990). Nocturnal Eyewitness Observation of Circles in the Making. North Wiltshire, 29 June 1989. *J. Meteorology*, Vol. 15, 5–7: HARRIS, P. (1990). Do. East Kent, 10 August 1989. *Ibid.*, Vol. 15, 3–5.

MEADEN, G. T. (1990). Crop Circles. *New Scientist*, Vol. 126, 47–9, 23 June 1990.

RANDLES, J. and SKINNER, R. (1989). The Mowing Devil. *J. Meteorology*, Vol. 14, 381–9.

Chapter 4. The Mark of the Goddess

BARNATT, J. and MOIR, G. (1984). *Proc. Prehist. Soc.*, Vol. 50, 197–216.

BURL, A. (1976). *Stone Circles of the British Isles*, pp. 43–4, 56, 58, 205–8.

CUNNINGTON, M. E. (1929). *Woodhenge*. Wilts. Arch. Soc., Devizes.

HEGGIE, D. C. *Megalithic Science*, p. 42.

KENDALL, D. G. (1974). Hunting Quanta. *Phil. Trans. Roy. Soc., London. A*, Vol. 276, 231–66.

THOM, A. (1955). *J. Roy. Statist. Soc.*, A Vol. 118, 275–295.

THOM, A. (1967). *Megalithic Sites in Britain*, pp. 28–30, 46, 62, 73, 77.

THOM, A., THOM, A. S. and BURL, A. (1980). *Megalithic Rings*, 131–2, 308–9.

Chapter 5. Pathways to Heaven

ASHBEE, P. (1984). *Wilts. Arch. Mag.*, Vol. 79, p. 62, of pp. 39–91.

CASE, H. (1952). *Proc. Prehistoric Soc.*, 18, 148–59.

CAWDOR, Earl and Fox, Cyril (1923–4). Excavation of the Beacon Hill Barrow, Barton Mills, Suffolk. *Camb. Antiq. Soc. Communications*, Vol. 26, 19–65.

Excavation of Four Round Barrows. *Proc. Prehist. Soc.* (1960). Vol. 26, 343ff (p. 365: elliptical Shalbourne barrow, axial lengths 80 and 68ft).

Fox, Sir Cyril (1941). Dateable Ritual Barrows in Glamorganshire. *Antiquity* 15, 142–61; see also *Proc. Som. Arch.*, Vol. 29, 46, 1883; *ibid.* v 42, 2–23, 1896.

GRINSELL, L. V. (1959). *Dorset Barrows*, p. 17 ff. Longman.

HARRISON, Jane. *Prologema to the Study of Greek Religion*. 125 and 68. 2nd edn 1908, Cambridge University Press.

PETERSEN, F. (1972). Traditions in Multiple Burial. *Arch. J.*, 129, 22–55.

ROBERTSON-SMITH. *Lectures on the Religion of the Semites*, p. 436.

STUKELEY, W. (1740). *Stonehenge*, p. 44.

Chapter 6. The Cult of the Round Barrow

ASHBEE, P. (1956). The Excavation of a Round Barrow on Canford Heath, Dorset. *Proc. Dorset Nat. Hist. Arch. Soc.*, 76, 39ff.

ASHBEE, P. (1984). The Excavation of Amesbury Barrows, 58, 61a, 61, and 72. *Wilt. Arch. Magazine*, Vol. 79, pp. 39–91.

ASHBEE, P., BELL, M. and PROUDFOOT, E. (1989). *The Wilsford Shaft*. English Heritage, London.

FOWLER, P. J. (1983). *The Farming of Prehistoric Britain*, p. 112, Cambridge University Press, Cambridge.

GRINSELL, L. V. (1959). *Dorset Barrows*. Longman.

HOARE, Richard Colt. *Ancient Wilts, vol. 1*.

MEADEN, G. T. (1986). Sighting of a Wind-Devil in Mid-Winter in Southern England. *Weather*, 41, 336–7.

REID, R. W. and FRASER, J. R. (1923–4). Short stone cist found in Kincardineshire. *Proc. Soc. Antiq. Scotland*, 58, 27–40.

WARD, C. G. (1956). A Whirlwind on Pilsdon Pen. *Weather*, Vol. 11, 170.

Chapter 7. The Sacred Centre

CURWEN, E. C. (1934). A late Bronze Age farm and a Neolithic pit-dwelling on New Barn Down, Clapham, near Worthing. *Sussex Arch. Coll.*, 75, 137–70.

ELIADE, M. (1961). *Images and Symbols*, Chap. 1, 27–56 (the symbolism of the centre). Harvill Press, London.

GUILBERT, G. (1981). Double ring houses, probable and possible, in Prehistoric Britain. *Proc. Prehistoric. Soc.*, 47, 29–317. The author provides over 20 plans of certain, probable or possible double-ring structures from different sites.

JOBEY, G. and TAIT, J. (1966). Excavation on palisaded settlements and cairnfields at Alnham, Northumberland. *Arch. Aeliana*, 44, 5–48.

THOMAS, N. (1952). A Neolithic chalk cup from Wilsford in the Devizes Museum, and notes on some others. *Wilts. Arch. Mag.*, Vol. 52, 452–463.

THURNAM, John (1872). Round Barrows. *Archaeology*, 43, 285ff.

Chapter 8. Sacred Marriage

BRENNAN, Martin (1983). *The Stars and the Stones*. Thames and Hudson, London.

COPELAND, L. and HOURS, F. (1977). Engraved Bone Tools from Jiita (Lebanon). *Proc. Prehist. Soc.*, Vol. 43, 295–302, for zigzags on bone dating from 14000–16000 b.c.

HEMP, W. J. (1930). The chambered cairn of Bryn Celli Dhu. *Archaeologica*, Vol. 80, 179–214.

MORRIS, R. W. B. (1977). *The Prehistoric Rock Art of Argyll*. Blandford Press, Poole.

MORRIS, R. W. B. (1979). *The Rock Art of Galloway and the Isle of Man*. Blandford Press, Poole.

MORRIS, R. W. B. (1970–71). The petroglyphs of Achnabreck. *Proc. Soc. Antiq. Scot.*, Vol. 103, 33–56.

Chapter 9. Symbols of Divinity

ANON. (1866). *Arch. Camb.*, p. 537 [at SH 62602570 near Hendre Wadod].

BECKENSALL, S. G. (1974). *The Prehistoric Carved Rocks of Northumberland*, p. 76. [Also, (1984) *Northumberland's Prehistoric Rock Carvings*. Rothbury: Pendulum. 1984.]

BOWEN, E. G. and GRESHAM, C. A. (1967). *History of Merioneth*, Vol. 1. Dolgellau.

EOGAN, G. (1983). Bryn Celli Dhu. *Antiquity*, Vol. 57, 135–6 in which Prof. Eogan explains why the older idea that Bryn Celli Dhu began as a henge is improbable.

FELL, Clare (1972). *Early Settlement in the Lake Counties*, p. 35, Dalesman, Clapham, Yorks.

FORDE-JOHNSTONE, J. L. (1957). Megalithic art in the north-west of Britain: The Calderstones, Liverpool. *Proc. Prehist. Soc.*, Vol. 23, 20–39.

GRINSELL, L. V. (1957). A decorated cist-slab from Mendip. *Proc. Prehistoric Soc.*, Vol. 23, 231–2, plate XXVII; also p. 20 of *Barrows*, 2nd edn 1984, Shire Publications, Princes Risborough, Bucks.

HARDING. A. F. (1981). Excavations in the prehistoric ritual complex near Milfield, Northumberland. *Proc. Prehist. Soc.*, 47, 87–136.

HEBDEN (1960–62). *Proc. Soc. Antiq. Scotland*, Vol. 4, 185–6 [Eday Manse reference].

HEMP, W. J. (1930). The Chambered Cairn of Bryn Celli Dhu. *Arch.*, Vol. 80, 179–214.

O'KELLY, Claire (1969). Bryn Celli Dhu, Anglesey—a Reinterpretation. *Arch. Camb.*, Vol. 118, 17–48.

POWELL, T. G. E. (1966). *Prehistoric Art*, 146–7. Thames and Hudson, London.

SHARPLES, N. M. (1984). Excavations at Pierowall

Quarry, Westray, Orkney. *Proc. Soc. Antiq. Scotland*, Vol. 114, 75–125. [Also brief note in *Antiquity*, Vol. 55, 129–30.]

SMITH, I. F. (1965). *Windmill Hill and Avebury*. Plate XXI and p. 134.

Chapter 10. Symbolic Ornaments

CHILDE, V. G. (1930–31). Final report on the operations at Skara Brae. *Proc. Soc. Antiq. Scotland*, Vol. 65, 27–77.

CLARKE, D. V. [excavator] p. 56 in *Symbols of Power*.

DARVILL, T. C. (1982). *The Megalithic Tombs of the Cotswold/Severn Region*, p. 26. Vorda, Highworth, Wilts.

EDWARDSON, A. R. (1965). A spirally decorated object from Garboldisham. *Antiquity*, Vol. 39, 145.

EOGAN, G. (1983). A flint macehead at Knowth, Co. Meath, Ireland. *Antiquity*, Vol. 57, 45–6.

EOGAN, G. (1986). *Knowth*. Thames and Hudson, London.

EOGAN, G. and RICHARDSON, H. (1982). Two maceheads from Knowth, County Meath. *J. Roy. Soc. Antiq. Ireland*, Vol. 112, 123–138.

GERASIMOV, M. M. (1935). Raskopki Paleoliticheskoy Stoyanki v Sele Malte. *IGAIMK*, Vol. 118. Leningrad.

GREENWELL, W. (1890). Recent Researches in Barrows in Yorkshire. Wiltshire, Berkshire, etc. *Archaeol.*, Vol. 52, 14–16.

MARSHALL, Dorothy N. (1975–76). Carved Stone Balls. *Proc. Soc. Antiq. Scotland*, Vol. 103, 33–56; (1983) Vol. 113, 628–30.

PIGGOTT, S. in *West Kennet Long Barrow* comments on the emptying of the chambered long barrow at Stoney Littleton, Avon County.

POWELL, T. G. E. (1965). *Prehistoric Art*, 146–7. Thames and Hudson, London.

SMITH, Isobel. *Windmill Hill and Avebury*, p. 132. Two from pit 36, one from pit 37, 12 from primary levels, and 15 from upper levels.

SMITH, K. (1977). The excavation of Winklebury camp, Basingstoke, Hampshire. *Proc. Prehist. Soc.* Vol. 43, 31–130 [illus. 105 on p. 104].

WAINWRIGHT, G. J. (1979). *Mount Pleasant, Dorset: Excavations 1970–71*. The Society of Antiquaries, London.

WAINWRIGHT, G. J., and LONGWORTH, I. H. (1979). *Durrington Walls: Excavations, 1966–1968*. The Society of Antiquaries, London.

WEBB, J. D. C., ELSOM, D. M. and MEADEN, G. T. (1986). The TORRO hailstorm intensity scale. *J. Meteorology*, 12, 337–9.

Chapter 11. Nature's Spirals

ANON. (1986). *Current Archaeology*, Vol. 9, no. 101, p. 183.

AVERY, M., SUTTON, J. E. and BANKS, J. W. (1967).

Rainsborough, Northants, England: Excavations 1961–5. *Proc. Prehist. Soc.*, Vol. 33, 225 and 305–6.

BOWEN, D. Q. (1970). The palaeoenvironment of the 'Red Lady' of Paviland. *Antiquity*, Vol. 44, 134–6. The date is 18460 ± 340 radiocarbon years before 'present', say about 16510 ± 340 b.c.

CALKIN, J. B. (1949). *Proc. Dorset Nat. Hist. Arch. Soc.*, Vol. 69, 33→, and Vol. 74, 51.

CAMPBELL, J. (1973). *The Masks of God. Primitive Mythology.* 2nd edn. Souvenir Press, London.

CHETWYND, T. *A Dictionary of Sacred Myth*, p. 138.

CLARKE, D. L. (1970). *Beaker Pottery of Britain and Ireland.* Cambridge. Vol. 2, p. 574, plate 3.

COURTNEY, M. A. (1890). *Cornish Feasts and Folklore*, cited by E. and M. Radford, in *Encyclopaedia of Superstitions*, p. 313, Hutchinson, 1961.

CUNNINGTON, W. (1857). A Barrow on Roundway Hill near Devizes. *Wilts. Arch. Mag.*, Vol. 2, 185–8.

GIMBUTAS, M. *The Goddesses and Gods of Old Europe*, pp. 54–5.

GREEN, C. and ROLLO-SMITH, S. (1984). *Proc. Prehist. Soc.*, Vol. 50, 255–318. Fig. 27 Ae1 on p. 308.

HAWLEY, W. (1922). Third report on the excavations at Stonehenge. *Antiq. J.*, Vol. 3, p. 14 of 13–20.

HEDGES, J. W. (1984). *Tomb of the Eagles*, Plate 19 and p. 149. Murray, London.

HEMP, W. J. (1935). Bryn yr Hen Bobl. *Archaeol.*, Vol. 35, 275.

JAZDZEWSKI (1938). *Die Graberfelder der Bandkeramischen Kultur. Wiadomosci Archaeologi*, Vol. 15, 1.

MEREWETHER, J. (1851). *Diary of a Dean.* London. [Mistletoe in centre of Silbury Hill.]

OAKLEY, K. (1965). Folklore and Fossils. *Antiquity*, Vol. 39, part I, 9–16; part II, 117–25.

OTTAWAY, Barbara (1973). Early Copper Ornaments in Northern Europe. *Proc. Prehist. Soc.*, Vol. 39, 294–323.

PIGGOTT, S. (1954). *Neolithic Cultures of the British Isles.* Cambridge University Press.

POWELL, T. G. E. *Prehistoric Art*, p. 270, Thames and Hudson, London.

RENFREW, C. (1973). *Before Civilisation.* Cape, London.

SMITH, Isobel. *Windmill Hill and Avebury.*

THURNAM, John (1870). On Ancient British Barrows, especially those of Wiltshire. Pt. II, Round Barrows. *Archaeol.*, 42, p. 432–3. 'Single bone pins were found by Hoare with 18 interments, or about once in 20 graves. Relatively, they were half as frequent again with unburnt as with burnt bodies. They were more than twice as often met with in the barrows of Derbyshire and Staffordshire as in those of Wiltshire; but the relative frequency with unburnt and with incremated remains was more than reversed. Bateman records one pin to about every eleven graves: namely, one to 25 unburnt and one to seven burnt bodies. In Yorkshire and adjoining northern counties, Mr Greenwell seems to have found seven bone pins in about 125 graves, or five with unburnt and two with burnt bodies, which is nearly the same ratio as in the Wiltshire barrows.' Refer to p. 541 for Thurnam's statement on the snails in the Roundway Hill barrow.

WILLIAMSON (1836). *Description of a Tumulus at Gristhorpe.* 2nd edn 1836, p. 10; 3rd edn 1872, p. 15 (cited by John Thurnam above).

Chapter 12. The Secrets of Silbury Hill

ATKINSON, R. J. C. (1968). Silbury Hill 1968. *Antiquity*, 42, p. 299; (1969), vol. 43, 216.

BATEMAN, T. (1848). *Vestiges of the Antiquities of Derbyshire*, p. 31.

BURL, A. (1979). *Prehistoric Avebury*, p. 122, 123, 130, 135–6.

CASTLEDEN, R. (1987). *The Stonehenge People* (pp. 236–9 on 'harvest hills'). Routledge and Kegan Paul, London.

CUNNINGTON, R. H. (1955). Marden and the Cunnington Manuscripts. *Wilts. Arch. Mag.*, Vol. 56, 4–11.

DAMES, M. (1976). *The Silbury Treasure*, 70–1, 74–5, 83. Thames and Hudson, London.

ELIADE, M. (1958). *Patterns in Comparative Religion*, 99–102.

EVANS, J. G. (1968). Periglacial deposits on the chalk of Wiltshire. *Wilts. Arch. Magazine*, Vol. 63, 12–76.

EVANS, J. G. (1972). *Land Snails in Archaeology*, 265–7. Seminar Press, London.

HOARE, R. C. (1821). *Ancient History of North Wiltshire*, Vol. ii, p. 7.

MENDELSSOHN, K. (1976). *The Riddle of the Pyramids*, p. 140.

MEREWETHER, J. (1851). *Diary of a Dean, being an Account of the Examination of Silbury Hill*, pp. 12, 15–16. G. Bell, London.

NEUMANN, E. (1963). *The Great Mother.* 118, 226–33.

PIGGOTT, S. (1962). *West Kennet Long Barrow.* H.M.S.O., London.

STARTIN, D. W. A. (1982). Prehistoric Earthmoving. 153–6, in *Settlement Patterns in the Oxford Region*, ed. H. J. Case and A. W. R. Whittle. CBA Research Dept, no 44, 1982.

VATCHER, F. and VATCHER, L. (1976). *The Avebury Monuments*, p. 28, H.M.S.O.

WILLIAMS, D. (1976). A Neolithic Moss Flora from Silbury Hill. *J. Arch. Sci.*, 3, 267–70.

Chapter 13. Gods, Goddesses and Spirits

BARNATT, J. (1982). *Prehistoric Cornwall*, pp. 223–6, 248. Turnstone, Wellingborough.

BRENNAN, M. (1983). *The Stars and the Stones*, p. 177. Thames and Hudson, London.

BURGESS, C. (1980). *The Age of Stonehenge*, p. 36. Dent, London.

BURL, A. (1976). *The Stone Circles of the British Isles*, p. 163.

BURL, A. (1979). *Rings of Stone*, pp. 14–38.

BURL, A. (1987). *The Stonehenge People*, pp. 118–19, suggests that trepanning may have been intended to cure headaches, insanity, etc. My proposal goes farther in proposing that the effectiveness of the rite lay in the 'circularity' of the incision because circular holes expressly allow spirits to pass.

CHRISTIE, P. M. (1967). *Proc. Prehistoric Soc.*, Vol. 33, 336–66 [trepanned skull from Earls Down Farm, Wiltshire].

CIRLOT, J. E. (1971). *A Dictionary of Symbols*, p. 271 [on lightning, moon and rain]. Routledge and Kegan Paul, London.

CURWEN, E. C. (1929). Excavations in The Trundle, 1928. *Sussex Arch. Collections*, Vol. 70, 33–85.

DEANE, Tony and SHAW, Tony (1975). *The Folklore of Cornwall*, p. 141. Batsford, London.

ELIADE, M. *Patterns in Comparative Religion*, pp. 157, 216–27, and Chap 6.

GRINSELL, L. V. (1959). *Dorset Barrows*, pp. 74–5. Longman, Dorchester [cupmarks on cist-slabs in England, Scotland and Ireland].

HADINGHAM. E. (1974). *Ancient Carvings in Britain*, *Part 2*. Garnstone, London.

HALPIN, Claire (1987). Excavation at Irthlingborough. *Current Arch.*, Vol. 9, 331–3.

ILKLEY ARCHAEOLOGICAL GROUP (1986). *The Carved Rocks of Rombalds Moor*. Wakefield, W. Yorkshire.

LEEDS, E. T. and MUSGRAVE, C. (1938). Beakers of the Upper Thames District. *Oxoniensa*, Vol. 3, pp. 31–40 [unfinished trepanation].

MACKENZIE (1927). *Infancy of Medicine*, p. 219, London [quoting newspapers of 1923].

MORRIS, R. W. B. (1979). *Prehistoric Rock Art of Galloway and the Isle of Man*. Blandford Press, Poole.

MORRIS, R. W. B. (1981). *Prehistoric Rock Art of Southern Scotland*. British Archaeological Reports no. 86.

MORRIS. R. W. B. and BAILEY (1964–66). Cup-and-ring marks of South-West Scotland. *Proc. Soc. Antiq. Scotland*, Vol. 98, 172.

MORRIS. R. W. B. and MARSHALL, A. (1983). *Trans. Bristol Arch. Soc.*, Vol. 101, 171–4.

NEUMANN, E. (1963). *The Great Mother*, pp. 127–8. 'In the hieroglyphics, the water jar, symbol of the celestial goddess Nut, is also the symbol of femininity, "female genital", "woman", and the feminine principle'.

PARRY, T. W. (1921). The Prehistoric Trephined Skulls of Great Britain. *Proc. Roy. Soc. Medicine (Hist. Section)*, no. 10.

PIGGOTT, S. (1940). A trepanned skull of the Beaker period from Dorset, and the practice of trepanning in Prehistoric Europe. *Proc. Prehistoric Soc.*, Vol. 6, 113–32.

PIGGOTT, S. (1973). The Dalladies Long Barrow: North-East Scotland. *Antiquity*, Vol. 47, 32–3. [I-6113.]

SAINTYVES, P. (1936). *Corpus du folklore préhistorique en France et dans les colonies françaises*, Vol. 1–3.

SMITH, G. E. (1919). *The Evolution of the Dragon*, p. 182, 199. Manchester [identity of the pot with the 'Great Mother'].

TATE, George. *The Ancient British Sculpted Rocks of Northumberland*. Alnwick.

THOMAS, N. and THOMAS, C. (1955). *Wilts. Archaeol. Mag.*, Vol. 56, 127–48 (p. 135) [round cranial disc found lying alongside a cremation].

WAINWRIGHT, F. T. *The Souterrains of Southern Pictland*, plate XIII.

Chapter 14. The Legacy of the Spiral

ANON. (1851). *Life in London*, p. 5, col. 4, 30 March 1851.

ASPELIN, J. R. (1877). Steinlabyrinthe in Finnland. *Zeits. fur Ethnologie*, Vol. 9, p. 439.

AUBREY, J. (1719). *Ancient History of Surrey*, Vol. 5, p. 80, 136.

BORD, Janet (1976). *Mazes and Labyrinths of the World*. Latimer New Dimensions.

BRISTOL ARCHAEOLOGICAL RESEARCH GROUP (1972). Research Booklet, pp. 15–16.

CIRLOT, J. E. *Dictionary of Symbols*, p. 232.

COOK, A. B. (1914). *Zeus*, p. 489 [citing E. Krauze].

GOULSTONE, J. (1980). Stonehenge: the Shepherd's Crook turf carving. *Wilts. Arch. Mag.*, Vol. 80, 230.

KNIGHT, J. (1977). *Arch. Camb.*, Vol. 126, 60–4.

MATTHEWS, W. H. (1922). *Mazes and Labyrinths, Their History and Development*. London. Dover Publications, U.S. 1972.

MOUNSEY, W. H. (1858). *Notes and Queries*. 2nd series no. 115, 211–13, who also cites the Welsh book, *Drych y Prif Oesoedd*, 1740.

PLINY. *Natural History*, xxxvi, 85 [According to Pliny Egyptian and other labyrinths are not to be compared with 'what we see traced on our mosaic pavements or to the mazes formed in the fields for the entertainment of children.']

RICHARDSON, Hilary (1984). Number and symbol in early Christian art. *J. Roy. Soc. Antiq. of Ireland*, Vol. 114, 28–47.

RUDBECK, O. (1695). *Atlantica*, 1695–8. Tab. 35. Fig. 134.

STUKELEY, W. (1776). *Itinerarium Curiosum*, pp. 31, 97.

TROLLOPE, E. (1858). Notices of ancient and mediaeval labyrinths. *Arch. J.*, Vol. 15, 216–35.

Index

Pictures in the text are indicated by italics. CP indicates colour plate.